From Dean's List To Dumpsters

Why I left Harvard to Join a Cult

JIM GUERRA

ARPress
ILLUMINATING IDEAS.
EMPOWERING VOICES

ARPress
45 Dan Road Suite 15
Canton MA 02021

Hotline: 1(888) 821-0229
Fax: 1(508) 545-7580

Ordering Information:

Quantity sales. Special discounts are available on quantity purchases by corporations, associations, and others. For details, contact the publisher at the address above.
Printed in the United States of America.

ISBN-13:   Paperback   979-8-89676-425-0
            eBook   979-8-89676-426-7

Library of Congress Control Number: 2025911929

Contents

Dedication

I dedicate this book to my parents, Charles and Marilyn, who suffered greatly during my cult disappearance and had to live life not knowing if I was alive or dead; who received me back with unconditional love, and who loved me until their passing.

I also dedicate this to my wife, Luchy, who has faithfully supported me in my work and life; and to Rebekah and William, my two incredible children, who are smart, loving, and ready to conquer the world.

Epigraph

"Some of the smartest people there were also the most committed. Intelligence doesn't make you less prone to taking on bad ideas, it just makes you better at defending them to other people and to yourself. Smart people can believe some truly ridiculous things, and then deploy all the reason and logic at their disposal to justify them, because a belief doesn't begin in your mind. It begins in your feelings."

The Magnus Archives, Episode 153: Love Bombing, Written and narrated by Jonathan Sims

"Never bite a gift horse in the mouth."

Catherine N'Komba, Agile Software Development Coach, Project Management Consultant, and beloved sister to Jim Guerra

Introduction to the Second Edition

Since publishing this book in 2000, I have been pleased with much helpful feedback from my readers and have decided to incorporate these suggestions into a revised, and hopefully, more useful book. My experiences in following Jim Roberts, the leader of the Brothers, have been useful to many who have never themselves been involved in anything as extreme. They recognize whispers of abuse in their own lives, perhaps from a manipulative relationship, a legalistic preacher, or even in their own self-talk as guilt and a longing to be loved drive them. My ten years with the "Brothers" encompassed many kinds of psychological and physical abuse, all supported by Scriptural references, but not truly based on Scripture. By presenting this story, I hope you can relate to me as I was seeking to follow God with all my heart while being immersed in error. And if there is a villain in this story, it is not God.

My hope for my reader is that your discernment is challenged and strengthened, and that you allow me to make the mistakes for you so that you will not have to suffer for your naivete. I want you to read this intelligently, probingly, and with an eye to applying it to your life. Perhaps we all have had a Jim Roberts in our lives, though I doubt one as fully developed as my leader. He is a caricature of spiritual abuse, and my life the canvas of man who allowed himself to be painted upon by others with the cruel paint strokes of guilt and manipulation. As you will see, I went very quickly from being a confident Harvard student with a full life ahead of me to abandoning society into the cloistered and uber secret life of a cult. I traveled about 100,000 miles, hitchhiking and hopping freight trains, eating out of dumpsters, and only briefly contacting my family during the ten years I sought to serve Christ this way. The pain I caused others is incalculable; the damage done to the gospel is inexcusable.

Perhaps the greatest mystery is that God was with me in spite of the structures imprisoning me. I serve a God who looks past my circumstances and loves me anyway. I would not want anyone who walks with me through these pages (and might shout, "Jim, don't do it! Don't go with them!") ever to think this a book which only proves that Christianity is a scam. Quite the opposite. This book recounts the story of the distortion of Christianity through unaccountable leadership and unquestioned allegiance to mere men. It should in no way negate the positive experience shared by millions of people whom God has transformed by His grace, who now find freedom and joy in balanced and healthy relationships with God and fellow Christians. I am still healing now, but I am grateful to all the wonderful "normal" people who have taken an interest in my story and who have helped me reflect on my experiences and beliefs.

Sadly, Jim Roberts passed away of untreated cancer a few years ago. He sought no medical attention and suffered greatly until his death. The Brothers changed their leadership that year, and the restrictions on marriage and connecting with family and friends was lifted, and many of their damaging practices were ended so they did not have to carry the heavy yoke of man made religion.

Please feel free to email me at jimguerra1304@verizon.net if you have any questions about my experiences or would like to leave me some feedback. May God bless you as you go through the maddening book!

I

Section One: Fleeing From Babylon

1

The Capture of Sister Hannah

"It sure would be a blessing to get a ride," I thought, as I sat on the cold steel guardrail alongside Interstate 80. The lights of Rawlins, Wyoming, shined below in the valley. I glanced at my watch.

Almost midnight, I thought. Please Lord, get us a ride!

Shivering behind me was sister Hannah, wrapped like a mummy, but vibrating intensely to keep warm. Angry thoughts entered me like the Arctic wind blowing in our faces. The sister is just trying in the flesh to please God. She's not obeying God from the heart. She's just trying in herself to be godly.

I stared despondently down the interstate at the oncoming headlights. Blurred in the distance, they slowly came into semi focus, but dispassionately whizzed past, a rming my faith that hardened mankind was in his last days.

Here we are, hitchhiking at night, standing in freezing weather, and no one has enough love to pick us up! It was not God's fault. The driver who dropped us off a few hours earlier had offered to share his hotel room with us. I decided to hitch on, feeling obligated to use every minute of sunlight to get to our designated destination. Brother Evangelist told us to get there as quickly as possible, and I yearned to obey God's will in the voice of my leader. There were still about 1,500 miles left to go.

"Wild, Wonderful Wyoming" stretched before us like a monotonous speech - never varying, strikingly unoriginal, flat, unimaginative, and tediously long. Beyond Wyoming lay Idaho, Oregon, and finally the rainy coast of Washington.

We were bound for Everett, Washington, just north of Seattle, but we could not tell the police that. Satan used them to persecute the church. Too many people, especially our "flesh relations," were scouring the country to take away "the precious truth that God has given us."

Brother Evangelist, our Elder and example, had sternly warned me a few days earlier that Sister Hannah's family was looking for her to snatch her out of the Church. "Be very watchful with that sister," he admonished me in San Antonio before sending us together to hitchhike. "Be faithful not to let anyone take her and deceive her."

I felt honored that he had given me such a large responsibility. It was about time. I had done everything possible to win his approval and to escape the status of being a younger brother. I bowed my head and avoided eye contact when he spoke to me. I said, "Amen" to everything he said and rejoiced as if it were all fresh and edifying. I stood up straight, looked at the floor, and folded my hands together behind my back. I let him do most of the talking, which was usually brief and concise. He avoided "vain babbling" by letting his words be as scarce as the number of marriages he permitted. I nodded and crowed, "Yes sir," and then, "Praise God," at the appropriate pauses.

When he called me from the bedroom to speak to me privately, I felt an adrenaline rush of honor. He was going to tell me something important. Brother Evangelist only said important things.

"Be careful with that sister. A few weeks ago the Lord delivered her from the fowls. She was hitchhiking with Brother Garth and the centurions stopped them and checked them out. There was a missing person's bulletin out on her."

"Praise God for delivering her," I commented.

"The police could not keep her because she was of legal age, but they are still after her. Be diligent and make sure that you do not do anything to cause a situation. We don't want to lose a precious soul."

"Amen," I meekly replied. "She sure is precious. She has definitely been pressing in. She hasn't eaten for over a week." I admired her fasting, but her example fed my guilty conscience. I had been eating the standard two meals a day like the rest, but this new sister was really going all out to please God. She was fasting all the time, but she did not look too happy. She seemed scared and depressed.

The Elder continued. "If you felt led, you can ask the sister a few questions about the incidents on the road with Brother Garth. But do try to lift up the standard and limit your words to only what is needful. Some sisters, if you ask them a question, will go on and on if you don't cut them off." His "you-know-what-I-mean" look demanded my admiration.

"It really is a godly thing for a woman to have a meek and quiet spirit. Sometimes we have to help them to be quiet."

Back on the on-ramp my thoughts turned back to the beginning of our journey. I had decided to fast with Sister Hannah and to get some more specific information about her encounter with the police. Not only was I seriously concerned about protecting her, but it was a sanctioned opportunity to actually speak with a sister.

The Church forbade brothers to speak much to sisters. Those brothers in authority were allowed to speak in measure to particular sisters. If a brother and a sister had to speak at length, Brother Evangelist would require a third party to listen in to assure that nothing private or too personal was being secretly shared. This time was different, however. I had permission from the top!

"Lord willing, Sister Hannah, can you tell me about your run-in with the police when you were traveling with Brother Garth?" I asked.

She froze, mumbled something, and then went silent. "Sister, I worked it out with Brother Evangelist to talk to you. He said I could speak to you about this matter." I did not say it too confidently. I was afraid the sister was closer to God than Brother Evangelist was, and the Holy Spirit was telling her not to answer my question. Perhaps it wasn't really God's will for me to be talking to the sister. Maybe I was not being faithful to lift up the standard.

She looked a little more confident, breathed a silent prayer, and said, "Well," searching for the proper words and terrified she would say something wrong. She gave up in desperation and mumbled, "Please help me, Jesus!"

I was starting to feel very guilty for asking the question. She then carefully explained, editing her speech to be as frugal with her words as possible. "Lord willing, the police checked us out and my name was on that machine. They called my flesh relations, but the police refused to hold us. We went back out to the road, and the Lord got us a ride almost immediately. Praise God," she said, with the muted enthusiasm of one constrained by a mountain of guilt.

"Yes," I said. "The Lord is really merciful. He really delivered you." I took advantage of the liberty to speak to her, but I had to reassure myself constantly that it was okay. Her cold, short answers make me feel insecure.

On the second day of our journey, a man offered us lemonade to take away the cotton-mouthed smell we had gotten from fasting. He insisted, we refused, he persisted, we accepted. It took some time to decide if drinking the lemonade was breaking the fast and if we offended God by drinking it. After all, I had vowed to fast for three days if He would promise not to cast me out of His church, the minuscule vagabond Christian ministry I had dropped out of Harvard two years earlier to join. I did not want to leave the group because I did not want to go to Hell.

On the third day we arrived at Rawlins, Wyoming, around sunset. I wrestled furiously whether to try to go further that night, or to accept the kindly newlywed's invitation to stay with them in the Holiday Inn near the interstate.

Decisions were difficult to make. I had grown accustomed to older brothers making them for me since I had joined the group. What liberty, what security, knowing that you have older brothers who could make decisions for you that you do not want to make for yourself! No more would I have to bear such responsibility for my life. The older brothers were eager to lead me.

From Dean's List to Dumpsters: Why I Left Harvard to Join a Cult

The couple had picked us up about 250 miles east of Rawlins. They planned to stay in Rawlins for the night and take us on the next day. Unfortunately, guilt overpowered me as we went to their hotel room. I looked at it and realized there was no modest place for the sister and me to sleep. There were two beds, true, but brothers and sisters do not ever sleep in the same room. This was not lifting up the standard.

Taking a green waterproof nylon ground cloth and stringing it across the closet, I discovered there was not enough room for the sister to sleep in the closet. I was perplexed. How could I face Brother Evangelist and explain that I slept in the same room with a sister? Besides, there was still a little daylight left and I knew that I should always hitchhike until it was too late to do so.

I told the sister we were going to hitch on, and to get her backpack on and get ready to go. She meekly obeyed and without a complaint followed me out the door of the motel. As we crossed the parking lot I prayed, "If this is not your will for us to hitch on, please do not get us a ride." I then found a package of chocolate chip cookies in the parking lot and conveniently reasoned that since God had provided the cookies, it was all right for me to break my fast. I offered some to the sister and felt relieved but guilty when she refused. Relieved, because she did not want any of my cookies; guilty because she was still fasting and I was not.

We walked up the long ramp and stood under a light pole.

The bitter slaps of the wind made waiting difficult. We jumped up and down, walked around, sang, or whatever to keep ourselves warm. After an eternity of waiting I started to get frantic and to shake my thumb furiously at the hardhearted tourists who forsook us and did not meet our needs. "When were you hitchhiking Lord, and we didn't stop and give you a ride?" I would imagine them standing before the Lord on the Day of Judgment. I could not see that the Lord had answered my prayer by not giving me a ride. It was not his will for us to go on. This set me up for one of the most traumatic experiences of my life.

The frozen ground was patch quilted with snow. Below us in the valley were some large stone drainage pipes. They might be a good place to sleep. I began to get restless and obnoxiously waved my arm like a man hailing a freight train. No one wanted to stop. Then I looked again. An unmarked police car suddenly pulled over. Thrilled, I ran up to the opened door and asked him how far he was going.

"Do you have any ID?" he asked.

"Are you a policeman?" I queried.

"Yes. Let me see your ID. Where are you headed?"

"We're headed out toward Salt Lake," I blurted. The older brother in Everett would have severely rebuked me if I had told the police where I was really heading. It was a standard in the church not to tell anyone where we were truly heading. You never knew when you might encounter someone who was looking for the church who might follow us back to the "camp."

If I had told the police where I was heading and they found the group there and took someone back to the "world", I would have to give an account to God for that person's soul. It was a serious sin.

The first time a brother lied about where he was truly heading, I felt uncomfortable. "Isn't deliberately misleading somebody the same as deceiving them and lying?" I asked.

"Brother, you are just a babe and these things are hard to receive at first. We are just being 'wise as serpents' and 'awake to the warfare.' Samson told Delilah all his heart and the devil used it against him. Besides, when people ask us those questions, they are just vain questions to entice you into vain babble. Besides, there are better ways to respond."

"Like what?" I asked.

"Well, you can say, 'We are just traveling for the Lord,' or 'We are just like the wind.' Jesus said, 'The wind blows where it wishes, and so are those who are born of the Spirit.' (John 3:8). But the best answer is to tell someone you are heading toward that city; they just assume you are planning to stop there, although you didn't actually say that."

A few days after the brother had explained that to me, I saw it in action. Brother Joseph and I had gotten a ride with a man on Interstate 95 headed north toward Boston. Joseph was a gentle but strong farm boy from the Midwest; very soft spoken and meek, devoted to prayer and reading the Bible. He bore a quiet strength and integrity as a warrior might carry a shield to battle. Sadly, they instructed even Joseph to be dishonest.

"Where are you headed?" asked the friendly young man as we got into his car.

"Oh, we're just traveling," he evaded.

"Oh," he persisted. "Do you have any specific city in mind, or are you just traveling?"

"We're heading toward Boston," Joseph replied.

"Oh," he continued. "Are you going into the city?"

"Well, not exactly," Joseph squirmed. "We're going to the other side of the city."

The cat and mouse game continued. "Are you going far on the other side of the city?"

The man was beginning to unnerve Joseph. "No, not far." The cat's curiosity was satisfied, or distracted by our weird behavior. Either way, he asked no more questions.

A couple of days later I realized what Joseph meant by "the other side of Boston." [(Up to that point, I did not know where we were going. That was privileged information for the older brother in the hitchhiking group.)] Portland, Maine, was definitely on the other side of Boston, about five hours on the other side!]

The police officer shined his light on Sister Hannah. "Does she have ID?" he asked.

"Oh, yes sir,'" she replied. I had told the sister before the police stopped to cooperate with them and to tell them we were heading toward Salt Lake City if they asked. I felt since the sister did not know where we were going it would look suspicious to the police if she answered the question, "Where are you going?" by saying, "I don't know. The Brother didn't tell me." I wasn't stupid. I knew that would raise more questions than it would answer. It was also important that our stories matched. If I told the police we were on our way to Salt Lake, and she said, "Provo," they would immediately suspect us of being "on the lamb." Therefore, I briefed her and our stories matched.

"What are you doing out here on this freezing night? Don't you have a place to stay?"

"Well," I answered, "We are Christians and we live by faith. We are out trying to serve the Lord and travel to preach the Gospel."

"I see," he said. "The way you were flapping your arms and harassing the motorists wasn't very good. That's the reason I stopped." He wrote down our names and birth dates.

"Would it be alright for us to continue to hitch up here on the ramp? There is no traffic down there in the city there and it is late at night. If we hitch up here, we have a chance to get a ride. If we hitch down there we won't get anywhere."

The police officer smiled. "You can stay up here on the interstate if you promise not to harass the drivers and to stand in a safe place. I wouldn't want anyone to get hurt."

We smiled back, thanked him, and promised to do as he said. He drove on and left us in the cold dark night alone. I said to the sister, "Get you pack on. We should get out of here." The sister numbingly agreed, and we started to walk down the long on-ramp to the city far below us. I fixed my eyes on the storm drains, thinking they would provide us with decent shelter to bed down. I also examined the underside of the freeway bridge, but there was no flat cement shelf to lay our nylon ground cloths and foams on to bed down.

Returning to the ramp, I saw the police car backing up furiously with its dome light blinking and stopping where we had been just a few moments earlier. He turned on a search light and desperately scanned the area for us. Then, looking in his mirror, he spotted us down the ramp and backed all the way down to meet us. Meanwhile, two police cruisers from town came up from behind us and trapped us.

"Are you Cheryl Eastman, daughter of Carl and Sheila Eastman?" he shouted excitedly.

The question terrified her. Her hour had come. The devil's forces were surrounding her to pluck out the seed of God's word planted in her heart. Her eternal salvation depended upon never returning to the world and forever following Brother Evangelist. He warned us about these forces of Satan called the "police." In the name of her parents' love, the police were dragging her away to meet her persecutors. Fortunately for her she had been fasting and therefore could be assured of some help from God.

I was bewildered but exhilarated. Here was the test of my faith as a brother. The older brothers who had gone through the persecution in Tucson, Arizona, in November of 1975 had glorious war tales to share of the trying of their faith. Here, about three years later, was my chance to go through some tribulation for the Lord. This was my rite of passage, my stamp of approval. This was my opportunity to battle the system, using my natural intelligence to deliver the sister legally and become a hero.

"Did you have a history of mental problems, and did you use to get regular psychiatric care?" he asked.

Sister Hannah panicked and said nothing. Her parents used a false accusation to get her detained by the police. That shocked me and jolted my confidence a little. However, I knew she was not crazy. She was a precious sister trying to follow the Word of God. Besides, God gave all Christians the Spirit of power, and love, and of a sound mind. Her membership in the group assured both her present and future sanity.

The police officer handcuffed the sister and put her in his car. I stood and spoke to the other police officers. "What's going on?" I asked.

"Her parents haven't heard from her for over a year," he said.

She's of legal age, I thought to myself. "My parents haven't heard from me for a long time, either. That's not against the law."

"She has suicidal tendencies," he elaborated. "It's time something was done to get her back to her family."

What else could I expect? The police were on the side of the parents, and the parents were on the side of Satan, so what else could they do? I quickly thought about the legal options, but from my experience with the law, I realized that laws which were written and passed were not necessarily the laws obeyed and enforced. These local hacks could become little Hitlers if they wanted to and I was powerless to resist. What could I do when the police acted unlawfully - call the police?

I asked the officer what they were going to do.

"We're going to take her to the police station and call her parents.

"Then what?"

"After she talks to them she can decide what to do. If she wants to go on with you, she can. If she wants to stay, she can wait for her parents."

That sounded good. "Would you mind if I went with you to the police station?" He agreed and let me into his car after searching me.

"There's a little pocket knife in my front pocket. Would you like me to put that on the dashboard?" I asked, being as friendly and cooperative as I could.

"That wouldn't be necessary, he answered, "unless you plan to use it."

"No," I smiled. "I am a man of peace."

When we got to the police station, we sat in a main waiting room while the police went to call the Eastmans. The sister, trembling for the cold and the terror in her soul, looked down forlornly at the floor. I moved over to talk to her but she shrank away from me because I was a brother, and brothers don't get too close to sisters.

"Under the circumstances, Sister, it would be okay to get a little closer," I explained. She cautiously moved closer, and I took the role of spiritual instructor and supporter. I was the brother, and although she was not my wife, I was her "head" in the Lord. It was my duty to prepare her for her upcoming spiritual trial. Besides, it was an opportunity for me to share some wisdom and do some teaching and even speak to a sister legally. Someday she might even tell the other sisters what I had said and what a strength it was to her in the battle. A little glory, a little ego trip, a little recognition. Hers was the pain; mine was the glory.

"Sister, I encourage you to trust God in this. The devil is trying to pluck the precious seed from you. Be steadfast, and hold onto the Lord. You cannot endure this trial in your own strength. You need to trust the Lord to keep you. A sister once said she got through some of her greatest trials by just waiting on the Lord. Paul said, 'In the evil day, and having done all, to stand.' (Eph. 6:13) Do all you can, and then just stand."

As I spoke, the sister nodded her head and looked at the floor. She sadly went to meet her captors when the police took her away for questioning. Before departing from me, I told her what to do if she escaped. "If you are on the west coast and you escape, go to Portland, Oregon, and wait at the post officer. If they take you to the East Coast, go to New York City, and check Washington Square Park in Greenwich Village." She nodded and bravely entered the arena of her testing.

When I said goodbye to the sister, one of the lieutenants scowled at me out of the side of his eyes. I could sense the animosity in the officer. There was more going on than I realized, but I believed enough in the integrity of law enforcement officials to assume they were really going to let the sister do what she wanted. That was the legal thing. To my surprise, it did not work out that way.

The arresting officer drove me back to the hotel where the newlywed couple had invited me to stay. I asked the officer what was going to happen to the sister, he told me her parents were flying in the next day, and she would choose then whether to go with me or to return home with her family. I thanked the officer and went to the couple's room. They wearily let me in, tired but not grumpy, and I explained what had happened. They felt for me, but could not relate. The next day they drove me downtown and parted, wishing me the best.

Rawlins is a small Wyoming town that survives mainly on the oil business. There are a few oil wells there and the oil companies employ many of the local folks. The main downtown area has few buildings over three stores, a cluster of small businesses, and a lot of surrounding residential housing. If you walk a few blocks in any direction, you are out of downtown, and for what was about to happen to me at the police station, that was fortunate.

My mind was racing as I walked those streets alone toward the police station. I reviewed what I knew about the law, the sister's legal right to live as she chose, and my right as a citizen of the United States to exercise my freedom of religion without the government interfering. I examined their case. Legally they could hold the sister on the charge of hitchhiking because we were on the interstate, and Wyoming law forbids hitchhiking anywhere in the state. (The State Highway Patrol once commanded Brother Daniel to walk against traffic to the state line or spend a week in jail. A compassionate motorist stopped and gave him a ride anyway, and he escaped imprisonment.) They could hold her legally, and if they wanted, they could decide to arrest me on the same charge if I showed my face in the station.

I imagined myself as one of the older brothers who had gone through persecution in Tucson. I compared myself to them and prided myself on my wisdom and maturity. Before leaving the hotel room I had gotten rid of any notes that showed where the church had been, any veiled reference I had written down, and any maps that had routes drawn on them. It was important that I not only deliver the sister, but that I do not betray the group in the process. The Devil wanted everybody, and I could not risk sending so many people to hell by my slothfulness and lack of diligence in warfare.

I smugly walked down the street, one of the handfuls of people who knew the truth of God, and went to do battle with the Antichrist system that was trying to overcome my sister's faith.

It was a lonely feeling, too. I knew nobody in town. All the members of my church were in distant and unknown reaches. My family was in Washington, D.C., and I had forced them to the back of my mind. Remembering them threatened my faith, and I was in unbearable tension because I could not allow myself to love them instead of God. Brother Evangelist severely narrowed our choices: love God or love your family; love God or have a job; love God or get married. These were mutually exclusive. One could not do both.

As I meandered past the shops and office buildings, I said to myself, "Boy, do I need a friend!" As so often happens when I am desperately in need of comfort, God comforted me. The song came to me, "What a Friend We Have in Jesus." I smiled, "Yes, I do have Jesus." Just then, a young man working on his car looked up and asked me where I was going. This was no time for evasiveness. I began to pour my heart out to him, telling him how the police had taken my sister and how I was going to try to deliver her. He smiled and said he knew what that was like. He, too, had hitchhiked with a woman, and the police discovered on their computer that she was underage and a runaway. They arrested her and sent her back to her parents, leaving the man all by himself to travel. Here was my friend!

He took me home and offered me a bite to eat. I shoveled in all that he gave me, fully deciding to give up my fast and to make up for such a long period of abstinence. I washed up, hoisted on my massive backpack in the kitchen, and returned to the police station to rescue the sister. However, deep in my heart I needed to understand why God was putting her through this. Then my judgmental heart took over:

"The Lord is doing this for all her sins," I reasoned. "Whenever she says, 'Yes sir,' to me it sounds so phony. She isn't really reverencing me in her heart. She is just imitating the older sisters. Maybe God is trying to purge her out for being such a hypocrite." And so I went to rescue her.

At the main desk, I inquired about the sister. They told me her parents were coming for her. When I asked if I could speak to her, one of the secretaries replied, "She hasn't called or written to her parents for over a year. It's time something was done to clear up this matter. I'm a mother, and I know how badly I would worry if my children disappeared and didn't contact me. This isn't right." She choked back tears. Then the arresting officer spotted me in the station. He whispered something to the obese captain who then strutted up to me and fiercely shouted, "She's going back with her parents. You get out of town immediately and never come back!"

At that point, I dropped all my pretensions about being a skilled lawyer and instead grew chicken wings and flew the coop. I skipped and ran out of the building without looking back and walked a deviant direction to my friend's house, making sure no one was following me. I got to his house and called the bus station, inquiring when the next bus left town headed west. They told me one was leaving soon toward Ogden, Utah, and there was still a seat. I reserved a seat, rode to the station with my friend, and Greyhounded it out of town. We barely outraced a winter storm, and I scarcely escaped from the police. Had I hitchhiked, the police probably would have seized the opportunity to arrest me and show me the inner workings of their penitentiary system, my dream research project.

On the bus, I began to reflect on why they took the sister. She obviously was not pleasing the Lord; she was just fasting in herself and not God's strength. She did not really reverence me; she was just mocking me. The Lord was doing a good thing to purge her out. God historically had purged out those who were not doing well anyway. They did not submit very eagerly to the church leaders, and they often jested and talked a lot. Sometimes they failed to live up to what Brother Evangelist explained to us was holiness. Some people, Brother Evangelist told us, were foolish enough to leave the group and all its precious truth just to be closer to a refrigerator. God was not respecter of persons. If I did these same things, God would purge me out, too.

Obviously, the sword had fallen on the sister for her sins. I smugly stretched back in my seat watching the desolate scenery whir past. I imagined how pleased Brother Evangelist would be when he saw how diligent I was to try to rescue the sister. I had performed like an older brother and had not given away the location of any camps. I ate quite temperately, almost starving myself, so that no older brother could accuse me of gluttony. I also felt that somehow all my fasting and self denial was pleasing to God and would eventually save me. Life had become an endurance contest and membership in the group a condition for salvation. As brothers and sisters dropped by the wayside and left the group, we grew discouraged and thanked God He had spared us. We never knew if God would eventually cut us off by giving us a strong delusion as He had done to so many before me. Multitudes whom I thought would never fall became victims to the never-ending purge that left only those most dedicated to the group's goals and beliefs. Death stalked our camps, leaving few to stand. This God of grace was grudging, and hard, if not impossible, to please. Indeed, I had more compassion and mercy than the God the brothers portrayed. But on that bus ride the God of wrath, who ceaselessly cast frail and ignorant people into hell for misdemeanors, sat on my shoulder, listening to my thoughts.

When I disembarked from the bus on Interstate 80 just outside of Ogden, Utah, I stood and looked at the full stars overhead. They appeared fuzzy and indistinct because I was not wearing the glasses the brothers had instructed me to forsake two years earlier. "If you wear glasses it is a sign that you are not trusting God to heal your eyes," they explained. "Because it is not of faith, it is sin. It may be hard for you to receive now, but when your senses are better exercised, you will see that it is right. You are just a babe, and we have been searching the scriptures much longer than you have. The Lord even healed one brother at his baptism a few years ago. Just trust God to heal your eyes, and if it is His will, He will." I looked up through the squinting eyes wishing God had given me better vision.

As I stood there waiting, nothing happened; not a leading, not an inclination to go a certain direction, no sense of the presence of God, just aloneness, dreadful aloneness. I felt God-forsaken and rejected, without the precious consciousness of God's Spirit I had felt from the day I repented and turned to serve the living God. I felt a great blackness, like a child alone without a mother or father, terrified, hopeless, having lost his whole purpose and life mission in a twinkling of an eye. Something was wrong in the Cosmos. God was not with me. God had cast me off. God, where are you?

"You have been cut off," the voice said.

What? It can't be. "Oh God, let it not be!" I shouted to the heavens. Anguished, like a man facing an eternity of hell, my tears burned furrows in my cheeks. "God, where are you?" I bellowed.

"Has God really cast me off?" I wondered. I struggled down the embankment to the barbed wire fence, weeping bitterly, straining through the darkness of my despair for a glimmer of hope. After a few horrible moments, the presence of God returned and assured me that He had not left me. At that point, I was willing to do anything to keep Him with me forever, never to lose his companionship and comfort.

I stumbled into a nearby train yard and looked around for an empty car to ride in. Three cars looked very good, so I chose the one least desirable to sleep in. I did not want to displease God in any way by choosing not to suffer a little. I cringed and shook in fear that night. Emboldened a little, I asked God why this happened to me. I realized it was because of my evil thoughts against Sister Hannah. I should not condemn her for having problems with her family and with doing her works outwardly and not from the heart. She was a person, too, and needed our support and love. Who was I to assume that God was casting her out for hypocrisy?

The next day I arose at sunrise to hitch to Everett, Washington, as quickly as possible. Late that night I arrived, after getting about twenty-two rides of varying distances in one day, covering over 1,000 miles in 24 hours. Once, a man driving by saw me getting out of a ride, so he pulled over and gave me a ride! I got out of one car and jumped into another! By the end of the day, I was in Seattle, Washington. The next morning I arrived at the house and told Brother Evangelist the fowls had taken Sister Hannah.

At first, he seemed upset, but then he comforted me. I explained how I chose to hitch a ride rather than to sleep immodestly in a room with a sister. He reminded me that he had told me not to allow the police to check us out and that hitchhiking after dark was not wise. I felt awful that I had failed the brother. Then he comforted me with some good news.

A sister had reported a dream to him that the "fowls" had taken Sister Hannah, and that she had endured the ordeal and returned to the church. "It seems the Lord was giving her a great deal of grace to be able to fast," he commented. "She came through it okay in the dream. It was just through the mercy of God that she had some time to get rooted in the truth before the devil plucked her away to try her."

What a relief! This was God's hand, and the dream confirmed it. I just happened to be the unlucky one to get a taste of persecution myself and to be with her when the police arrested her.

When Brother Evangelist reported dreams to the church in the past, they were always significant. They told the future, gave direction to us, warned of persecution, and told us about "souls" falling away and leaving the group (with editorial explanations of why God had purged them out of the group.) Older brothers usually reported the dreams to the group after the event and used them to confirm that God ordained and had foreknowledge of the event.

When Brother Caleb had left a year earlier, Brother Evangelist shared a dream about Caleb and his family. "In this dream, Brother Caleb was in the back of a pickup truck and leaving the church. As he left, Caleb said, 'I'm going to go do things my way.' That is a fearful thing to say. We're supposed to do things God's way." We cringed and trembled at the warning. We would surely not let pride make us independent and think we could run our own lives. It was always safer to submit to God and Brother Evangelist.

When Brother Evangelist threw Brother Ezra out of the church two years later, he told me, "There was a dream about that brother smoking a cigarette and offering one to his sister. I believe the interpretation is that the brother was trying to defile his sister with slander against the older brother," which meant Brother Evangelist.

But when brothers came to him with dreams about marrying a sister, he acknowledged the dreams that were against marriage, but disregarded those in favor of marriage. "We can't be led of dreams," he would double standard. He would condemn brothers with dreams, but not permit marriage; he gladly used dreams to determine which brothers and sisters should be in which cities, but not in matters of love and marriage.

Nevertheless, here I was in a group of nomadic Christians, thinking we were the only true Christians, terrified and vowing never to leave the group or hold a job again. We were living under suspicion of our leaders and in fear of our families; hiding from police, parents and friends, and leaving behind Harvard University, my dreams, and my loved ones to follow a path of suffering, self denial, and alienation. The group culture had cloned me into a homogenized image of our leader. How did this happen? Two years earlier, I was enjoying my Christian life at Harvard.

Ten years later, I would shake my head in disbelief that an intelligent man like me would fall under the power of a charismatic leader and become a victim of a religious cult, throwing out my ability to think critically, and casting the responsibility for my life upon the group. I had earlier vowed never to join a cult, but when one came along it was everything I had been looking for.

2

The Harvard Years

I entered Harvard University in September of 1974, a few days before my eighteenth birthday. I had been a big fish in a small ocean at Frederick Douglass High School in Upper Marlboro, Maryland, where I was student government president, co- captain of the baseball team, and voted "Most Likely to Succeed." But as I surveyed the ivy covered walls of Harvard Yard, I sensed that I was now in the big leagues.

These were the best and brightest of my generation, young men and women extraordinarily gifted and motivated. I was among the future leaders of industry, government, medicine and finance. They came from all walks of life; Midwest farm boys who got up at 4:00 in the morning to feed their cattle and who still graduated at the top of their class; graduates of the top private schools in the world; and small town boys like me who dreamed big and worked hard. We had one thing in common: we were able to get into Harvard. As I stood among them, I felt profoundly unworthy of inheriting the honor as a member of that select fraternity. I assumed everyone there was smarter than I was, and all it would take was an unwise slip of the tongue and everyone would know that I was an intruder, not a privileged guest. By no means was I unique in feeling this way; I discovered later that not a small portion of the incoming Harvard class felt equally under-qualified.

My freshman year I lived in Holworthy Hall, one of the four story brick dorms that were at the end of the Yard, just a stone's throw from the Science Center. I felt so unworthy of my seat in the freshman class of 1978.

My roommates were stellar. One of them had two middle names and a Roman numeral at the end, and had written speeches for a U.S. Senator at the age of nineteen. Exceptionally well-bred, he proceeded from a wealthy Chicago family with New England roots going back generations. He was politically conservative and religiously liberal, smoked a pipe, drank sherry from his custom decanter, and attended prayers every morning at Memorial Hall, led by the Right Reverend Peter Gomes. He was destined to become a federal judge and head of the Federal Elections Commission and a personal lawyer for Stephen Colbert.

My immediate roommate, Tim, was an unpretentious son of a Connecticut oil executive, a straight A student, and very friendly and level headed. Rogers, the son of a progressive architect, also was a straight A student at Harvard, destined for a career in academics and a full professorship at UCLA.

All three of us had been student government presidents in high school, but I was the only one professing to be "born again."

Harvard was an intimidating place to me. In high school I could usually state my opinions on any subject, whether I had any knowledge or not, and use such elevated language that my classmates actually thought I knew something. At Harvard, I discovered that people not only understood me, but they disagreed with me. They scrutinized my words, challenged me to prove my statements, offered me alternative ways to look at things, and generally left me feeling stupid.

Harvard has a unique testing system. In high school, I had grown accustomed to expecting a test every week or so. At Harvard, I would go weeks without any tests. This encouraged slothfulness, because I am the kind of person who works best under pressure. At the end of every semester, there is a three week span called "reading period," when classes are not held and students prepare for final exams. This fed right into my play ethic, as I could procrastinate during the semester, make up for it by studying slavishly for three weeks, and pass my exams. This lack of daily structure was one reason I joined up with Brother Evangelist's group. I knew I could only perform well if I received pressure from others holding me accountable daily to do my best.

I moved into Lowell House my sophomore year and continued my strong relationship with the Harvard-Radcliffe Christian Fellowship. Harvard modeled its housing system upon the British system. Each "house" was a separate college within the college, with its own library, cafeteria, and recreation facilities. The students elected their own o cers to run the affairs of the house and selected a faculty member to live there as the "House Master." He and his wife gave a weekly tea and invited the two hundred students who lived in the house.

A large bell tower crowned the entrance of Lowell House and faced the Harvard Lampoon Castle. Lowell House consisted of a series of interconnected dorms in the shape of a square figure eight, creating two enclosed courtyards. The library was in the entrance next door to mine; underneath my room was a squash court, and across the courtyard was the dining hall. My room had two bedrooms, a private bathroom, a living room and a fireplace. Tim, Rogers, and I shared the room our sophomore year.

I was a member of the Harvard-Radcliffe Christian Fellowship, an interdenominational group that met Friday nights at the Freshman Student Union for a speaker and singing and divided into small group Bible studies during the week. It was during my sophomore year that the seeds of my conversion to the cult began to be planted.

It began with my prayer to grow in faith. I did not want just an intellectual Christianity; I wanted to experience the supernatural. I had read in the Bible how God intervened miraculously in history and in people's circumstances and delivered on His promises, leaving His quiet footprint wherever He found faith. I wanted to see that for myself.

Second, I had done a great deal of reading about miracles that God had done for people who were in positions of great need. I wanted to experience those things for myself. I hungered to see miracles, to sense and experience the supernatural. I felt that by being in a place of great need where only a miracle would save me, I could see miracles in my own life. Of course I had experienced the power of God's forgiveness and seen my desires and interests change for the better, but this was not enough. I wanted to see God rain down peanut butter and jelly sandwiches on my front lawn. I wanted to see God in an extraordinary way.

Early that Fall I read Foxe's Book of Martyrs. The martyrs' accounts of unswerving faithfulness to Christ in times of persecution deeply moved me. I read stories of Roman emperors feeding Christians to the lions and being amazed at the Christians' courage as the lions tore them in pieces; of men and women refusing to compromise their faith and being put to death by burning, wild beasts, and boiling oil. The rulers hacked them to death with swords, stoned them, and chased them from city to city. I began to think these were the true Christians, and I was not anything. I was ashamed to share my faith with others. I hid the fact I was a Christian from people I wanted to impress. Once, when standing outside the dining hall and giving away New Testaments, I hid my embarrassment behind my jokes. As I handed them out I explained, "Youth for Buddha."

My eschatology also played into my vulnerability to the cult. (That's a big word for "study of the end times.") I had read some unbalanced books about the Second Coming of Christ and believed that He was coming before 1988, just a few years down the road! It seemed logical that the only reasonable actions would be to drop everything and preach the gospel. Other authors suggested it was useless to build up a future here when Christ was coming so soon. I began to believe that the Biblical signs of Israel becoming a nation in 1948 and the increase in earthquakes, famines, false prophets, and war all pointed to a Second Coming in just a matter of years. Working hard and getting a degree seemed ridiculous considering Christ's imminent coming.

One Wednesday in March of 1976, I sauntered over to Chris Weinhold's room for our weekly Bible study. I was reluctant to go, having just spent the whole night up scratching out a paper, with another paper due in two days. The long awaited Easter vacation began that Friday, and I had plans to spend it in D.C. with my parents, family, and a few special high school classmates. I dreaded facing another "all-nighter" to finish my term papers and to please my academic taskmasters.

When I entered the room, a very somber feeling overcame me. I had arrived at the door laughing at some joke I was telling myself, but when I entered my laughter ceased and I felt tension and gravity upon us all. I then noticed that we had two visitors, young men about our age, with scruffy beards, baggy pants, and long shirts covering the crotch areas of their pants. I introduced myself and sat down across from them, eyeing them suspiciously, but not certain there was anything wrong. When the others arrived I began to question them. "Where are you all from?" I asked.

There was a pause.

"We're just traveling for the Lord and living by faith," Richard replied. He was the spokesman. Robin, the other man, sat quietly by him and stared at the floor, saying nothing, looking a little like a young Andrea Bocelli.

"Do you all live around here?" I asked, trying to break the ice and normalize the tone in the room.

There was a pause…sweat…and silence. Nervous anxiety filled the room as their awkward behavior increased. Finally, Richard cautiously replied, "Well, we're staying outside of town. We came into Boston to witness and met this brother here, and he invited us to stay with him and to come to this Bible study." He pointed at a freshman. I later learned that Richard and Robin had seen a banner in the freshman's window that said, "REJOICE IN JESUS", and had gone up to introduce themselves. He invited them to stay and go with him to our Bible study that night.

"Well, I said, "Welcome to our Bible study."

We probed some more about their lifestyle and Richard skillfully avoided direct answers to our questions, and instead began to quote Bible verse after Bible verse in Elizabethan English, speaking first in generalities and a rming many of the scriptural principles that I had already believed in. There was nothing new or radical at first. I felt like saying, "Yes, we know this. Can we please go on to something new?"

Then Richard got specific, painfully specific. "Jesus said, 'No man can serve two masters, for either he will love the one and hate the other, or he will hold to one and despise the other. You cannot serve God and mammon.' (Matt. 6:24) If you are serving mammon, a job, you cannot serve God."

"Are you saying that it is wrong to work and have a job?" I asked in disbelief.

"No, I'm not saying it's always wrong to work a little here and there for money. But our primary work must be in the Gospel, preaching the truth to the lost before Jesus comes back. God is tearing down this wicked world, and He doesn't want us building up what He is tearing down. There are scriptural conditions also in determining the types of employment that are acceptable for Christians."

"Like what?" I was intrigued. Here was a man who transcended the realm of principle and could specifically apply the Bible to real life. Here was somebody who could tell me concretely and practically what to do to be closer to God. I had asked my friends beforehand what I could do to be closer to God, and the answers I got were foggy and useless: "You need to love your neighbor, and ask God to help you in ways to be loving, and so forth." These were lovely sentiments, but worthless counsels. Richard was being specific.

"The Scripture says not to be a partaker of another man's sins. (1 Tim. 5:22) You may not do work that makes you sin, or in which you are helping someone sin. For example, if you work in a grocery store, you have to sell ungodly magazines and cigarettes. John said in the Book of Revelation, 'Come out of her, my people, lest you share in their sins, and lest you receive of her plagues.' (Rev. 18:4) If you share in her sins, God will plague you, too. He is no respecter of persons."

This put some fear of God in me. I was so critical of my friends' spirituality at that point (and mine), that the idea that the devil had wholesale deceived us did not seem strange to me.

"The call of the hour is to come out of the system and serve God with His true believers, those who have heard the call to forsake all and follow Him. We must not be as Lot's wife, who fled from Sodom but looked back. (Gen. 19:26) We need to flee and separate ourselves before God pours His wrath out upon the vast majority of mankind."

"The vast majority?" I asked. What was this new worldview? My Bible teachers had been assuring me that many would be saved in the end time, and that we were facing a time of great revival. I had heard of thousands accepting Christ worldwide and God pouring out His Spirit in marvelous ways. What did they think?

"Jesus said that the last days would be like the days of Noah. (Matt. 24:37) In the days of Noah only eight people got onto the boat: Noah, his three sons, and their four wives. Jesus also said, 'Strait is the gate and narrow is the way that leads to life and few there be that find it.' (Matt. 7:14) So it won't be a vast multitude, but just a handful of people living right that are going to be saved, those who have forsaken all." (Luke 14:33)

They challenged me and fascinated me. There was a Bible verse to support everything they said. They were not greedy, covetous cult members. These men had given everything up for the Lord and were living in poverty, selflessly dedicating themselves to preaching the Word, suffering in the elements, and taking a strong stance against sin.

And deep down there was something appealing about their doctrine. It was a call to suffer, to sacrifice, to adventure, to life; a call that appealed to my idealism, my romanticism, my martyr complex. Here was a cause, a fight, a high calling. Rocinante was ready to carry young Don "Guerraxote" to fight his windmills. But above all, here was a price to that calling.

It had long bothered me that becoming a Christian in twentieth century Christian America seemed so much easier and inexpensive when compared to the cost in blood and suffering that Christians in other countries and in other centuries, have had to pay. It was more in vogue to join the "born again club," paste a "Honk if you love Jesus!" bumper sticker on your Ford Pinto, and continue to live a life radically conformed to society. Where was the persecution, the lions, the racks, the boiling oil, the imprisonment? Where were all the hard sayings that offended some of Jesus' earlier halfhearted believers? Where were the rich men who walked away from Christ, unable to pay the price? Why weren't American Christians persecuted by the world? There was something bogus here that had bothered me for a long time.

"Do you think God calls every Christian to forsake all to travel and preach?" I queried.

"Jesus said, 'Whosoever of you that forsakes not all that he hath, he cannot be my disciple.' (Luke 14:33) Acts 11:6 says, 'The disciples were first called Christians at Antioch.' So to be a Christian is to be a disciple and vice versa. You cannot be a Christian without giving up everything you have. The early Church sold everything, and laid the prices of the things that were sold at the Apostles' feet, and distribution was made to every man according as he had need." (Acts 2:44, 45)

"Jesus meant to forsake everything in your heart," I replied.

"Aren't you glad that Jesus didn't just go to the cross "in his heart'?"

"You're saying that I am not a Christian?" I asked, bewildered.

"I don't deny that God has worked in your life, but there's more you need to do. It's not God's will for you to get a carnal education here."

"What do you mean?"

"Wouldn't you agree that this place is highly esteemed among men?" he challenged.

"Why, yes," I confessed. Just a day, earlier God had convicted me for gloating about Harvard's superiority over Yale (which is still true until this day!).

"Jesus said, 'That which is highly esteemed among men is an abomination in the sight of God.' (Luke 16:15) God doesn't send his people to abominations."

Touché! A coup de grace of fine logic and twisted Scripture, too subtle for me to detect.

I was almost hooked at this point, but cautious. I did not want to join a cult, so I thought I would test them further. "Do you guys believe in marriage and eating meat?" I asked. If they answered negatively, I would know they were an end time cult. If they passed this test, they were bona fide believers. I knew there was a Bible verse somewhere that warned about false teachers coming and forbidding certain foods and marriage. (1 Tim. 4:13)

"Yes, we believe it's okay to eat anything you want, and that marriage shouldn't be forbidden. We believe the Catholic Church has fulfilled that Scripture by forbidding their priests to marry and forbidding meat to be eaten on Friday.

We spoke until 2:00 in the morning and then agreed to go to bed and meet again in eight hours. I was definitely in their crosshairs and they did not want their quarry to escape. Their message was fascinating but world shattering; it portended some radical life changes and difficult decisions, decisions that could affect the rest of my life. They both intrigued and irritated me. They now represented a romantic but bitter path, and like the Apostle John's apocalyptic vision, it was sweet in my mouth but bitter in my belly.

Chris invited them to stay in his room. When offered the couch to sleep on, they politely refused. Instead, they rolled out their ground cloths and foams, and chose to sleep on the floor. When they undressed, the paleness of their flesh repulsed me; other than their hands and faces, their bodies had not seen sunlight for years. They could have been the poster children for Vitamin D sales.

I rushed to my dorm and hopped into my bunk. The next morning, exactly eight hours later, they rapped on my door. I was irritated but polite, not wanting to face the decision I had to make.

Nevertheless, it was exciting to think about living by faith and seeing God provide. I had thought that by putting myself so at God's mercy I would see more miracles and discover how real God was. I also felt the immediacy of Christ's coming and the urgency to share the Gospel. But the Brothers weren't done with me yet.

"So, where are you guys staying?" I asked. "You did say there were more of you, didn't you?"

"We are staying just outside Boston with some friends, "he replied.

"Nearby?"

"Not far. What do you think of the things I shared with you last night?"

"Well," I hesitated, "it seems that everything you shared was scriptural. I really agreed with what you said about this place being an abomination to God."

"Would you like to come out today and meet some of the brothers and sisters, and kind of try the spirits?" he urged.

"Thank you, but I don't know. I need some more time to think about this. Could you come back tomorrow, and I will let you know?"

"Lord willing, we can come back. We'll give you a call tomorrow and come and see you. Just be careful not to let the devil pluck out that seed the Lord has planted in your heart. Oh, and be careful to obey the Lord. We have seen that the longer people wait to do the will of God, the harder it is for them to do it. This is your chance to go on with the Lord. Be wise and do not lose it. Remember Jesus said, 'He that doeth the will of my Father which is in Heaven, the same is my brother, and sister, and mother." (Matt. 12:50)

They spoke a few more things and departed, promising to call me the next day. I took the day to count the cost. The thought of leaving my friends and family was devastating, but the thought of my crushing academic load was not particularly appealing either. I wanted to grow spiritually, but I also wanted a Harvard degree. I wanted to live by faith, but I also wanted to positively influence my society. I felt called on and held back, torn by the risk of leaving but drawn by the thrill and romance of adventure. I slipped into a very somber and reflective mood.

The Brothers' words were poltergeists to my mind, haunting, shaking their chains, opening and slamming doors of thought. Like a pair of glasses made for someone else to wear, their words distorted my vision of reality.

That day I went to visit a friend at Salem State College in Salem, Massachusetts. From the moment I hopped on the Red Line at Harvard Square until I arrived at North Station, I observed a world that appeared suddenly filthy. Perhaps I was now divinely enlightened.

Looking out the bus window, I surveyed the garbage heap of society; the people hopelessly overcome by sin; and strangers without power or moral conviction, appearing as beasts without brains.

Sickened, I turned my thoughts to the choice I had to make. To stay in the world meant to become corrupt like the world…and what did the brothers tell me? "Come out of her my people, and be not partaker of her sins lest you receive of her plagues." (Rev. 18:4)

Yes. The society was plagued. I needed to come out of it and join with those seeking to live holy and separate. I needed to change my life and become a bold testimony against this fallen, corrupt world. If I did not, God would punish me with the world. Jesus was coming so very soon and having a career did not matter if He was going to destroy the whole world. The important thing was to preach the Gospel and try to save the endtime remnant. However, I had to be part of the remnant myself before I could draw in others.

I greeted my friend Betty at the bus stop in Salem. She hugged me and explained that she was very concerned about her fellowship. There had been a prophecy that the Lord was going to purge her campus fellowship, and she trembled and wanted to know what to do to survive. As we walked through the town, she pointed out where the witches were known to congregate, and she talked about the howling noises that often filled the evening air - howls that pierced her heart and made her fear; subhuman but of human origin. "The Lord is greater than them," I reassured her, "For greater is he who is in you than he that is in the world." (1 John 4:4)

She escorted me to Salem State College where she introduced me to her friends. The president of the Christian fellowship was pu ng on a cigarette when we walked in. "Praise the Lord," he said in an effeminate voice, and limply shook my hand. Another woman came over and hugged me warmly but sensuously. "Hi, brother!" she said. Then the humor began.

Had I been in a bar with no women around, I might have been able to laugh. Had I been anesthetized on an operating table the humor would have been bearable. But there was something about this collection of witticisms that seemed wholly inappropriate for those claiming to be

Christians. I fled the room with Betty to get some fresh air. This was further proof that the world was fallen. Even the church was corrupt.

I returned that night to Lowell House, crossing the street next to the Harvard Lampoon Castle, through an entranceway past the security o ce, and through the courtyard to my room. I knew what I was going to do; I just didn't want to do it.

The next morning the phone awakened me. Richard wanted to know if he should still come. I said yes and went back to bed, assuming that it would take them a long time to hitchhike the fifty miles to get to Boston. About an hour later they were at my door. "That was quick," I mumbled.

"The Lord got us here quickly," he replied.

He had brought Brother John with him, a kind and humble speaking man from Waco, Texas. We talked for a while and it became apparent that John believed everything Richard believed. This stunned me. Every Bible study I had been in was filled with disagreement about interpretations of Biblical texts. Sometimes they erupted into violent disagreements and shouting matches. But here were two Christians fully assured of the truth. They worked together, thought alike, and insisted that God had shown them the truth.

At last some unity! Finally, someone had figured out the complex and controversial Bible. Why did God bless them to understand the Bible correctly?

"Have you ever read the parable of the pearl of great price? Look here: 'Again, the kingdom of heaven is like a merchant man seeking goodly pearls, who, when he had found one pearl of great price, went and sold all that he had and bought it.' (Matt. 13:45-46)

Notice, there was a price to obtain the pearl. If you do not pay the price for something, you cannot obtain it. The price is to sell everything you have. Then, and only then, will the Holy Ghost reveal the truth to you.

We all agree on what the scripture says because the Holy Ghost has revealed the true meaning of the Bible to us. The reason the false churches don't understand the Bible, the reason there is so much division, is because they have never paid the price to obtain the truth. It says in Proverbs, 'Buy the truth and sell it not…' (Prov. 23:23) There is a price for the truth, and the false churches don't have the truth and can't save you because they insist on holding onto their worldly things, like their houses and jobs, their stereos and televisions, their fancy chariots and vain wardrobes. God has not shown them the truth. They are deceived and following the false prophets."

That was a mouthful of convincing rhetoric. Perhaps more convincing was that they were so confident of themselves and their teaching.

I had a problem, though. Staring me in the face and smiling was my long-awaited spring vacation that was to begin that day. My mother was in Washington, D.C. waiting for me with tickets for the inaugural ride of the Washington Metro train, the newly completed subway system. Some friends from the Harvard-Radcliffe Christian fellowship were coming down with me and we were going to celebrate collectively. However, the brothers had other plans for me.

"What do you think about what we've shared?" they pressed.

"I can't argue with a thing you're saying," I replied. "It's all out of the Scriptures."

"Yes, and to follow God is to follow the Word of God. The Spirit will never lead you contrary to the Scriptures. The Spirit will always lead you to obey the Scriptures."

"Amen." I agreed.

"And the Scripture exhorts us to be doers of the Word and not hearers only, deceiving our own selves (Jas. 1:22). Do you think you would like to come out and meet some of the brothers today?"

"Well, I would like to, but I have a vacation beginning today for which I have been waiting a long time. Could I get in touch with you again in a couple of weeks after I have had time to think about it and speak to my family about it?"

The brothers panicked. John winced and inhaled deeply through clenched teeth.

"What's wrong?" I asked.

"That's just the devil trying to pluck the seed!" He looked terrified for me.

"That's the devil?" The thought was terrifying. I thought it was my reason, but they were certain the devil was planting thoughts in me to turn me away from the truth. I began to get worried. What other thoughts of mine did the devil inspire?

"Are you sure the Lord would have you go on this vacation? He has already shown you the truth. You just need to obey and walk in it. Let me share a Scripture." He turned to Hebrews, Chapter 11. "By faith, Noah, being warned of God of things not seen as yet, moved with fear, prepared an ark to the saving of his house, by which he condemned the world, and became heir of the righteousness which is by faith."

"How does that apply?"

"God is warning you, and by faith you need to obey and save yourself. Noah didn't hesitate. When the angels told Lot to flee from Sodom, he tarried, but God had mercy on him and took him by the hand and carried him out of the city. We have often seen that when people hesitate it is because they are not awake to what God is doing. Some have hesitated and missed their chance."

"I still need some time to think about it," I pleaded. "Maybe one of us can come down to D.C. with you and speak to your family, and then you can leave and come with us."

"You would have to ride down with my friends, and I don't think they would like you." My judgment was probably correct. "Would you guys, um, brothers, mind if I spoke to some of my friends about this and got their counsel?" I was looking for a way out, although I knew they had trapped me.

"Not at all. Just make sure it is godly counsel. A true Christian will always encourage you to obey the Scriptures."

I could not think of anyone who could give me godly counsel. They were all in the world and caught up in school. But the brothers were sold out and living for Christ.

I crossed the courtyard to the dining hall and ate lunch. At the salad bar I made a couple of egg salad sandwiches to smuggle back to the brothers. Before I got back, however, I stopped at the room of a friend in the fellowship. I knocked at the door and waited for him to come. Inside I could hear someone typing, but he seemed impervious to my rapping. I persisted, but there was no answer. Finally, I walked back to my room, confident the Lord did not want me to speak to my friend.

They pleaded with me more. "One man said to Jesus, 'I will follow thee whithersoever thou goest.' Jesus replied, 'The foxes have holes, the birds of the air have nests, but the Son of Man hath not where to lay his head.' (Matt. 8:20) We don't believe that following Jesus is a life of luxury. You must be willing to follow him and forsake all. Jesus didn't have a place to lay his head, and he said, 'The disciple is not above his master, nor a servant above his lord.' (Matt. 10:24) But if you look at the churches, they live far above their Master."

"That's true," I admitted. "But I still think I should speak with my parents first about what I am doing so they won't worry."

John replied, "Have you ever read this verse? 'And another also said, 'Lord, I will follow you, but first let me go and bid them farewell that are at my house. But Jesus said to him, no one, having put his hand to the plow, and looking back, is fit for the kingdom of God." (Luke 9:62)

I hated that verse because it trapped me.

"Remember Jesus said if we sought to save our lives we would lose them, and if we lose our lives for His sake, we would find them." (Matt. 16:25)

Another nail in my con.

"Jesus said, 'A man's foes would be they of his own household.' (Matt. 16:25) Although your family may never throw you to the lions, since God is dealing with you about coming out of this evil world, and since He is not dealing with them, there is no way they'll be able to understand what God is calling you to do. They will try to persuade you to stay at Harvard and you will not be saved unless you obey the light you have been given."

The Gospel depressed me for the first time in my life. Decision weighed on me like a Goliath, and pressed me like a screaming baby demanding immediate pacifying. What had begun as an idle curiosity about some itinerant Christian's lifestyle had evolved into a life and death decision that would determine my eternal existence.

Out of the arsenal came the final arrow, a magnetic thought. I was idealistic. I loved adventure. I was drawn to do noble deeds and sacrifice for a cause. The internal martyr jumped for joy at the thought of dying for God's purpose.

"By faith Abraham obeyed when he was called to go out to the place which he would afterward receive as an inheritance. And he went out not knowing where he was going." (Heb. 11:8)

"God's people throughout the ages have suffered. It says in Hebrews, 'And others were tortured, not accepting deliverance, that they might obtain a better resurrection. Still others had trials of mocking and scourging, yes, and of chains and imprisonment. They were stoned, they were sawn in two, tempted, were slain with the sword. They wandered about in sheepskins and goatskins, being destitute, afflicted, tormented - of whom the world was not worthy. They wandered in deserts and mountains, in dens and caves of the earth.'" (Heb. 11:35-38)

"You can see that God's people did not live comfortable lives. They suffered, and all who will live godly in Christ Jesus will suffer also."

"I hear my Master's voice," I admitted. A true Christian life was never easy. My life at Harvard was too easy, and therefore something was wrong. These young men had really paid the price and God had blessed them with an excellent understanding of the Bible.

I, however, was out of whack with the Universe. They were not afraid to confront the hard sayings as my friends were. They were living by "…every word that proceedeth out of the mouth of God." (Matt. 4:4)

Here was God's answer to my heartfelt cry to know Him deeply and intimately. It was time to flee Babylon, the world, to go to Zion, the Church.

3

Stepping Back Into The First Century

I reached for my contact lens case. Richard smiled. "You won't be needing those." Reflecting on the harsh manner of outdoor life I was facing, I realized that maintaining contact lenses was a little unrealistic. No money to buy chemicals to clean them, the possibility of losing them… No. Glasses made more sense.

As we walked past the Jesus Bookstore toward U.S. 1 to hitchhike, I felt apprehensive but excited. I was free at last, with no more term papers to write and no more Ivy League pretensions. Tramping out into the unknown and unfamiliar, I embraced the thrill. Then I asked Richard, "Do the brothers and sisters wear glasses?"

"That's between you and the Lord," he replied. "Most of the brethren trust God to heal their eyes. When the church baptized one brother, his glasses fell off when the older brother dunked him in the river, and when he came out of the water, his eyesight was restored. He wore real thick classes, but the Lord honored his faith and healed him. He hasn't worn glasses since then."

I was uncomfortable with that answer, but I was willing to do anything the Lord wanted me to do. "Oh, well, I guess we walk by faith and not by sight," I half-joked. Richard politely smiled, but did not laugh. That raised another question.

"Do you guys believe in joking - I mean, like spiritual joking? Sometimes I use Scriptures in funny ways. Is that okay?" I was the eager but inexperienced disciple trying to understand the group's social norms so I would fit in. I also felt they understood righteousness better than I did and their insights could make me a better person.

Richard smiled. "Sure, we rejoice in the Lord. But we prefer to rejoice in spiritual things."

I was not ready to give up my sense of humor and I think he realized it. To them I was just a carnal little spiritual baby they would have to babysit until I grew up to their maturity. I was beloved, but annoying; put up with until I learned the group's ways and could become like them. A little joking could be tolerated and even expected. However, the brothers would have to carefully watch me to make sure that my personality did not provoke others to such degrees of "foolishness."

"You said you were an older brother. How long have you been with the group?" I asked. I had been a Christian for about two-and-a-half years and I wanted to figure out where I would fit into the group's pecking order. If Richard was in a place of authority, and I was a Christian as long as he was, would I be required to have some authority in the group when I joined? Would they expect a lot from me? Don't they understand there are a lot of things I don't know?

"About three and a half years," he replied. "Are you one of the older brothers?"

"There are several older brothers in the group. One brother has been in the group for about five years. He is really a blessing, a true servant."

"Who is the leader?," I asked.

"The Lord is the head of the Church."

"Yes, I know, but don't you have a leader or a pastor or something?"

"We do have a number of older brothers who are good examples to us. The older brother is a very good example to us. He would be willing to die for the brothers. He lives just like the rest of us. If there is a warm sleeping bag and a bag that is not as warm, he will give you the warm bag and sleep cold. He always sacrifices for the brothers." I wanted to follow that kind of spiritual leader.

We pushed on to Route 1 and proceeded to hitchhike north. To my right, I noticed a huge water tank, and the word "GRACE" painted in huge letters across its face. It was a sign from God. He was showing me grace, and by His grace, I was going to go through with following Him. Sure, it was difficult. Wasn't it supposed to be? Here I was, following this young man to an unknown destination, leaving everything I had worked for and loved, feeling like God had specially selected me to know His truth.

We got about three rides, and the last driver let us off a block from a small apartment building in Fitchburg, Massachusetts. Richard had witnessed to some of the drivers, not being pushy, but willing to make a stand for his faith. In my mind, though, he was not adamant enough with the great truth he had.

We walked up to the door and a kindly man opened the door and very warmly said, "Praise God," and let us in. I said, "Praise God" back, but felt awkward. We entered a large room that had two long wooden tables that filled it like an over furnished tree house. Seated at the tables and standing around the room were a variety of men, all dressed in shirts hanging down to their loins, sporting beards and sober countenances. My first impression was that I had stepped back nineteen centuries to New Testament Palestine or across the continent to the Rockies, and had found a convention of mountain men.

From Dean's List to Dumpsters: Why I Left Harvard to Join a Cult

One by one they approached me and introduced themselves. "Praise God," they each said as they shook my hand, or "Lord bless you, brother." Richard told me their names, each name adorned with the title "brother." They were enthusiastic about the Lord adding me to their group and very encouraged that He still was able to bring "souls" out of the world in such a late hour. The Lord's coming was just around the corner and the door to salvation was almost completely shut. Few were willing to hear the true Gospel message, and when someone did, the good news went viral through the group.

We entered the kitchen and what I saw shocked me.

Standing around a large cauldron were two young women in long dresses, happily stirring the evening's stew and peacefully enjoying each other's company. Their faces spelled "submission," and they seemed quiet, but content. They saw me out of the corners of their eyes, but said nothing. Then Richard, contrary to all group etiquette, introduced me to them. They smiled, nodded, and said, "Praise God," and turned back to their stew, eyes floorward, obviously pleased but a little embarrassed that Richard had drawn them into an infraction.

I was mesmerized by them, staring and taking in the beauty of what I saw. Their long dresses reminded me of Amish women I had seen, but they did not wear what I considered the hideous Amish coverings over their hair. Esther was fifteen and beautiful, playfully freckled and shy, her overflowing black hair cascading past her waist. Joanna was sweet and glowed with a warmth and meekness, a tough Midwestern farm girl who had cheerfully adopted the way of the group and who was devoted to principle and service, truly one of the finest women I have ever known.

Perceiving my interest in the women, an older brother tried to get me out of the kitchen. I would not move. He indirectly suggested I should go into another room, but I assured him I was happy there. Then Richard asked me if I wanted to help bring some food in, and I agreed. The car had arrived with about four brothers in it, the trunk filled to overflowing with boxes of vegetables, fruit, yogurt, bread, donuts and potato chips. I wondered where it had come from, but that did not matter. These people were well organized and e cient. They knew what they were doing, and I trusted their experience and resourcefulness.

I walked into the kitchen loaded like an uncovered dump truck with a large wooden box of canned goods Sister Eunice, Esther's mother, met me with a smile, and our relationship began with the words, "May I help you?" She was like a mother to the group, the hardiest and strongest woman on the far side of midlife crisis I had ever met. Like Esther, her daughter, Eunice's hair was long and thick, silver streaked at the temples. Being of Native American descent, Eunice was adorned with the high cheekbones and large brown eyes of her Winnebago tribe. She and Esther, I later learned, had joined the group a few months after Eunice's older son, Silas, met the group in a park. Silas persuaded almost the entire family to come to the group. Eunice left her husband behind because the brothers had convinced her that her marriage was really adultery since her husband was previously married, and they would go to hell if they continued the relationship.

I asked Eunice where to stack the food. She was a bit embarrassed because I put her in the awkward position of telling a man how to do something. I was later instructed that this was contrary to the order of God and the group. She understood that I was a new brother and she just waited until an older brother intervened and directed me to the place.

I sensed that there was an order in the group that brothers just did not talk to sisters at will, so I began to look for excuses to speak to them. I asked them harmless questions just to speak to them. The older brothers tolerated this for a short while, but soon made it clear that I needed to cooperate and reform my behavior.

The whole experience was a culture shock. I saw a couple of brothers lying on a mattress in a dark hallway, appearing to be sleeping, but really meditating and praying. Opened Bibles were being read everywhere. Brothers and sisters had written Bible verses on large sheets of butcher paper, cardboard, and paper plates and had nailed them to the walls. I squinted across the room and examined the kind man who had opened the door. No one had to tell me he was the Elder. His whole being emanated power and authority.

I turned to Richard and asked nevertheless. He was the leader. Something set him apart. All the others were miniature versions of this prototype. He scared me, but did not repulse me. He represented strictness and righteousness. He appeared as a pillar, a stern but loving father, a surveyor who could set the boundaries for my chaotic life, an enforcer of goodness, a lion not to be provoked by evil doers. If I behaved, he would be a lamb; if I did evil, a lion, confirming my developing view of Christ as both Judge and Redeemer.

That night I heard him preach for the first time. The brothers and sisters oozed out of the woodwork of the apartment, some awakening from their sleep, others entering with their heads low in deep meditation. Before we ate dinner, we gathered for our spiritual food. We mobbed together, brothers on the inside and sisters on the periphery, to worship, sing songs, and hear testimonies of what God was doing in the church. One brother told how he had been addicted to a medication and had tried to get off it, and that the Lord, through the brothers' counsel to forsake the medication, had healed him. The brothers and sisters shouted, "Praise God," and applauded. We sang a few Bible verses and hymns a cappella, and then, after a subdued pause, Brother Evangelist began to preach.

"Let's pray that the Lord anoints his word to our ears tonight." We all prayed silently. "Open your Scriptures to First Corinthians 3:17-19. Could someone please read those verses?" He nodded to a brother who read, "If anyone defiles the temple for God, God will destroy him. For the temple of God is holy, whose temple you are. Let no one deceive himself. If anyone among you seems to be wise in this world, let him become a fool that he may become wise. For the wisdom of this world is foolishness with God."

After nodding slightly with his eyes closed, appearing to listen carefully to the Holy Spirit, Brother Evangelist began, "There is a train of thought here. We are the temple of God, and if we defile ourselves, God will destroy us. One of the ways people defile themselves is with the wisdom of this world. If you go about and fill your mind with the teachings of man, and defile yourself, you will become carnally-minded and God will destroy you. You can search and search the books of man, but you won't find any salvation in them. They are all carnal and foolish. We need to study the Word of God. Universities fill men and women with the wisdom of this world that is just foolishness with God. Why would anyone study a bunch of foolishness?"

The brothers and sisters listened and nodded in agreement, some taking notes, no one dissenting. I trembled. God would destroy me for studying at a university? It's a good thing I found this out. I was on the way to hell, thinking I was a Christian. What mercy God had shown me by bringing me to this group! It didn't occur to me that this doctrinal arrow was deliberately shot my way!

We then turned to the meal. We stood in rapt attention as the older brother "doing the camp" announced the portions. "Lord willing, there will be one cheese bagel apiece on the table, and one cup of salad. Raise your bowl when you are ready for dessert, and the sister will bring your dessert. Brothers can be seated first in the large room, and the sisters can eat in the kitchen."

The men filed in an orderly fashion and sat down on long benches at the large tables. I sat down at the end, and immediately noticed there were no napkins. I asked Richard about this. He said brothers carried their own handkerchiefs, and almost in agreement with a plan, a brother pulled out his handkerchief, blew his nose, and put it back in his pocket. An appropriate dinner napkin, I thought sarcastically. Then I remembered everything else that had happened, and that God had truly spoken to me through these people. I'll get used to it, I thought.

Shortly thereafter, a brother farted. I smiled and was about to make a joke of it like I always did, but I noticed I was standing alone in amusement. Farting must be a normal and acceptable practice in this group, I surmised with a smirk. There was so much to learn. On the table there were three one-gallon milk containers containing water, but no cups. I turned to Richard, "How do you drink water without cups?"

"Straight out of the bottle." "Everyone?"

"Sure."

It took me until the end of the meal to get up the guts to drink out of a community water bottle, and when I did, it was not as bad as I had envisioned. Richard seemed pleased that I was willing to drink out of the communal trough; however, I still did not like the snotty napkin practice.

Because these men and women represented righteousness to me, I was willing to believe the ordinary manners and social customs which the group ignored and sometimes flagrantly violated were just "worldly customs" that were "vain." The group showed no favoritism. Anyone could fart without being laughed at.

After the meal, I asked a brother how many people were in the group. He responded, "There are about a hundred, but there were a lot more a few months ago. The Lord has really been purging the church."

"What do you mean?" I trembled.

"We recently went through some fierce persecution, and a number of souls could not endure it and fell away. They were dragged away by the police and did not have the foundation to stand. They turned away from God and went back to the world."

I trembled again. God had "purged" the church. People who had been saved were now rebels against God and were going to hell - people who had these great revelations about how to separate themselves and serve God as an endtime remnant. How privileged they had been, and how lightly they had taken the truth!

The word "purged" especially bothered me. I had always associated "purging" with men like Stalin who rounded up the innocent in the middle of the night and marched them off to firing squads. I did not like to think this of God. However, in time, the preaching I heard transformed my concept of God. The loving and merciful God I had known became a cruel oppressor who made salvation unreachable and damnation almost inevitable.

A little later Richard told me that Brother Michaiah wanted to talk to me. I was nervous as I went to confront him, not knowing what he wanted. Michaiah greeted me with a winning smile and an authentic kindness that inspired me to want to be like him. I could see in his eyes a clarity and honesty and joy that attracted me to holiness, and confirmed my decision to join the church.

"Richard told me you were thinking about being with us. He also mentioned you wanted to call your mother and explain what you are doing."

"That's right."

"Do you think you would like to be with us?"

I nodded. Just looking at this brother's holiness convinced me this group was everything I had been looking for.

"It should work out to go and call her. Richard will go with you."

I wanted to explain to my mother why I was not going to show up that night in Washington as expected. I knew she was not going to understand my decision. She couldn't. God was working with me and revealing things to me that He had hidden from the rest of the world. She probably would think I had joined up with some cult, and I wanted to assure her I had joined a legitimate group. These people were fantastic. They had so much love and were so obedient to God. Their passion was to serve God, and this was my opportunity to give up everything for Him.

From Dean's List to Dumpsters: Why I Left Harvard to Join a Cult

As we left, a brother assured me he would pray for me while I spoke to my mother. they had all gone through the pain of breaking off from their families, and he knew how hard it was. At the time, I did not intend to leave my family forever; I was just telling them about my decision to join the group and would contact them later.

As we walked to the pay phone about three blocks away, Richard encouraged me not to tell her where I was, because in her frenzy she might drive up to Boston and snatch me away from the truth. It was better for my soul to give her as little information as possible. I reluctantly obeyed.

The phone call was short and curt. I began to deny my emotions that night, stung them deep and rationalizing my selfish choice. My sister answered the phone and I asked to speak to my mother. She replied, "Why, Jim? Is something wrong? Aren't you coming home?" I had to cut her off. I did not want her to become hysterical before I spoke to my mother. "No, Catherine. I'll explain it all to Mom. Let me speak to her." She protested briefly and then finally yielded.

"Hi, Mom. This is Jim."

"Jim, where are you? Is something wrong?" "No, Mom. I'm not coming home."

There was a shocked gasp and bitter tears at the other end. "Why?"

"I've met a group…"

"What kind of group?" she snapped.

"A Christian group. They are unlike any other group I have ever met. They are really filled with the fruit of the Spirit."

I could hear her gasps of disbelief. Was this really her son?

What was he getting himself into?

"Mom, I have examined this group and they are really following the Word of God. Don't worry about me. God will take care of me. Just trust the Lord." I had no idea what I was asking her to do.

She laughed sardonically. "Don't make me laugh. What God?" (My mother had converted to the Christian faith a few months earlier, and my harsh handling of my leaving shook her weak faith. She recovered a few weeks later after pulling herself out of deep emotional shock at my decision.)

I assured her that I loved her, that I would stay in touch, and not to worry. She tearfully told me she loved me, and we hung up, neither being able to endure the grief we both felt.

I was shattered. I had no idea my decision would affect her this strongly. As I walked back with Richard, I felt angry at God for requiring so much. In my heart my fist was clenched against Him in defiance, while I bitterly thought, "This had better be worth it!

I began to weep bitterly. Richard offered me his handkerchief. Fortunately, it was clean.

It would be a decade before I would return to my home, freed from the control and indoctrination of the group. That night I thought I would never leave. (And if not for the prayers of my family and friends, I might still be there.)

4

Come Here, Wife!

The next morning I was startled out of my sleep by the morning wake-up announcement.

"Lord willing, the camp is getting up now. There will be a meal in thirty minutes, Lord willing."

It had been a nightmarish night. A dream plagued me all night that the brothers were sexually molesting me. It was just the devil fighting me, I realized the next morning. He did not want me to go with the Brothers and serve God.

I resurrected myself from the cramped mattress, reached for my clothes, and waited to know what to do next. Around me, brothers were bent prostrate in prayer, doubled together like rocking inchworms, covered by their sleeping bags. Gradually the room was filled with the activity of men putting away ground cloths, opening Bibles, and arraying themselves for the day.

After breakfast I asked if I could take a shower. Since there were about thirty of us sharing one bathroom, the older brother told me to wait. A little later, Brother Justus shoved a paper plate under my nose on which he had written, "Lord willing, you can take your shower now." I wondered why he didn't just tell me and it wasn't until many months later that I fully understood. He was not mute; he was "speech fasting." Brother Evangelist had taught that it would be better for our souls to write down our communication than to always open our mouths and speak. After all, in the multitude of words there wanteth not sin. Justus happened to believe him and take him literally.

After my navy style shower in which I quickly wet down, turned off the water, soaped up, rinsed, and dried myself, I was told to get ready to leave. "Where am I going?" I asked.

"There are some brothers camped outside of town here that you haven't met. We are planning to leave the city soon, and we need to make more room in this apartment."

Later that afternoon we loaded up in the brothers' car, and headed east. In the car ride out to the woods I watched the beautiful New England houses as we rolled past. The adventure was just

35

beginning. What lay next? Would someone drive up and give me food? Would we see miracles? What great things was God going to do for us?

We turned off the main highway down a long dirt path through some thick woods. I disembarked from my "Mayflower" and entered the woods to meet the noble savages that inhabited them. I was surprised to see at the center of a clearing a large tent about twelve feet tall, and women standing around it. Nearby a campfire burned as the women were preparing the evening meal. Scattered to the right about twenty yards away were the brothers, standing around their own campfire to stay warm. Richard led me away from the sisters' camp to the brothers', and they came over one by one to greet me. I bubbled over with questions and admiration for what I saw: real Christians suffering and paying the price for their faith.

"This is Brother Matthew," Richard said.

"Praise God," said Matthew.

"This is Brother Jason."

"Now none of that," Jason said as he lumbered over to me to hug me. He wasn't about to limit his affection to a mere handshake. He grabbed me in a warm, brotherly bear hug, rolled his eyes to heaven, and said in unfeigned joy, "Praise God! Good to have you with us!" With the ice broken, I felt free to hug the remaining brothers.

Jason was from the Great Lakes area and had been with the group for three years. His Friar Tuck appearance and simple speech made him as non threatening as a teddy bear. He was the supreme woodsman. Girded in sandals and thick woolen socks and carrying a large Bowie knife, he would make a lean to from the surrounding firs, or carve a stirring rod for the kitchen cauldron. He carried a woolen blanket wrapped up in polyethylene, and slung over his shoulder like Big Foot carries dead deer. The comparison stopped there as I imagine his manners were much better than our Yeti friend.

As I released from the embrace of each of my new brothers, I could see the same love in each of their eyes (except for one young man, and he left the group a few months later.) I could sense the brotherhood in the group, although with it came a bit of elitism.

Later, I came upon a group of brothers "fellowshipping," and I decided to listen in and glean more of their wisdom, but at the outset, they sounded quite smug.

"Did you hear about the cosmonauts that Russia sent up in their spaceships? One of them mocked and said, 'I don't see any God up here.'"

"Whew," snorted one brother in disgust. "They'll discover there's a God when they are in the Lake of Fire!"

"Yeah," agreed another. "By then it will be too late. God is going to pour out His wrath upon them for their disbelief."

"Then they'll know there is a God," chortled another. They seemed happy in the apparent justice of the damnation of the ignorant Communist. I was troubled by their attitude.

"They just don't understand, "I pleaded. "Until I met you guys I thought I was saved, and I was really trying to please God."

It was as if I had raped the Pope in Saint Peter's Cathedral. Silence the weight of seawater flooded the forest. I had rebuked my older brothers. They did not like me rebuking them. I had to bear their silence.

I slowly walked away and found Richard. I wondered what I had done wrong. The silent treatment and the displeasure I received for speaking my mind was a signal that there was an authority in the group against which I was not to speak. The proper way to handle my dissension in an orderly way was to go to an older brother and ask him a question. He would straighten me out and I could reconcile my gut with my mouth.

"Richard, aren't they judging the poor cosmonauts who just don't believe? Doesn't the Bible say that we are not to judge?"

Richard looked down and smiled. "I am not in a place to answer your question because I am not an older brother. You have to ask an older brother."

"Well, who are the older brothers?" I asked.

"They are Gary and Robert. They're both married brothers, and they can answer your questions." Richard went away and a few moments later came back and led me to Robert.

Robert was an unusual man. Standing about five feet six inches, he had incorporated into his mind practically everything one could know about anything. Raised in New York City, he devoured encyclopedias like most kids ate ice cream. He loved to read and his mind cherished knowledge more than a guilty politician his paper shredder. In spite of his vast knowledge, there was a nonchalance and earthiness to him that made him fun to be around. In his humility he often assumed that you knew as much as he did.

Robert took my question about judging seriously and explained that we need to judge in order to discern between good and evil. We were not to judge by our own standards, but by the Word of God. If we judged by the Word, we were judging righteous judgment. So to judge others was okay, as long as you were judging them by the Word. I was relieved that I could get the discord out of my system by asking, and it wasn't long before I succumbed to the judgmental spirit of the group.

All along I was feeling the pressure to get rid of my glasses. I knew the group did not approve of them, and it was obvious some should fear the farmer's wife if they valued their tails. It was another step in a long battle of unsound faith against my common sense, and the desire to be accepted by the group prevailed. I took my glasses out of the backpack they had given me and tossed them reluctantly into a snow bank. How metaphorical of my new life; my sight thrown into a snowbank!

I spent that day reading the Bible and getting a better understanding of the group's doctrines. When I had a question, I would ask a brother at random, and they told me each time, "You need to ask an older brother." Brother John, who helped Richard bring me to the group, continued to teach me things about the Bible that day. A younger brother overheard him and told an older brother. In mid sentence his name was called.

"Lord willing, Brother John. Could you come here a moment?"

"Yea, brother," he said. He tucked his tail between his legs and shu ed off to be rebuked. He came back a few moments later with his head down and shoved out an apology.

"I'm sorry, brother, for being so proud. I'm really not in a place to teach. It was okay to witness to you and bring you to the Brothers, but my teaching role ended after you decided to follow the Lord." After that I only asked him a few questions. I was afraid of the older brothers and did not want to talk with them until I was certain they were merciful and benevolent.

Later that day I helped the brothers carry water in five gallon plastic buckets from the stream across the road to the kitchen area next to the tent. One of the younger brothers thought it would be charitable to carry my bucket for me, but I was offended because I felt old enough to carry the bucket for myself. He backed down and apologized. "Sorry, brother, I just wanted to help. Praise God."

That night we gathered for the evening meal, and Brother Gary led the evening gathering. We sang a couple of Psalms, which delighted some members, but seemed dry and unmelodious without accompaniment. Gary opened his Bible and preached a message about "pressing into the Kingdom," which meant praying more, reading the Bible more, and witnessing more. I felt the same power from his words that I felt listening to Brother Evangelist, and I marveled. "Boy, all these brothers are anointed," I muttered to another brother.

After dinner some of the sisters went off a distance and began to sing together. I looked around to see angels and to my surprise saw only women. Their sweet, polished harmonies wafted through the air and flooded me with the beauty of their sacrifice. What talent and grace they had! How lovely if Brother Evangelist had allowed them to sing at our worship services and do their own special numbers. However, he did not permit that. They could sing along with the men but not alone; they were forbidden to speak at gatherings. Obviously, that included singing special numbers. After hearing the croaking of some brothers who could make a joyful noise but nothing musical, their music would have been a subtle reminder to the men that the women had something to offer, too.

That night Brother Jason tried to explain to me how to put my blanket inside the cotton sleeping bag they had given me to sleep in. I listened with a puzzled look until he finally broke down and did it for me. It made me feel like a secure child again, being cared for by a number of wiser, older brothers. I snuggled in and slept soundly, content and peaceful in my new life of sacrifice and devotion to God.

The next day the fire fell. Brother Gary got us together and strongly exhorted us to get off our duffs and go witnessing. Although we were out in the woods about sixty miles from Boston, he said, some brothers had gone into town and reaped a new brother (me). The harvest is plenteous but the laborers were few. If more brothers did not start going out to win souls, the older brothers would talk to the offending members one by one to assure compliance.

I trembled. I did not want any of the older brothers rebuking me. I would obey. Fortunately, I was told to go on the road the next day as the Elder decided to leave the Boston area to go to other cities. At last, I was to see the country and begin my adventure by faith!

That day a brother drove us back to the apartment to prepare to leave. When I went to bed, I decided I wanted to travel with Brother Jason because I liked him the most among the brothers I had met. He was willing to speak to me at length, and at times, he seemed almost like a long lost older brother.

The next morning Brother Jason came to me and said, "Lord willing, pack up your things. You'll be traveling with me." I was amazed. How did Brother Evangelist know that was who I wanted to travel with? I concluded that God truly led him and had shown him to pair Jason and me together to travel. God wanted to bless me by giving me what I wanted.

Gary, Jason, and a few others gathered around a U.S. map from the American Automobile Association in a small room in the apartment. Wordlessly, Gary pointed at Buffalo, New York, and told us to meet at the Student Union of the State University of New York at Buffalo. A brother divided up the "road food" (food that would not perish on the road and was easy to carry), and gave each group a few things to carry. A brother then drove us out of town to a good spot to hitchhike on the interstate.

Brother Larry was traveling with Brother Joseph. Larry, in his previous life, had done time for burglary, but had faithfully renounced his old ways. He appeared eternally sad, but was really a deep thinker who had a lot of integrity and love for the Lord. Watching him one might think he was lost and bewildered, but speaking to him you would see that he had wisdom far beyond his nineteen years.

The brother let the four of us out and we split up into pairs, Larry commenting about the "rain trial" we were to have by hitchhiking in the rain. They walked a ways down the on-ramp and hitched apart from us. Soon a young woman stopped for Jason and me, and we asked her to pick up Larry and Joseph. She took us about fifty miles while the brothers witnessed to her. The brothers' boldness embarrassed me. However, the other brothers' silence was more embarrassing. When the woman tried to change the subject, the brother refused to speak about other things. To discuss anything but the Bible was "vain babbling."

Toward the end of the day we were walking on the freeway when I asked Jason if I could step into the woods for a moment. He said okay and I began to ask him what kinds of herbs the brothers gathered to eat. After all, since we lived by faith and did not have much money, we obviously lived off the land.

Jason smiled and said the Lord provided, and then he showed me a small bag of tea leaves he had gathered and wanted to dry. My stomach petitioned my mouth to plead its cause, and I began to ask Jason more fervently about food.

"Can we eat now," I pleaded. "I'm hungry." "We'll eat when we get to town," he said.

"Okay," I acquiesced. But my belly revolted the rest of the day.

That night we stopped in Albany, New York. "Now we'll find something to eat," Jason said. As we walked, I looked around at the buildings lining the street and Jason noticed a bakery.

"Wait here while I go to get you some food," he smiled. "But that place is closed. You can't get any food there." "Just wait here. I'll get it around back."

"Around back?"

"Yes," he said. "These stores often set their leftover food around back."

"I didn't know that," I exclaimed. So I waited until I became anxious and feared something had happened to him. Suddenly he appeared with a big smile on his face, carrying a cardboard box in his Yeti arms across the street to me.

"Is everything okay?" I asked. "What took you so long?" "Nothing. Look what I found." He pulled out some nice

wheat bread, some rye bagels, peaches, yogurt, and cheese. "There's nothing wrong with this nice piece of cheese, is there?" he asked with more enthusiasm than I was able to muster.

"They just set that stuff outside for people to pick up?" "Well, not exactly. You have to go looking for it."

"You didn't steal it, did you?" I asked.

"No," he admitted. "I got it out of the dumpster." The food looked fine and I had no problems with that, and he was careful to wash it with water from his bottle before we ate it.

I ate what I could, and we devoted the next few hours to finding a place to sleep. We checked out abandoned boxcars, but I refused to sleep there, afraid we were trespassing. We got into the back of a rental truck, but I did not like the corrugated steel and aluminum floor and was afraid we would be caught.

Finally Jason acquiesced to my suggestion that we sleep on the top of picnic tables in a small city park near the freeway. He had misgivings about the police who patrolled the park, but I assured him all we had to do was to explain to the police that we were passing through and just needed a place to hang our heads for the night. God protected me in spite of my divine naivete.

At about four in the morning the police found us snoring skyward in their sacred city park and came over to check on us. "What are you doing here?" one patrolman asked.

"We were just passing through the city and needed a place to sleep," I said.

"What's your destination?" "Buffalo."

"Where are you coming from?" "Fitchburg, Massachusetts." "What's in Buffalo?"

"Oh, we're just going there to witness. We are Christians traveling for the Lord."

The officer shrugged his shoulders and wished me good night, assuring me that no other police officers would bother us that night.

"Be careful. There are a lot of idiots out here," he counseled as he drove off.

"Who was that?" Jason asked from beneath his wool blanket.

"It was the police. They said we could stay here and that he would tell the other police to leave us alone."

"Praise God. He sure kept us from those centurions."

I went back to sleep, not quite sure why the brothers distrusted police so much. I guessed I would understand in time. In the morning, we finished off what food remained and went back up to the freeway. That night we arrived in Buffalo, New York, and went straight to the agreed meeting place, the Student Union building of the State University of New York at Buffalo.

We climbed the stairs of the modern facility, looking more like interlopers than students. Upstairs sat Joseph, quietly studying his Bible, staring off in deep meditation, startled only back to planet Earth by our sudden appearance at his table. I sat down with him while Jason disappeared to find the older brother for further instructions.

"Did you have a good journey?" he inquired, searching for acceptable words that older brothers would not label as "vain babbling."

"It was a real blessing. But the rain the first day was kind of hard to take. It was a real trial."

Joseph hung on my every word as if what I had to say was the most important message he would hear that day. He nodded his head, praised God, and went back to reading. He was laboring to keep his mind stayed on God and I didn't want to distract him. Soon Brother Larry came over. He looked sad, but deep down he was battling the most important issue in life, the salvation of his soul.

Larry was from El Paso, Texas, and had a criminal record for burglary and other minor crimes. After joining the group, he was arrested and tried for some crimes he committed before his conversion to the Brothers. Larry's trial was a laughingstock. Because Larry was unable to afford a lawyer, the court appointed him one. Larry then refused the counselor's help because the brothers had assured him that lawyers were the "arm of flesh" and that he should go to court armed only with the Lord. This offended the appointed lawyer, so he proceeded to outdo the District Attorney (DA) in prosecuting his own client until the DA finally protested, "Objection, your honor! Counsel is badgering his own witness!" Larry turned to the judge and said, "Amen." The judge acquitted Larry and he returned to the group.

Soon Jason returned and we gathered up our traveling gear and left the Student Union building. We took a bus across town and got out near a small public works building. Away in a distance off the road was a large patch of woods and a smaller patch beyond it after a small clearing. Jason gazed across the field toward our oasis of trees and pointed, "That's where we are going."

By then I was cold and hungry. There were patches of snow on the ground, and my leather boots seemed permanently glaciered. My frozen toes screamed for relief and finally spurred me to ask Jason if we could build a fire when we got to our campsite.

"Lord willing, that won't work out."

"Why?" I pleaded. I'm cold and my clothes are wet."

"It wouldn't be wisdom. The police might see us and check us out."

"But can't we make a small fire and shield it from everyone?"

"The police might see it from the sky. Police have used airplanes and helicopters against us in the past to find our camps. Besides, the older brother told us not to have any fires. It's not wisdom."

I resigned myself to my situation and followed morosely on. This was all part of serving Christ, I guess. He suffered for me and I must suffer for Him, and I must be willing to endure hardness as a good soldier. Safety was more important than comfort.

When we entered the woods, Jason found two trees about eight feet apart and began to clear out all the underbrush from between the trees. He was suffering patiently, mumbling to himself quietly, assuring himself that I would be less of a burden after I got out of my spiritual diapers. This he did not tell me. He was far too kind a man to hurt me or discourage me.

Jason strung a cord about shoulder high from the trunk of one tree to the other and then began looking for small pebbles about the size of marbles. He found about eight of them, and tied them in corners of a very large sheet of polyethylene which he stretched over the cord tied to the trees. Finding a few sticks, he made stakes and tied strings to the pebbles in the corners of the plastic. When he finally staked the whole conglomeration to the ground, I had my first polyethylene palace, a shelter from the rain and snow, a protective plastic pup tent, a humble abode that rivaled only a manger in meanness. I snuggled into my sleeping bag cold, and during the night my body heat dried the clothes.

When we woke up the next morning we discovered that several other brothers and sisters had arrived and had pitched their tents near ours. There were a few married couples sequestered a "modest" distance from the rest of us, and the sisters were off to themselves a distance from the single brothers. The older brother in the camp, Gary, woke us up with the traditional wake-up call, brighter and earlier than our tired bodies wanted. "Lord willing, the camp is getting up now. There will be a meal in an hour, Lord willing."

The men gathered in a small circle with the women on the perimeter. Gary moderated. "Let's thank the Lord for getting us here safely." We clapped, praised the Lord, sang a song, and listened as a brother announced the portions of the meal. The brothers lined up to receive a bowl of hot vegetable stew, and the sisters followed.

Halfway through the meal, I spotted a young woman with wavy blonde hair. Seeking an opportunity to speak with her, I went over to the "table" (which was nothing more than a piece of plastic spread on the ground) and asked her if I could have more stew. She said nothing, but motioning with her eyes, looked back at the three gallon bakery grease can in which the stew was cooked. Her behavior seemed odd, but I was undaunted. I needed contact with the opposite sex, even if we only spoke one word to each other.

Later, I asked a brother if there was going to be a dessert. He told me the brother had already announced it, and that I'd better hurry over to the pot if I wanted any. I asked the sister for dessert and she nodded, silent as a whisper, filling my bowl with a fruit and pastry delight.

After the morning meal, I scanned the sisters' area, wanting to know the names of all the sisters, married or single. Turning to a brother, I began to ask him the names. "The tall one with the thin face, what's her name?"

"Uh, Sister Phebe." "The sad looking one?" "Sister Hannah."

"Brother Andrew's wife? The one he addresses as 'Wife?'" "Sister Deborah. Why do you ask?"

The brother was getting suspicious of my questions because it appeared I was scouting out a potential mate. This was perhaps somewhere in the back of my mind, but not my chief reason for asking. When one camps with a group of people whom you call "brother" and "sister", you want some idea of who they are.

When I later asked Andrew the name of his wife, he scowled and answered coldly, "Deborah." From then on I realized that a proper brother ignores the sisters.

We gathered and teamed up to go witnessing. The older brother selected me to go with Brother Bob and Sister Phebe.

Gary paired older brothers with younger brothers, and each group left the woods in five minute intervals. The three of us tramped through the frozen field to the State University of New York shuttle bus stop. The bus was packed with students riding to the main campus. Like a young chimpanzee emulating the older males in the herd, I did as the older brother, staring at the bus floor and avoiding looking at the attractive coeds standing in the aisles or seated in front of me. New and angry thoughts filled my mind. Look at these women. They are all dressed like a bunch of harlots. They paint their faces so men will lust upon them and make them fall into sin. I can't wait to get off this bus.

We disembarked at the main campus and went to the Student Union building at the quad. Facing the building was a large plaza where students would study and eat lunch. Two long sidewalks on each side of the plaza linked it to the Student Union. Because there was such a large amount of student traffic there, we positioned ourselves beside the sidewalks and attempted to witness.

"Brother Bob, I'm not ashamed of the Lord or anything, but I feel kind of strange about witnessing. I haven't done it very much."

Brother Bob's eyes twinkled with understanding. He had been a younger brother himself, and he knew how awkward it was to approach people with the Gospel. "Don't worry, Brother Jim. You just pray while I witness."

Sister Phebe asked permission to go off and witness by herself and Brother Bob let her, agreeing to meet her back there in an hour. Meanwhile, we stood by the flood of students flowing to the Union, trying to grab their attention by saying, "Seek the Lord," or, "Seek Jesus while there is still time." After about twenty minutes of our holy posturing, a young lady finally stopped to listen to us. Brother Bob witnessed long and hard, quoting Bible verse after Bible verse, assuring the woman that Jesus was coming soon and that it wasn't God's will for her to be studying at a university. She was a sincere person, and listened intently and politely while Bob tore down her lifestyle, ambitions, and assumptions about life.

When Bob finished, I began: "I really want to encourage you to see God if it's His will for you to be going to a carnal university. I just dropped out of Harvard to serve the Lord and he has really blessed my decision by giving me peace and joy and a sense of purpose. He's really shown me that the wisdom of this world is foolishness with Him, and that we need to be studying His word day and night to enter into His kingdom." I flushed with pride when I mentioned Harvard.

When it was over, she said she would pray about it and would meet us the next day to know her decision, if she was going to serve the Lord or not. We further exhorted her to pray and fear God and do what the Scriptures say. She smiled, said she would, and departed.

Our work there finished, so we started to search the campus for someone else to teach. When we returned to where we were to meet Sister Phebe, we spotted a large crowd gathered near the center of the plaza laughing and pointing. I grew curious and went over.

From Dean's List to Dumpsters: Why I Left Harvard to Join a Cult

In the center of the circle were two medium-sized dogs, male and female, locked in mortal intercourse. The intercourse was completed but the dogs were still locked together as they struggled in vain to separate. Howling in pain, facing in opposite directions, spinning on their anal axis, they were uncertain what to do. A grinning student stepped in to help, poured a bucket of cold water on the canine junction, and separated the dogs immediately. They scampered off in opposite directions, howling in pain about as loudly as the students howling in laughter. I smiled, but realized it would be ungodly to comment upon the situation. I needed to labor to remain sober.

The day was over, and we rode the campus shuttle bus back to the woods. Upon disembarking, we found Brother Jason struggling with a heavy backpack and some large banana boxes filled with dumpster food. We rushed up to him and took a box, and he thanked us. Standing by the side of the road until there were no more cars coming, we made a beeline into the field.

Jason told us the police had stopped him earlier and asked him why he was carrying the boxes. "I told them I was gathering the food for some sheep," he grinned. "But I didn't tell him it was for God's sheep!"

That evening we needed to get some water for drinking and cooking, as there was no well or running water in the woods. Brother Gary asked four of us to take the five-gallon buckets we had found in the Dunkin' Donuts dumpster and get water at the public works garage at the edge of the road. "But use wisdom, brothers, Gary warned. "We don't want any situations."

This was exciting! We were going to sneak into a fenced enclosure at night, fill some buckets, and sneak away without being seen - just like on television and in James Bond movies. I chortled with excitement as we neared the facility.

We passed through a hole in the fence and made our way to the outside spigot, which we had spotted earlier in the day. No one heard us as we filled each bucket, eight in all, and loaded three on a pole to carry back on our shoulders. We must have looked like a band of natives carrying back a gazelle we had killed in the hunt, though it was not too pleasant to be sloshed with the cold water splashing out of the swinging buckets.

That night a freeze hit the town, and we huddled together in our plastic shack for warmth. When we awoke, I saw a new face in our camp - a young man named Garth - beaming from head to toe, fascinated with the group. I approached him and asked, "Are you a new brother?"

He smiled and introduced himself. "I'm Garth." Over near the single brothers' area was a large footlocker in which were a hatchet, some socks and underwear, flannel shirts, bungee cords, and various other paraphernalia suitable for outdoor life. Garth was donating everything he had to the group and, having decided to leave school, happily teamed up with the "brothers."

A few days later, Brother Gary announced that everyone should pack up and be prepared to leave that day. Some of us were sent to the house of one of the older brothers' parents, while a few stayed in the woods. While I was leaving with Brother Larry, I noticed the field was full of small garter snakes writing and twisting. I asked the brother if this was a sign from God that trouble was coming, but he rebuked my superstition. Later that day, Brother Gary showed up at the house telling us that the police had come into the woods and found only a few brothers, and that God had been impressing him before the police came that it was time to leave town. I marveled at how led by God the brothers were. It even confirmed my superstition about the snakes.

The next day I paired up with Brother Bob and Sister Phebe

to hitch to Columbus, Ohio. Our journey was terrapinical, as we waited for most of the day in front of the toll booths at Hamburg, New York. We bedded down that night in some woods a short distance from the New York Throughway and awoke early to the crystal dew of a bright spring morning. Almost immediately after eating our meal, we got a ride headed toward Columbus. The driver was a young man in his mid-thirties, blue collar - the kind that could appreciate a cold Budweiser and a rocky trout pool.

As I sat in the back seat with the sister, the man showed his proclivity toward Budweiser by turning and graciously asking me to pull one out of the ice chest at my side. I smiled and began to comply when Brother Bob's arm shot across the front seat and grabbed mine, pulling it away from the cooler.

"Uh, brother, we can't give the man his beer. We would be partaking of another man's sin."

I felt odd and excessively uncomfortable in the man's presence. He had gone out of his way to help us, and now we were rudely rewarding him by refusing to help him.

He seemed a little surprised, but was gracious enough to get the beer himself. The car swerved as he turned around in his seat to reach for it, but he later let us out when we arrived in Columbus, and we parted in peace.

That peace was not going to last long.

Two sisters "laboring with a sould."

5

The Fowls Awaken

We walked a while downtown and then boarded a bus that took us out to some woods near the Interstate. A shallow stream about twenty yards wide bordered the woods on one side, running underneath the freeway and towards town. We saw Brother Larry jump on the bus after us with a backpack of food foraged from the local Kroger's. He smiled and wisely disassociated himself from us while we were out in public. We did not want to attract attention or let on that we were part of the same group (although our fashion sense indicated we were together!). There were too many people out looking for us to risk being noticeable in public.

When I saw Larry, love flooded my heart as I realized that home is where the family is, and not a particular piece of real estate that had become dear through familiarity. Although nothing else was familiar in the strange city of Columbus, Ohio, I was secure with the brothers and sisters.

In the woods, we greeted the brothers with hugs and the sisters with holy indifference, and set up our tents where the older brother told us. After a couple of days on the roads, it was so refreshing to be back in the order of the camp, with the kitchen area set up in the center of the tents and the married couples a distance away from the single brothers and sisters. We chatted awhile with the brothers, and when we had talked enough, we sat around and read our Bibles, waiting for the evening meal.

A couple days later Brother Andrew and Brother Aaron went to an evangelistic meeting sponsored by the local college fellowship. A Jewish Christian was preaching to the Jewish students to receive the Messiah Jesus. A very zealous young man named Shor, about twenty four years old, asked the preacher why he was not using the Bible to persuade men like Saint Paul did but was using human reason instead. When Aaron and Andrew perceived the astuteness of Shor's question, they decided to speak to him alone after the gathering. As Shor was leaving, Aaron caught his attention and began to witness to him, exhorting him to leave the world and live by faith and preach the Gospel to the entire world. Shor loved the Word and decided that night to come out to the camp.

The next morning I awoke to Shor's smiling but unfamiliar face. "Who was he?" I wondered, hoping that some sinister persecutor had not infiltrated our Eden. An older brother introduced him as a new brother and was to be received into the brotherhood. I smiled back and said, "Praise God," and he nodded his head quite profoundly and said, "Amen."

That night we were eating our meal when some brothers came back and told us we were leaving. Hastily we packed our bags and began to prepare for a late night escape from the city. "What's going on?" I asked, clueless to why the older brothers seemed so anxious to leave. "Just get ready, brother," was the curt reply.

When we had thoroughly packed up the camp, buried the garbage, strewn leaves over the abandoned tent sites, and hidden the stakes we had made out of live tree limbs, we escaped across a broad field under the cover of night. It was exhilarating. Something exciting, something dangerous, something significant was happening. I turned to Jason and asked why we were fleeing.

"Caw, caw," he replied, imitating a crow.

"Caw, caw?" I asked, wondering why he was responding to me in bird talk.

"Fowls!" he said, taking out his Bible and turning to Matthew 13. "When anyone receives the Gospel, and doesn't understand it, immediately the fowls of the air come and try to pluck away the seed. That new soul has received the Gospel, and there are professing Christians after him trying to pluck the Gospel out of his heart."

He was referring to Shor. His friends from the college ministry were afraid Shor had gotten himself involved with a satanic cult that had taken him into the mountains to sacrifice him to the devil. Because the brothers had instructed him to be vague about his plans and the nature of the group he was joining, his friends became afraid for his life, frantically trying to save him. However, the brothers were convinced that the devil had stirred them up and was using them to persecute Shor and drag his soul back to the world. Therefore, we had to protect our new brother in Christ and get out of town before they found us.

We waited in the field under the cover of darkness while

Gary went to a public pay phone to call Brother Evangelist. When he returned, he paired us up to flee the town that night. I was sent with Brother Joseph, the quiet, lanky southerner who spent most of his time reading the Bible and praying.

We traveled late that night and finally decided to bed down on the side of a steep, wet incline next to the freeway. Joseph, in characteristic humility, offered me his coat to sleep on. "Thank you Brother Joseph, but I have enough. Is your coat extra?"

"Lord willin'," he drawled. "You can use it if you like." "Would you have anything to sleep on?"

"No, but I would be okay."

I marveled at the man's love, willing to give me what he needed to sleep on while I had more than enough.

6

The Arctic Baptism

The next day we arrived in Ann Arbor, Michigan, where we met the brothers at the Student Union building at the University of Michigan. They directed us to a small patch of woods about half a mile from campus. We stepped through some underbrush and were startled to find a camp with about fifteen tents filled with brothers and sisters. Among them was Brother Evangelist, whom I hadn't seen since I was in Fitchburg, Massachusetts.

The brothers came over and warmly greeted us with hugs. We turned our "eating gear" (bowl and spoon) into the kitchen area and sat down on a log. Soon a tall young man from Southern California briskly walked over.

He looked like a thin faced version of the Cowardly Lion in the Wizard of Oz. His manner was stern and militaristic, with a dash of friendliness. "Praise God, Brother Jim," he smiled as he embraced me.

I like him. Some had told him my name. "Lord willing, do you have any laundry?" he asked.

"Lord willing, yes. What should I do with it?"

"Just bring it here and put it on the log." I did so. Then the brother, whom I later nicknamed "Sergeant Louis," looked at my pile and extracted the underpants I had put on top. "Brother," he explained, "it wouldn't be edifying for the sisters to wash those underpants. Brothers usually wash their own shorts. It may cause them to have ungodly imaginations about the brothers."

I agreed. Sergeant Louis was a man who had no problem with taking authority of a situation. He had discipline, integrity, a heart devoted to obeying the standards of the group, and a burning desire to mother hen those under him on the ladder of seniority. He was not afraid to rebuke someone, but would refuse to allow disagreement from his pecking order inferiors. Around him I felt secure. I knew if I were subconsciously erring in the faith, he would detect it and straighten me out. He was an animal of Brother Evangelist's stripe - a kitten when obeyed, a lion when crossed.

That night Brother Evangelist gathered with us to warn us of the great spiritual war we were fighting. "Brothers, we are in a war for our souls. There are many souls who once walked among us, who once knew the glorious truth, who fell away and went back to the filthiness of the world. As the Scripture says, 'It would be better for them not to have known the way of truth, than having known it, to turn from the holy commandment delivered to them. But it happened to them as the true proverb, the dog has returned to its vomit, and the sow that was washed to its wallowing in the mire.' (2 Pet. 2:21-22)

We dropped our heads and tensed ourselves to receive some bad news. Whenever he spoke of falling away, it was usually about a member recently leaving the group. Everyone who left the group was bound to go to hell.

"We are living in a time of great falling away. Over the years, I have seen many, many souls become offended in the straight and narrow way and turn back. Some have left because the love for their flesh relations had been so strong. Others have left because they have not been able to abide persecution. Others have not been able to remain humble and submit themselves to God's ministers. When you get rebellious, brother and sister, and resist the older brother, God will resist you.

"Sister, when you cease to walk meekly and lowly before the brothers, when you lose your shamefacedness and begin to smirk like the harlots of the world, you need to get on your knees and pray. Our humble sister Mary was content to be a handmaiden; she was not lusting after power in the church, and God mightily used her to give birth to Jesus. There has been too much talking in the sisters' tents, just babbling and babbling away. In the multitude of words there wanteth not sin. If you want to cut down on your sin, limit your words."

"There has been a shaking in our midst. As you know, some brothers went into a library a few cities ago and were deceived. Those places are the pits of the devil. Those books have a spirit to them that says, 'Read me, read me!' Well, the brother that read those books is no longer with us. He was deceived into thinking that the resurrection was already passed. Woe unto you, brothers, if you let the devil deceive you like this."

"So we need to keep our hearts with all diligence. There will be storms to try our love of God and his church, people trying to drag us back to the world. Make sure you are rooted in the truth, and let no man take your crown."

We stared at the ground until the preaching was over. Some nodded their heads and knit their brows to cushion against the discouraging blows, fearing for their salvation, taking every word to heart and wondering if they would be the next to fall.

"But brothers, if you keep your hearts with all diligence and watch and pray, 'a thousand shall fall at thy side, and ten thousand at thy right hand, but it shall not come nigh thee.' Let's pray that the Lord keeps us humble so that we might receive the grace to endure in this war we're in."

We closed the gathering with a song and scattered, some into their tents, others off by themselves in the woods, to pray and relieve their fears that they would be the next to fall away. I still felt a little special, that God still had some patience left for me, and that He was not as strict with me as with the others who should know better. But I also dreaded that perhaps I was just ignorant of how strict God really was, and that I was only deceiving myself that I was standing in His grace.

The next day we gathered and the older brother told us to prepare to go on the road. We packed up and drove north to Brighton State Recreation Area where the older brothers had arranged for us to camp legally. It was almost deserted since it was the off-season. The camping area bordered a large clear lake plentifully stocked with all manner of trout, bass and carp. The waves of the lake licked the beach like a dog savoring a bone, lending a tranquility and beauty to our environs. An oval pavement connected the various campsites like pearls on a necklace, each campsite being flat and without vegetation, appearing more like parking spaces than the repose for the holy church of God.

Coming up to greet us when we arrived in Shor's car was Brother Byron, a tall, cheerful Oklahoman with a red-tipped nose and a heavy wool jacket. He hugged me and led me over to show me his tent. I have never seen such a large tent since Barnum and Bailey had visited the Washington Coliseum! It could seat about twenty brothers comfortably, had standing room for even the tallest brother, and seemed able to hold all their backpacks besides. Byron began to share some things, looking over his shoulder not to be rebuked for talking too much, explaining how happy he was that the Lord had led him to the group and how the group was definitely the Lord's endtime church.

"I had a dream a couple of years ago that I was going to be serving God, and that He was going to send me His people. It was a year later that I met the brothers and sisters and I knew He had called me to serve Him with the brothers." It was a compelling testimony and reinforced my faith that I had made the proper decision.

Later that day the brothers asked me if I had been baptized. I told them that I had, and that a sister in Christ had baptized me. They smiled but felt it was shameful that I had let a woman baptize me.

"Do I need to be baptized again? Was the first baptism good enough for the Lord?"

"If you're not sure, it might be better to be baptized just to be sure. It 'becometh us to fulfill all righteousness,' by being baptized. There are some brothers who were baptized when they were in the world who did not feel they were completely immersed in water, and therefore they didn't fully crucify and bury the old man. By the way, when you were baptized, were you baptized in Jesus' name, or in the titles?"

"I'm not sure. What do you mean, 'in the titles'?"

"When she baptized you, what did she say? Did she say, 'I baptize you in the name of Jesus', or did she say, 'I baptize you in the name of the Father, and of the Son, and of the Holy Ghost?'"

"In the name of the Father, and of the Son, and of the Holy Ghost."

"Jesus is the name of the Father, and of the Son, and of the Holy Ghost. The false churches don't understand this, and they are baptizing people the wrong way. There's going to be a study later for the new brothers if you're interested in being baptized in the name of Jesus."

A little later Brother Andrew gathered Brother Garth, Brother Shor, and me, took us to a quiet spot away from the rest of the brothers and sisters, and proceeded to share the church's teaching about baptism with us. I listened to his teaching style, wondering why it wasn't more like the popular dynamic preachers I was used to hearing in the fellowships I was in before meeting the group. With no humor, very little depth and faulty grammar, he expounded only the most obvious points, adding very little to what was already apparent to even the most ignorant and unlearned of babes. I wondered why he finished every other sentence with the phrase, "Praise God," why he felt dropping a few words from a verse was the same as explaining it, and why he was in a position to teach when I myself could have entertained and preached much better than he.

"Brother Garth, could you please read for us Matthew, Chapter 3, verses 13-15?" (Brother Garth? I was the older brother! I should be asked to read first!)

Garth scanned his Gideon's, fingered the verse, and began to read: "Then Jesus came from Galilee to John at the Jordan to be baptized by him. And John forbade him saying, 'I have need to be baptized by you, and do you come to me?' But Jesus answered and said to him, 'Permit it to be so now, for thus it is fitting for us to fulfill all righteousness." Then he allowed him."

Brother Andrew paused deep in thought and began to expound. "Praise God. Here Jesus comes to John to be baptized by him in the Jordan River. John forbade him, but Jesus said it was fitting to fulfill all righteousness. So John baptized him, praise God. Since it is fitting for us to fulfill all righteousness, we need to be like our Master in everything and be baptized, too. Praise God. 'He that says I know Him ought himself also so to walk even as he walked.' (1 John 2:4, 6) So if we say we know Jesus, we ought to walk just as he walked and be baptized, too. Praise God."

The study droned on with no interaction or discussion between the teacher or the disciples; all the communication was one way, and all questions reserved to the end when each of us was allowed to express privately our doubts to the brother giving the study and get our questions answered. We were told not to discuss the study among ourselves because being unstable in the faith, and feeble-minded, we might unwittingly deceive another younger brother or sister by bringing the "leaven" of a false doctrine into the Church. We had brought a lot of false doctrine in from the world when we came. It was vital that we humble ourselves and learn of the Lord, that we might be cleansed of the filthiness of the false churches and receive the unleavened bread of truth from the brothers.

Andrew left the main thrust of the study to emphasize a doctrine I had not yet accepted. The brothers did not believe in the Trinity, but in the Oneness of God. Trinitarians say God exists eternally as three distinct Persons, yet comprise one God. However, the group taught that there was only one God who held three offices, but was not three distinct Persons. Simply put, God is Jesus, Jesus is our Father, and Jesus lives within us as the Holy Spirit. "Father, Son, and Holy Ghost" are titles for one God, just as a man can be called "a devoted husband, father, and employee," and not be three distinct people. Consequently, when Jesus commanded his disciples to baptize in the name of the Father, and of the Son, and the Holy Ghost, His disciples did not blow it when they baptized in the name of Jesus in the Book of Acts. So the proper way to baptize was "in the name of Jesus."

His argument was persuasive, and I decided I wanted to be baptized as soon as possible in the name of Jesus. Later that afternoon an older brother announced there was going to be a baptism that day and we should all get ready to gather at the lake. Garth, Shor, and I got our towels, dry shirts, and sandals and marched down to the water where the brothers and sisters were gathering for the baptism.

Brother Gary led the baptism. He smiled and began: "There was a prophecy that the church was going to blossom in the Spring. Today we see that has come to pass. We have three brethren ready to be baptized and to become new creatures in the Lord. We know that baptism does not save us by the washing of the filth of the flesh, but by the answer of a good conscience toward God. Let's thank the Lord for this baptism and these new brothers today."

The brethren began to clap and shout praise. They were joyful that we were taking this step of faith, preparing ourselves to live a new life of sanctification and obedience to the Lord. Gary began a song and the others joyfully followed.

There's only one, one, one One way to God
There's only one, one, one One way to God
There's only one, one, one One way to God
Baptized in Jesus' name!

It's by the Holy Ghost and Fire One way to God
It's by the Holy Ghost and Fire One way to God
It's by the Holy Ghost and Fire One way to God
Baptized in Jesus' name!

When we finished that song and had praised some more, we began to sing another:

The Mighty God is Jesus, the Prince of Peace is He
The Everlasting Father, the King Eternally
All wonderful in Wisdom, the Lamb for Sinners slain
The author of redemption, All Glory to His Name.

Jim Guerra

It's all in Him, it's all in Him
The Mighty God is Jesus and it's all in Him.
It's all in Him, it's all in Him
The Mighty God is Jesus and it's all in Him

The Alpha and Omega, Jehovah, Lord of hosts,
The Ever present Spirit that fills the universe;
Our Advocate, the High Priest, our Righteousness and Power
Yes all we need is Jesus we find this very hour.

The praise and the singing were exhilarating, and we felt very joyful as we prepared to be baptized. Garth was first, and an older brother took him aside to explain the process. He smiled and took the wallet and other valuables from Garth's pocket to keep them from becoming waterlogged during the baptism. Garth gingerly stepped into the freezing water while I looked on, a little offended that they had chosen to baptize the brother with less seniority before they baptized me.

The water was icy. Gary slowly inched his way out into the lake until he found a spot deep enough to immerse the brothers. He trembled and breathed shallow breaths. Garth was noticeably shocked by the temperature of the water, but greater things beckoned and every disciple was called to suffer to fulfill God's will. Garth moved delicately out toward Gary who was trembling in the cold.

When they met, Gary privately instructed Garth a little more, smiled, and shouted, "I baptize you in the name of Jesus Christ for the remission of your sins," and then proceeded to dunk him in the water. When Garth resurfaced, he gasped for breath but seemed truly filled with joy for having been baptized. I followed next, went under the glacial waters, and arose joyfully, although fully jolted into another dimension by the frigid temperatures. Shor followed and came out shouting for joy. On the shore the brethren and sisters shouted for Joy and clapped their hands when each of us was dunked, crying "Praise God! Hallelujah! Thank you Jesus!"

When we climbed back to shore the brothers greeted us with hugs and a dry towel, while the sisters quietly filed back to the camp. We did not expect the sister to say anything to us on this occasion, though it was supposed to be the greatest moment of our lives. It would have been out of order for them to have said anything to us, or to have hugged us to congratulate us.

Back at the camp we stood around a great fire that the brothers had started in a fire pit, and we huddled together to dry ourselves and unfreeze our battered bodies. The very next day it snowed a couple inches, and we were thankful that we got the baptism over with before the storm arrived.

56

7

A Twentieth Century Judas

A few weeks later we arrived in State College, Pennsylvania, hometown of Penn State University. The journey had been long, and when we arrived at the main library, the appointed meeting place, we saw the brothers' vehicle disappearing around the corner on its final pickup run of the day. Jason groaned in disappointment knowing we had to find a place to camp ourselves and would not be able to meet the brothers until morning.

The next morning the vehicle drove around the library and the brothers spotted Jason sitting near the main entrance. Rejoicing to see him and embracing him, the brothers asked where I was and told Jason to fetch me and bring me to the car. As usual, the older brother stashed me in the bushes with the backpacks until we were ready to leave the meeting area. It was important to keep a low profile in a strange town.

The brothers dropped us off at the edge of some thick woods a few blocks from the campus and drove back to check the library for more arriving brothers. Another brother was waiting for us to show us the way back to the camp. Through thorn and thicket we trudged over mound and gully, dodging nettles and sludge, to the camp sequestered in the woods. When we arrived the brothers smiled and rose to greet us. The sisters smiled and looked discreetly away, putting their hands on their mouths, wanting the brothers to notice that they appreciated them, but not to notice too much. We set up our tents and after resting for most of the day, awoke to the dinner announcement.

Dinner that night consisted of cottage cheese for the appetizer, cottage cheese for the main course, and cottage cheese for dessert. The more mature brothers were able to shrug contentedly and thank God for providing this bounty. However, we younger brothers found it hard to appreciate the cottage cheese that sat as solitary on our plates as a hermit in a cave, especially since it was the first meal after a long journey in which the older brother decided how much and when we would eat.

The next morning Brother Joseph and I were sent out together to witness. Joseph, tall and lanky, was dressed in a long gray coat that had a hood over it and it had all the appeal of a prison garment. I had a shirt made for a brother larger than me, and it sagged and drooped like a shoplifter's coat. Together we walked out toward the clearing leading to the main road to campus.

As we stepped out of the woods, a State College policeman on patrol drove by us very slowly, riveted his head in disbelief and fear at what he saw, turned the car abruptly around, and sprang out of his car, pointing both barrels of his 20/20 shotgun at us. We were astonished and froze, compliant and still.

"Put your hands over your heads and keep your hands out of your pockets. Do you have any I.D.?"

Joseph replied, "Yes sir. Excuse me sir, what is this all about?"

"Just let me see your I.D. What were you doing in those woods?"

Joseph stood there waiting on God for an answer that would get us out of this situation without exposing the camp to the fowls. Married couples and children were there as well as some members that the fowls were after. To reveal the location of the camp to the police meant betraying Christ and His Church, both nearly unforgivable sins. Joseph waited for wisdom from the Lord.

I interpreted Joseph's silence to mean he was not in control of the situation, and that it was my duty by default to step in and save the day. "We're just Christians traveling and living by faith."

"Were you camped in the woods?"

"Well, we're just passing through and we sleep wherever we can find a spot to lay our heads. Jesus said, "The foxes have holes, and the birds of the air have nests, but the Son of Man hath not where to lay his head." (Matt. 8:20)

He mellowed a little although we had not answered his questions. "Do you have some identification?"

"Uh, yes. But I left it there."

"Where?" he snapped. I grimaced because I knew that I had just put my foot into my mouth.

"Back there, in the woods."

"Take me there." After taking down our names and radioing in for reinforcements, he put us in the car and drove us part of the way up the hill to where we were camped. In the meantime, the police used their National Crime Information Computer to see if there were any warrants out for our arrest.

"May I ask you a question?" I ventured. "Sure."

From Dean's List to Dumpsters: Why I Left Harvard to Join a Cult

"What is going on? We are only strangers here and we haven't done anything. Why did you point your shotgun at us?"

"There was a jailbreak about five miles from here last night. Two of the inmates escaped, and we haven't apprehended them yet. When I drove by and saw you guys coming out of the woods looking like escapees, you fit the description of the missing inmates in those clothes. By the way, you guys have nothing to fear. I'm a Christian, too.

As we drove up the hill we came across Brother Larry walking out to go witnessing. Immediately the policeman stopped him and asked me if we were together. I acknowledged it, and the police o cer searched Larry and gave him over to the reinforcements that had just arrived. Larry would not speak a word, nor confirm that there were any others encamped on the hill. He quietly muttered to himself, "Jesus have mercy." Larry just sighed deeply and prepared to receive the wrath of the police o cer for not being cooperative. The reserve o cer put Larry in the car and began to question him. We left him there and began to walk the rest of the way to the camp.

By now I felt like a Judas leading the mob to Christ. What would Brother Evangelist think if he were in town? Immediately after I pondered this we found ourselves in the camp, amazing the police to find so many of us crammed into a neatly ordered camp. After standing everyone in a line, he asked who the leaders were, and Gary stepped forward. The police recorded all the brothers' and sisters' names and birth dates and radioed back to the crime computer to see if any state had issued a warrant for the arrest of any of the members. Everyone came up clean, and after ordering us to leave as soon as possible (because the locals who lived nearby were afraid of us) they kindly wished us the best and departed.

About five minutes after they had departed, I heard a loud whisper. "Have they left?" Someone turned around and said yes, and Brother Joel came scurrying out from under a bush, wiping the twigs and dust out of his clothes and waist long beard..

"Brother Joel, where were you?" I asked, astonished. "Over here, under this bush," he smiled. "I heard the radio and knew it was the fowls, so I hid myself so they couldn't check me out."

"Are there any warrants out for your arrest?"

"Not that I know of, but in this warfare we need to be wise as serpents and as harmless as doves." (Mat. 10:16)

We packed up and left the woods. Some went on the road to another city while I stayed that afternoon and all the next day with a few brothers. I knew that I had done wrong by leading the police into the camp, but I was a younger brother and did not know what to do. I just feared running into Brother Evangelist and getting a sharp rebuke from him.

The next day Brother Evangelist arrived and met us in a large park filled with green grass and picnic tables. We had been spending our day there awaiting instructions about where to go next. I was afraid to look him in the eye, but he smiled very meekly and kindly to me, being absent of malice and supernaturally concerned about my feelings. He spoke at length privately with Brother Gary and then sat by himself for a while to consider the situation.

I guiltily slunk over to him, waiting to get my tongue lashing over with, but he only smiled and said graciously, "It can be very unnerving when those centurions point their weapons at you. We've had it happen to us before. It can be a frightening thing."

I felt the warmth and kindness radiating from his heart. "I feel like I've betrayed the Church by leading them back to the camp. But I told them my I.D. was 'back there', and by then I realized I had said too much. I did not know what to do so I led them back."

He listened attentively, fishing for some way to reassure me that I had been forgiven without a rming my mistake. He smiled, "It doesn't seem like anything came of it. The Lord did seem to keep the Brothers. Praise God for his deliverance."

"Praise God," I said, departing with a stronger love for Brother Evangelist.

Three brothers with bikes meeting in a park. Note the untrimmed beards, long shirts, and day packs.

8

The Fowls Arrive

The police in State College, having ordered us out of town, later spotted some of us from a helicopter as we prepared to bed down the night before we left. We slept there anyway, trusting God to keep us until the morning. The next day we packed up and hit the road for Amherst, Massachusetts, the home of the University of Massachusetts (affectionately known as "UMass") and Amherst College. Most of us arrived that night and we met in some woods east of the city, far from the madding crowd, nestled halfway up one of the hills of the Berkshires. Being in a large college town, we felt we might be able to find some disillusioned adolescent who might appreciate our witness.

We were not disappointed. The next day a few of us went to the UMass campus to witness, and after a while we found some people to speak to. Brother Joseph and I approached a young man and he said he would stop and listen. Joseph began to talk to the man, word by word, pausing and waiting for the Spirit to give him holy utterance, while I grew exasperated by his verbal pace. I piped in and took over. The man was going to think we were weird if we waited ten to fifteen seconds after every question he asked us to formulate an answer.

"We don't have a name," I said. "We just travel and live by faith."

"Do you work? I mean, how do you get your food?"

"Jesus said, 'Take no thought for your life, what you are going to eat…'" (Matt. 6:25) I droned on, the man obviously more curious about us than about Jesus.

"Why do you guys stare at the ground when you talk? Why don't you look me in the eye?"

"I hadn't realized I was staring at the ground," I replied (although I did it because I was emulating Joseph.) "It's just part of being humble. We don't have anything to hide. 'God resists the proud but gives grace to the humble." After pointing out to the man how humble we were, we dismissed ourselves, asked the man if he wanted to talk more about Jesus sometime (which he really didn't answer), and left. Near the Student Union we ran into Brother Aaron, extremely enthusiastic and exulting because he had run into so many "hungry souls" that day.

A little later we boarded the Sunderland bus, a shuttle for UMass students, and rode back to the 7-Eleven that bordered the hill where we were camped. On the bus we spoke with Brother Aaron about his day.

"Boy, this place is full of hungry souls! Three different people came up to me and said, 'Are you a Christian? How do I become a Christian?'"

"Praise God," I said. Finally someone wanted to hear the truth.

Little did we know what was really happening.

When we got off the bus in Sunderland, we met Brother Samuel walking back to camp. We found the narrow dirt path that led up the hill and slowly made our way up the trail. Suddenly we came across a young man in his mid twenties, tall and serious looking, peering through the bush in the general direction of our camp. He seemed startled to see us and gave us the general look of disgust we often got when someone didn't like us or trust us.

"What are you doing?" Samuel asked. "Bird watching?" Samuel suspected something and didn't trust the intruder.

"I'm waiting for some friends … up there," he said, motioning with his head toward our camp.

We continued up the hill and when we entered the camp we saw the brothers and sisters lined up and a plainclothes police o cer and a fireman questioning them. They were examining the brothers' identification and radioing in their names and dates of birth.

Meanwhile, Shor and Aaron met at the agreed upon time and prepared to come back together in his car. (When Shor joined he brought his vehicle, and the brothers had not sold it yet.) However, as Shor and Aaron were leaving, a carload of Shor's friends from Columbus arrived and tried to drag Shor away from the Brothers and truck him back to Columbus. They had sent fliers around to the various camps Christian groups warning them about us. They also asked each group to keep watch for Shor, whom they felt we had kidnapped to sacrifice to the Devil. A campus minister had spotted us and alerted them that we were on the UMass campus. They immediately clustered together and drove all night to arrive in Amherst the next morning. To find where we were camped, they pretended to be "hungry souls" itching to be recruited, hoping to be invited back to the camp to find Shor and save him from the Devil.

In the process they spotted Shor and Aaron and tried to follow them. When the two brothers realized they were being trailed, they drove around until they could find a brother and explain what was happening. They did find Brother Gary and, after explaining to him the situation, offered Gary a ride back to camp, agreeing to meet in front of the 7-Eleven with the car at 7:30 that night. The chase was only beginning.

As Shor pulled up to a tra c light, one of the pursuers jumped out of their car and flung the hood of Shor's car open, flailing his arms and grasping for the spark plug cables, trying to shut the car off so they could grab Shor. Shor panicked, put the car in reverse and floored it, barely eluding his captors. Gary jumped out and shut the hood and the two of them peeled off onto the highway to escape.

Meanwhile, back on the hill, the policeman asked me for my identification and Social Security number. Although I knew it was standard in the church to forsake our Social Security numbers, I still had my card. After surrendering it to the policeman, I sheepishly took it back when he was done looking at it, and destroyed it in the fire. The police o cer waited for the crime database to expose any warrants listed for us, and after it cleared us he told us we had to leave. "This land is public property and no camping is allowed on it. Also, the fires you have been having are illegal. We have strict fire ordinances around here to protect the forest."

"How did you know we were up here?" I asked.

"We received numerous complaints about smoke coming out of the woods up here, and we observed your campfire so we thought we would investigate."

It turned out that Shor's friends, having driven up all night from Columbus, Ohio, called the police and complained about our camp. The young man we encountered in the woods led them to our camp, and consequently we were forced to leave town.

"Pack up, brothers and sisters," an older brother ordered, taking charge until Gary returned a few minutes later. We followed our typical routine, disassembling our tents, burying our garbage, throwing excess food to the forest critters, scattering leaves where tents had scarred the forest floor, and tossing green wooden tent stakes cut from live trees into thick forest brush to mask any environmental damage we had done.

We trudged down the hill, hurried by Brother Gary to be at the meeting place by 7:30 p.m. I was thrilled at the smell of battle, joyful to be worthy to suffer persecution, and thinking of sarcastic and bitter thoughts against Shor's misguided rescuers. "His friends smelled the smoke all the way in Columbus, Ohio, hundreds of miles away, and drove all night just to come and make a complaint to the local fire department about our campfire. What hypocrites! Those guys are real unjust!" (Later it was revealed that they had told the police that Shor was in a group that sacrificed innocent people to the Devil, and that if they opened the trunk of his car, they would find a body. The police did stop the car and gingerly opened the trunk, prepared for the worst, only to be shocked by the gruesome specter of a spare tire.)

When we got to the road, Brother Gary exhorted us to lay low in the ditch along the road, and be ready to jump into the car as soon as the car stopped. A few minutes later we saw the lights on Shor's car driving into the parking lot with the fowl's car about fifteen seconds behind him. We sprang up, Shor unlocked the trunk, we quickly shoved our backpacks into the trunk, piled in and began to drive off. Unfortunately, this extended pit stop allowed the fowl's car to pull up behind us and one of their leaders sprang out and dashed furiously alongside Shor's car to thwart our getaway.

He then did a desperate thing. Knowing that the right front window of Shor's car did not work properly, his pursuer began to drum with his fists against the pane while he shouted, "Don! Don! Why are you running from us? We love you, Don!" Just then the window collapsed into the door and the man catapulted himself across the three brothers crammed in the front seat, elbowing one brother in the groin, and maniacally grasping for the ignition keys. He made driving impossible for Shor, so Shor stopped the car, only to be lynched by the rest of the Columbus cavalry. Swarming around Shor like a frenzied mob attempting to do justice to a papal assassin, they dragged him out of the car and tried to shove him into their awaiting car.

The brothers leapt out of the car and began to take defensive measures. Samuel raced to the waiting car and locked his hands on the back car door to hinder them from putting Shor inside the car. Meanwhile the mob was yelling Scriptures at Shor, locking arms like a rugby scrum fighting for the ball in the middle of the huddle. Shor was silent and relaxed.

"Don, Jesus said, 'My yoke is easy and my burden is light,'" one of them pleaded.

"We're saved by grace through faith, and not by works," (Eph. 2:8) another proclaimed.

"These men are following Captain Jimmie Roberts, ex marine and wig salesman!" revealed another.

At this point, an older brother came over to me and told me to sit in the car. I was not ready for this spiritual warfare yet. I obliged but wanted to be in the thick of the batter there in the Sunderland 7-Eleven parking lot.

I watched from the window. One of the members of Shor's former fellowship lifted Samuel up and down like a merry go round horse, but Samuel would not get angry nor relinquish his grip on the car door handle. Brother Joseph, the lanky and quiet Oklahoman, quietly walked up to the pack and meekly said, "Here, Brother Shor, give me your hand." He did so and Joseph, after humbly bowing his head like a tame ox might receive its harness to plow, proceeded to drag Shor and the whole mob across the parking lot away from the escape vehicle.

The employees at the 7-Eleven, terrorized by this sudden rumble in their parking lot, phoned the police. A few minutes later, the local police arrived and took control, segregating the two factions and sending them to opposite ends of the parking lot. After hearing both sides, they decided it was simply a religious matter between two rival religious sects to be worked out peacefully by the concerned parties. Brother Gary and the opposing leader agreed, and they took Shor into a nearby pizza store and talked it over, agreeing to abide by Shor's final decision.

The police waited a few minutes, and soon the three appeared. The police were content that the leaders had resolved the matter and bade us to live peacefully and not to brawl on their soil again. As the police were about to drive off, I begged one of the o cers to please stay until we had gotten away because I was sure they would not honor Shor's decision to stay with us if that was what he had decided. The o cer was convinced that everything was under control and drove away. But for us, the fun was just beginning.

As they were leaving, the three appeared from the pizza shop, Shor seeming conciliatory and kind toward his former churchmates, but disposed to stay with us. Shor got into the front seat and listened to a little more pleading, smiling sincerely when the leader said, "We love you, Don. We really do!"

"Don't believe them," I shouted at Shor, angry at the unjust manner in which they had attempted to kidnap him. Shor had chosen to be with us. If they loved him, why didn't they honor the choice? Shor smiled and waved goodbye as we headed out to the highway, certain they would attempt to follow us.

Soon after we got onto the road, we looked behind us and saw their car in the distance chasing us. Matthew looked behind us and could tell by the headlights that it was their car.

"They're following us back there," he said. "I would suggest you get a ways ahead and try to ditch them."

"There's a barn just up the road on the left," a brother said. Shor saw it, pulled behind it, and turned off the headlights. A few minutes later the other car raced by, pursuing us like a possessed posse. We smiled and got back on the road heading in the opposite direction, pulled into a closed gas station, and parked again with our headlights off. They were obviously persecuting us because we had the truth and the Devil wanted to pluck the seed from brother Shor's heart. (This never happened when you join the Presbyterian Church!)

Soon the fowls returned, flying desperately past us the opposite way, cleverly trying to catch those who had outsmarted them. We waited a few minutes and got back on the road again heading the opposite direction, and pulled over several miles outside of town. We hugged Shor and encouraged him to continue, assuring him that the Lord would keep him if he was faithful to God. "Amen, brother," he smiled, and hugged me like we were members of a band of brothers serving in 'Nam together. We had won the battle, but the war was not over...far from it.

View to the Boston's Back Bay from Boston Common. Photo by Sean Sweeney on Unsplash.

We fled from there to Boston, and several days later met in the Boston Common. Historic Park Street Church shadowed us as we sat watching the pigeons scurrying for popcorn thrown at them by the middle school children returning to take the Red Line home. It was an unseasonably bitter cold day, and not being allowed to go into libraries to warm up didn't make things easier. I looked around the Common to see if I recognized any of my school buddies from Harvard going down the subway steps to catch the Red Line back to Harvard Square. There were none. In my pocket were the room keys to Lowell House Room D5, my dorm. I was tempted to go back there and use them. Deep down, I wished there were another way to be saved, but since there wasn't I had to repress the rebellious thoughts I had about leaving the Brothers.

Lingering with the bitterness of what I had to suffer to be saved was the sincere longing to see my former roommates and my family. Perhaps they could tell my mother I was all right and relieve some of her worries.

We regrouped in Boston to hide from the fowls and to decide our next destination. Brother Evangelist had sent us to wait in Boston for his word. Not knowing how long that would take us or where we would sleep that night, the older brothers scattered, looking for food and a place to sleep. Those of us not mature enough to handle these tasks were told to sit in a park overlooking the Charles River next to the Massachusetts Avenue Bridge. We huddled in the cold, read our Bibles, and pleaded with the brother in charge to let us go inside somewhere because of the cold.

"I know it's a real trial, brother, but try to endure it. It is still a standard in the Church that we don't go into libraries. Remember what happened to the brother who read a deceitful book recently and got a strong delusion."

"Couldn't we just go in and promise not to read any books?

66

I just need to get out of the cold."

That was it, the answer. Nothing I could say could change the law. Apparently the standard was more important than my health. That night we bedded down under the Harvard Bridge and ate a simple meal of tuna fish and fruit. The next morning I got nauseous just in time to hitchhike to Champaign-Urbana, Illinois, a thousand miles west on Interstate 90.

John W. Weeks Bridge and clock tower over the Charles River at the Harvard University campus in Boston, MA.

9

Let's Throw Them Into The Bushes

I was chosen to travel with Brother Samuel and Sister Hannah. The journey progressed and so did my sickness. I could not keep food down, and I suffered dizziness and nausea. Even the thought of food made me sick and I refused to eat. After two days I desperately needed a doctor, but that was not of faith.

One night, as we were riding in a car, I earnestly longed to spend the night in a house. Sleeping by the side of the road in bushes and high weeds was not the balm I needed. My body required the comforts of civilization. Small chance, though. In the two months since I had forsaken Harvard, no one had invited me home to sleep.

The driver was a fatherly type who had taken a real liking to us. Samuel had shared some of his faith in God to provide needs, and the man seemed impressed by our devotion. As we approached his freeway exit, he asked, "Where are you guys going to spend the night tonight?"

Samuel responded, "We're not sure. Do you have any suggestions?"

"As a matter of fact, I do," he said. "Just over there is an abandoned house where you could stay. It's not much, but it will keep you dry and, by the clouds, it looks like it's going to rain. I would take you home, but I'm not sure how my wife would react. You understand?" he smiled with a flash of guilt.

"Sure, praise God!" O looked to the heavens and blessed God for a dry place to stay. Right then I sensed that God personally knew my needs and was willing to bend some of the suffering so that I might be able to endure. It was an intimate moment. I was experiencing the love of God.

Like so many other places I had slept since joining the group, it was su cient though not fancy; a manger, not an inn. But it was enough for my needs and it was free.

We finally arrived a few days later after cars stopped and sped away from us when I startled them by rising out of the long grass to join the other two approaching the car. It came across like an ambush! I must have scared a dozen drivers who thought they were stopping for the brother

68

and sister only. I was laying in the thick grass out of sight trying to get over my sickness. Samuel hitchhiked and Hannah, fifty pounds lighter than me, added my backpack to her own load and carried my gear almost the entire trip. After several days we arrived in Champaign.

The Brothers met us in Shor's vehicle and carefully loaded me into the back seat. I was weak, my mouth smelled bad, and I had no energy. To my surprise, Champaign-Urbana was not our final destination. Nellie, the kindly Christian owner of a farm in Niles, Michigan, invited some of the brothers to live on her farm, just north of South Bend, Indiana. The farm had a large wooden barn with swinging red doors in which the brothers set up camp. Some of the married couples placed their tents around the barn to be separate from the single brothers and sisters.

By the time I arrived there I was miserable. I still could not eat or drink. The brothers made a special room for me in a semi opened shed next to the barn, where I lay on my foam for three days, unable to eat or drink. I began to really stink. Nellie's dog came sni ng over to me and recoiled its head when it caught a whiff of my odor. She scampered away for her life and left me in my misery. My sides ached, I didn't have the strength to rise and use the bathroom. Occasionally brothers would come over and try to encourage me to wait on the Lord, that He would get me through this trial.

After three days I began to regain strength. Brother Evangelist came over to comfort me a number of times. He seemed very concerned about my health, and told me that if I needed anything to let him know and he would get it. Other brothers told me how charitable Brother Evangelist was to those who were sick. He would buy soup and juice for sick brothers and deliver it himself. He would pray and fast and worry until the sick brother or sister was healed. And he would make sure that others realized the need to pray for and support the sick.

One afternoon Brother Richard came running into camp. "Where's the Elder?" he panted. He explained to the older brother that something had come up at the Catholic Charismatic conference being held nearby at Notre Dame. I heard whispers, but when I asked Richard later about what happened he told me very little. Later a brother explained. Shor and a few brothers had been trying to witness at the conference and had been spotted by some Christians who knew Shor's situation with his friends in Columbus. They telephoned the "fowls" who drove all night up U.S. Highway 30 from Columbus to South Bend to recapture Brother Shor. When the brothers realized what was happening, they ran with Shor back to his car, hotly pursued by his former church brothers. One of the pursuers flagged down a police car and told the policeman that the brothers were kidnapping Shor to sacrifice him to the Devil. The police, riled up and deceived, gave chase and pulled Shor's car over. When Shor explained the situation to the police, they turned and rebuked Shor's persecutors, telling them never to involve the police in their private affairs again.

Meanwhile, six of the brothers who were witnessing at the conference jumped into the car with Shor, and the fowls continued to chase them in their car. They drove awhile and then decided to split up and confuse the fowls. Shor stopped the car and let two brothers out of the car, and the fowls did likewise, hoping to tail them back to the camp. A little farther down the road, Brother Michaiah and Brother Evangelist climbed out and the fowls let out two more to tail them. Finally Shor and another brother parked the car and ran.

Meanwhile, the folks following Michaiah and Evangelist found themselves on a narrow railroad bridge. When he was halfway across, Brother Evangelist turned around and began to walk toward the men, loudly condemning them with Bible verses. "When in the Book of Acts do you ever read about Christians persecuting Christians?"

The men gawked at him like they had seen the Wolfman, convinced they were in the presence of an evil mad man. They eased back slowly, terrified at the apparition, but still resolute to find Shor. When Brother Evangelist backed off, they regrouped their wits, and continued to pursue them across the bridge and down a narrow path.

Evangelist soon became weary of the aggravation of these two fowls tailing them like they were escaped prisoners. He turned to Michaiah and said, "Let's grab them by the seat of their pants and throw them into the bushes."

Michaiah was shocked. Didn't the Bible teach passive nonviolence, to turn the other cheek, and love your enemies?

When then did Brother Evangelist want to deal violently with these men?

They eventually escaped their tails, and returned to the camp in safety. Meanwhile, Shor and another brother were hiding in some tall grass, waiting for their pursuers to give up the chase. Shor began to cry bitterly, wanting to be freed from this persecution and to be left alone to serve God.

Elsewhere, Brother Dave was being tailed by a man who felt it his privilege to test the sincerity of Dave's faith. "The Bible says, 'Give to him who asks of thee, and from him who takes away thy coat, let him have thy cloak as well.' (Matt. 5:40) If you're a Christian, let me have your backpack!" he challenged.

Dave replied, "All right, but you're taking the part of the evil man. Jesus is speaking about not resisting evil, and you're being evil!" The man walked away.

10

Instructions For Raising Children

A few days later we found ourselves in Portland, Maine, crammed into a spacious nineteenth century mansion about two blocks away from downtown on Congress Street. It was to be the last time the whole Church would gather together in one house in one city, but none of us knew it then. Filled from basement to attic with brothers and sisters - perhaps about seventy five to eighty men, women, and children - the house seemed to rejoice with us that we were together again after so long.

Brother Evangelist had split up the Church after the persecution in the fall before I joined the group, and brothers and sisters smiled broadly to see others they had not seen for months. Brothers hugged brothers as they arrived through the high arched doorway, and sisters were ushered upstairs to anxious and expectant sisters whom they had not seen for eons. Some of the sisters who had been there for a while helped the arriving sisters off with their backpacks, while arriving brothers greeted the resident brothers with hugs, kisses on the cheeks, and warm words. An older brother briefed those arriving, showing where the separate prayer rooms were, about the bathroom rules, where they could lie down and take a nap after their journey, the time of the evening meal, and to which brother to give your dirty laundry to so he could distribute it to an appropriate sister to wash.

The Elder had to quell some of the enthusiasm at the evening gathering as he warned the brothers, but especially the sisters, that although it was a blessing to fellowship, they must labor to keep their words few. Proverbs 10:19 instructs, "In the multitude of words there wanteth not sin: but he that refraineth his lips is wise." A few sisters hung their heads as they realized they had spoken more than they should, and decided to be more faithful next time.

As I awoke one morning, I noticed a brother killing mosquitoes in the room. I was grateful for the relief. However, another brother took note of the insect massacre and rebuked him. "Don't do that, brother. It hasn't done anything to you. It's not right to kill those things."

I was a little uncomfortable with his judgment, and confused about whether the brother was correct in his assessment of God's will about killing mosquitoes. Fortunately an older brother later explained that what the brother said did not reflect the general feelings of the more mature brothers in the church and that it was not a church teaching.

Around this time I began to notice many of the brothers had their hair clipped razor-short, except for their neck hairs, which they left shaggy because the Old Testament commanded that a man should not "mar the corners of his head, nor round the corners of his beard." (Lev. 19:27)

To me, the brothers looked hideous with their hair that way, but after persuading myself that I was just being proud and vain to worry about my personal appearance, I asked a brother to cut my hair. All the brothers' haircuts that day were done in the same style and coincidentally were identical

to the hair of the brother playing barber that day. Each brother's hair was cut in the image of the barber. Fortunately, he cut my hair short, but was willing to shave my neck, though I felt guilty asking.

Later, as I was speaking to Brother Nathan on the sidewalk that bordered the house, one of the four year old children came walking up by herself. Brother Nathan beamed and said to the child in child talk, "Praise God, sister! Have a blessed day! Amen, sister."

I smiled and enjoyed having the little child with us, feeling like I was part of an inter-generational family. Brother Evangelist was watching the interaction, and as the spiritual enforcer of the church standards, he reminded Nathan saying, "Brother Nathan, we shouldn't be fellowshipping with the little sisters. It's still the standard in the Church that brothers should not be fellowshipping with the children, because in their little hearts they might start thinking they are older brothers and sisters. It is charitable not to speak to them because it helps them stay humble."

Nathan dropped his head in shame and said, "Yes, sir," with his slight Mexican accent. The Elder left and sent the child back to her parents. Nathan tried to save face.

"Amen, brother. That brother is real faithful. I knew I shouldn't have acted carnal with that little sister. Lord, help me! It's hard for me since the children are so cute. But the Lord has set up that standard, and I need to pray to be more faithful."

After that, Brother Nathan had no spirit left. He was discouraged. He had acted carnally, in the flesh and not in the Spirit. Shoulders drooping, he praised God, and went to the prayer room where he cried out that God would help him be more faithful. I, too, needed grace to be delivered from the temptation to enjoy the beauty, wonderment, innocence, and sincerity of childhood.

11

Confronting Flesh Relations

My notebook continued to grow, filling up with scriptures from the Bible studies, notes from my personal study, letters to my family in which I was working fervently to bring them to the light, a small journal of my travels, and some words to songs the group sang. Brother Luke noticed the list of cities I kept in a notebook, some in code, and he questioned my wisdom for having such a list.

"Well, I just wanted to remember where I have been, that's all," I explained.

"Has the Lord shown you anything about it, if He thinks it's wise?"

"Not really," I mumbled. "What has He shown you?"

"It's not wisdom to keep a list like that. I used to keep a list of who gave the studies and where they were given, but after the persecution, I realized the fowls could get hold of them and persecute the Church. And besides, many of the souls who gave me the studies have fallen away and no longer walk with the Lord. What sense is there to remember them?"

I resisted his advice but later did what he said, and got rid of all the references in my notes as to where I had been and who had given the studies. I later learned it was a safety precaution, instituted because many people had left the group and taken their notebooks with them, which listed the doctrine and names of the leadership of the group, as well as indicating where the group was likely to be.

I traveled with Brother Robin from Portland to Springfield and decided to take advantage of our passing through Springfield, Massachusetts, to stop and see a cousin who was a Christian to witness to him. He was a faithful believer, and we had been close in previous years. Robin agreed to go with me, and we called him from a pay phone a few miles from his home. He came immediately, but his obvious discomfort quenched his normal jovial and punning manner.

I began quoting scriptures to him as we drove and explaining what I had learned by living with the group. He countered and questioned my harsh interpretation of the Bible, agreed on some points, and confronted me with the obvious uncomfortable questions that haunted my own troubled conscience.

"Why did you leave this way? Don't you think your parents would have let you do this if you really wanted to? Why are you hiding? No one is after you."

I knew David was right, but I had to be faithful to defend my leader's reasoning. Already the Church had suffered much persecution, mostly by parents, and Jesus had prophesied, "A man's foes shall be they of his own household." (Matt. 10:36)

"We used to keep in communication with them until some parents started hunting down their children and dragging them out of the group. It was the parents' fault. We wouldn't be running if they weren't chasing us."

David continued, "I know your parents. They are only worried about you. They don't know where you are, who you are following, how your health is, or if they are ever going to see you again. Don't you think this is a very unloving way to treat your parents? Why can't you even write to them?"

I knew David was right, but I could not admit it. I had been thinking the same things, but at that point I had less and less faith in my own thoughts, as I relied more on what others told me than on what I thought for myself.

"Please don't tell anyone I'm here. If Uncle Jim found out I was here, he might try to drag me out of the group."

My uncle was very fond of me and treated me like a son. He lived only about fifteen minutes away. Weary, Robin and I headed to the basement to sleep.

The next morning when I came upstairs, I received a great shock. My aunt had dropped in unexpectedly and saw me before I could recover myself and hide. She melted with compassion and said, "Jimmie, look at you! You've lost so much weight. You look so thin. Oh, come here! Are you all right?"

"I was sick a little while ago and lost a few pounds, but before I joined the group, the doctor told me I needed to lose a few pounds."

"Your father has been so worried about you since you left school without telling anyone. You're not with the Moonies, are you?"

"No, Aunt Frances. I'm with a small Christian ministry." "Does your group have a name?"

"No," I recited. "We don't have a name. Churches take on names because they only want to glorify themselves. The Bible says, 'If my people, which are called by my name…' (2 Chr. 7:14) We are to be called by His name: Christ… Christians."

From Dean's List to Dumpsters: Why I Left Harvard to Join a Cult

"Well, who's your leader? Every group has some sort of leader. There's nothing wrong with having organization. The Catholic Church is organized. It has to be to function. I don't understand what you have against the organized churches."

I remembered that one of the older brothers had instructed me not to mention Brother Evangelist's name to anyone so that they could not find him and persecute him. A lot of people were out to get him, and his safety, and the safety of the flock, continued as long as we remained anonymous. Besides, journalists had written dishonest and sensationalized newspaper and magazine articles against him and the group, so it was better that people did not associate us with those articles. Anonymity was the key to survival. That some churches seek to exalt themselves through their long and flattering names was really a secondary consideration.

"There are several leaders. The Lord ultimately is our head and leader. The Catholic Church follows the Pope; we follow Jesus." I had already voiced my belief that the Catholic Church was the great Whore of Babylon mentioned in chapter seventeen of the Book of Revelation, and the Protestant churches were her daughters. Dave also agreed that the Catholic Church was corrupt, but he wouldn't go so far as to say that every church was corrupt except ours.

I'm sure that Aunt Frances recognized my answer to be evasive and unsatisfactory, but I had to be faithful.

"Jim," she pleaded, "give your father a call. It is okay to call him, isn't it? He has been so worried about you. He doesn't know if you're dead or alive. You know, he's been taking this quite hard. Why didn't you talk with him about this before you decided to go with this group? I don't know the Bible like you do, but doesn't it say to honor your father and your mother?"

"God is my father and the church is my mother," I parroted. Any more parroting and I would be issued my own cage and bird feeder.

I knew she was right, but I was afraid of what the brother would say if I were to call my mother. When I asked him, he replied, "Obey the Lord," which at the time I thought meant letting God decide for you and you would determine His will, but I later realized it meant, "Leave me out of this decision." I considered what I thought the Lord would have me do, and I called my mother.

My mother answered the phone and broke into tears when she recognized my voice. "Jim," she gasped, "is that you?"

"Yes, Mom."

"Are you okay?" she wept. "Where are you?" "I can't say, but you'll find out in a few days." "Are you in Massachusetts?"

"I can't say. I just want you to know that I am safe and happy."

"Who are you with? Can you say?"

"I'm with a traveling Christian ministry. We don't have a name. We just follow Jesus." My answers sounded hollow even to me. A lump arose in my throat as I fought off my emotions and love for my mother. She was hurting so badly but I had to follow Jesus in this path of self denial, and be a testimony against her worldly living. She had a job, lived in a house, and had not forsaken all.

At the same time, I was desperately trying to relieve my guilt for putting my family through so much worry and fear.

"Did you get my letters?" I asked.

"Yes, I did. Thank you for writing them."

"Did you read the one I wrote to Chris Weinhold?"

"Yes. He sent it to me. He wants you to contact him if you can. He had some questions he wanted to ask you about the doctrine."

"Were the letters a comfort to you?"

"Yes, they were," she said. My conscience was partially relieved.

"I want you to know I have plenty to eat and I'm safe and happy."

"Thank God!" she replied. She seemed much more concerned about my well being than I was about hers, and I was the only one truly following God!

"Does your group follow the Bible?"

"Yes, Mom, we do. I checked out our doctrine thoroughly before I met the group. They are right on with the Word of God."

"Will I ever see you again?" she asked with terror in her voice. To them I was neither dead nor alive at that point. For them it would have been better if I had been one or the other. If I were dead, they could grieve, complete the mourning process, and go on with life. But I was in limbo, neither fully alive and in communication with them, nor dead and totally given up on. Their lives could not go on until the issue of Brother Evangelist was resolved, and Mom wanted to resolve the issue.

"I don't know. I would like to visit, but it might be awhile. I need to get more rooted in the Bible before I would risk something like that."

"If you are so sure about your faith, why is it a risk to come back?" she asked.

"Because I don't want to be swayed from my faith by the weak, carnal emotions. When I am stronger, I would like to visit."

"When would that be?" she asked.

"I don't know. But perhaps soon. I love you, Mom. I've got to go. I'll send you a long letter with my scriptural reasons for doing what I did."

"Please keep in touch," she pleaded with tears. "Promise me you'll write to me?"

"I'll do what I can. Bye Mom."

I hung up the phone and struggled to hold back the tears. I was wounded. David had raised some questions that shook my young faith, and my mother had brought me face-to-face with the love I still had within me for my family, a love that I had to deny continually, brand as carnal, reject, and shove to the deepest recesses of my sickened heart.

Aunt Frances left, promising not to tell anyone I was there until I had gotten a two-day jump on anyone who might try to follow me. David drove Robin and me to the road, shook our hands goodbye, and drove back to his house, disgusted with me and the trap into which I had fallen.

Outside of Springfield, Massachusetts, the brothers found a state park where we could camp, and we moved in. A car shuttled us out to the woods, and an older brother led us to a large area they had cleared out for us to camp. An icy stream passed through the foot of the campground, and the trees shaded the tents scattered on the slight slope down toward the water. A large fallen tree served as a bench for some of the brothers to sit on, and brothers were quietly scattered around the camp reading their Bibles, praying, resting, or talking quietly. The sisters were off sewing, singing, and cooking. It all seemed so peaceful.

To my joy, Brother Shor was there. We had not seen each other since April, and it was May already. We hugged each other and sat down to fellowship. A couple of minutes later, Brother Chris came walking by.

"Brothers, you know it is not in order for younger brothers to be fellowshipping."

"Yes, I did," admitted.

"There's a reason, brothers. You are both young in the faith, and being yet carnal you may easily speak things that are not sound, and one of you might end up deceiving the other. It has happened a few times where a couple of younger brothers start talking, and they talk each other right out of the truth. Even if that doesn't happen, younger brothers often just get into too many words which lead to sin. I have seen brothers start off fellowshipping in the Spirit, and the next thing you know they are laughing and being carnal."

We knew it was useless to try to continue talking together after that exhortation, so we split up and went back to our tents. Later that night, we found ourselves alone again, this time with no other older brother around to shut us up.

"What has the Lord been showing you, brother?" he asked. "All kinds of neat things," I began.

"It sure is a blessing to see you again." "You too."

"Do you have any water?" Shor asked.

"Right here. Take a look at the diameter of that spout," I said, showing him the wide mouth water bottle I had.

"Wide mouths sure are a blessing," Shor smiled as he began to drink.

"On water bottles!" I clarified. We both burst into laughter and looked guiltily around, trying to stifle our amusement, neither really believing that joking was a sin, but aware that those over us felt it was. We soon dispersed and went to bed.

The next day, Brother Evangelist gathered the brothers and sisters together to exhort us. He waited for perfect silence, surveyed the circle briefly, and stared through his beard back to the ground.

"We live in a late hour, brothers and sisters. We're living in a time of great falling away. I remember one soul who said, 'If it comes down to everyone having left but the older brother and me, I still won't desert the Church!' That soul got married, started desiring a ministry for himself outside the Church, and announced to me one day that he was leaving with his wife. A couple of days later his wife left him, and he wandered around the streets in such shock that they ended up putting him into a mental hospital. The devil painted a picture of how nice it would be to leave the Church and go back to the world, and he took the bait."

"Don't let the devil deceive you into thinking that life is better outside the Church. That brother probably never guessed what the devil had in store for him when he left, a divorced wife, a mental hospital, and possibly he lost his walk with God; it's a serious thing to leave the house of God."

"It's in the house of God that the table of God is…that's where the bread of life is, only in His house. This is where the true God is, fear to cause us to depart from evil. In the world the parents are not raising their children up in the fear of God, but in the fear of Santa Claus, Donald Duck, and Roadrunner."

At this point Shor did his best to mu e a laugh, but it exploded through his nose. Brother Evangelist knew about Roadrunner? This holy man who rarely used a word not found in the King James Bible said "Roadrunner"? Brother Evangelist's eyes snapped up, spied the transgressor, and in an act of mercy looked down and said nothing. I, too, could hardly restrain myself.

The next day Richard came up to me. Smiling broadly, he showed me the new backpack the sisters had just finished making for him. Considerably larger than his older frame pack, the new one had been patiently hand-stitched, every seam double-stitched and reinforced, every nylon edge melted with a candle so it would not fray, and every seam allowance at least three quarters of an inch. It was a masterpiece of design and production, and Richard knew it.

"Look at this, Brother Jim," he pointed out. "It looks like a machine sewed it."

From Dean's List to Dumpsters: Why I Left Harvard to Join a Cult

I smiled. Richard had bought the material, with my permission, from the funds I had brought to the group when I sold my typewriter.

"It's real nice, but I don't want to be guilty of worshiping the works of my own hands," I remarked, remembering what another older brother had said to me when I had complimented him on some of his own handiwork.

I continued. "What can I do since I do not have the room to stow my fruits and my goods? I will tell you what I am going to do. I will tear down the barns and build greater barns, and there will I bestow my fruits and my goods." (Luke 12:1718)

"Heavy," Richard smiled, ignoring my not-too-subtle rebuke.

Later I saw Richard sitting in his tent recopying page after page of Bible verses which he had organized into studies. He meditated on each verse as if driven by a great purpose.

"What are you doing?" I asked, seeking out some company because I was bored laying around all day and trying to be spiritual.

"Getting ready to go witness to someone." "Who?" I meddled.

"A woman I want to marry. I'm going over these verses because I want my spiritual sword to be sharp when I witness to her."

Richard explained that before joining the group he had known a woman with whom he was deeply in love. He had gone to witness to her once before and she had shown no interest in Christ at the time. He felt drawn to go witness to her, bring her to the Church, and marry her.

"Does Brother Evangelist know you're going to do this?" I asked.

"I've spoken with him about it."

"Is he going to let you go to see her?" "It's about fifty-fifty."

"What will you do if he doesn't let you go see her?" "I'm going to go anyway."

"But that's rebellion. The Lord isn't going to honor that." "Brother Evangelist doesn't understand. I love her!"

That finished the conversation. I was horrified. The brother who had brought me to the group was planning to leave. Satan was drawing him away and he didn't know it.

12

A Wedding And A Murder

On Independence Day that year, we packed up a new brother's car and drove from Springfield, Massachusetts, to the Lower East Side of New York City. On 10th Street, between Avenues D and E, Brother Michaiah and Brother Barnabas had found a burned out and dilapidated six-story tenement house. When we entered, the brothers who arrived a couple of days earlier to prepare the building greeted us. They carried banana boxes filled with chalky plaster rubble they had shoveled off the floors, broken wooden slats from the walls, and assortments of dung and urine-soaked newspapers where the homeless lay their burdens down.

"This is it?" I asked, as I surveyed the six-story carcass.

The brothers smiled and led us up to the floors they had already cleaned, which were still dusty but being mopped down by the sisters who had arrived earlier. Across the street was an open water hydrant where we got our water, and down the street was a city park where we could dump the buckets of collected urine and feces. The toilets were not yet installed and the brothers were still using buckets with tight lids on them as toilets. Early every morning a crew of brothers were sent out with the bucket to dump them either in the park or down the street in the sewer.

One afternoon I noticed Sister Faith, full-grown but somewhat strange, speaking across the alley from the fourth floor window to a Puerto Rican woman hanging her laundry out on a line.

"Jesus…is…my…best…friend!" she babbled.

The woman smiled back, looking like she was humoring a lunatic until the authorities arrived. I smiled and got a brother and showed him what was going on. Laughing, he rejoiced aloud.

"Praise God! Hallelujah! Out of the mouths of babes and children…"

"Yes," another brother cautioned, "we are to become as children to follow the Lord, but not childish."

From Dean's List to Dumpsters: Why I Left Harvard to Join a Cult

We stayed in New York from July 5, 1976, until September 22, 1976. I learned some very important lessons there that year. One day I went witnessing with an older brother, and the subject of the day was how wicked the women of the world are. All day long, I only focused on how wickedly women dressed, baring their thighs, cleavage, and beautiful feminine form. They were becoming a stumbling block to my spiritual growth.

As Brother Luke later explained, they were my enemies, unwitting tools of the devil, being used by Satan to paint their faces to make men lust and commit adultery in their hearts. All day, I strove to keep my eyes on the sidewalk, never looking a woman in the eyes, fighting my natural attraction to the opposite sex.

Brother Nathanael was with me. He grew indignant and decided to do something to improve the situation. He began to condemn women as they walked by.

"Put some clothes on!" he shouted at one angrily. "That's disgusting!" he shouted at another.

I began to get uneasy. Was this really what we were supposed to do?

When we got home, I went to the prayer room. It seemed so right to get angry at the world for their sins. Didn't God hate sin? Weren't they doing great evil by dressing like harlots and tempting men? Everywhere I turned I became bitter. Why wasn't anyone obeying the Lord and dressing modestly? Although I felt quite justified to be angry, I had no peace in my soul. Then, the Lord taught me something.

I was wrong to be angry at them. I was judging and condemning, something He had commanded me not to do. How was I any better than them, being filled with hatred and wishing Christ would come soon and judge the world? Was I so concerned about others being righteous that I had grown to hate them and become unrighteous myself? I had become a hypocrite, trying to win people with the love of Christ, but instead I was hating them for what they could not control, and for doing what they did not believe was wrong. I looked out the window and saw the people and felt that God was saying to me, "I love these people and want to reach them. I want you to bring them to me so I can heal them. They are what they are because they don't know me. You should love and forgive them."

"They're sheep!" I said to myself in tears. "They don't know what they're doing!"

I learned my lesson and escaped the hatred for a while, though our daily gatherings reinforced the judgmental spirit I was trying to escape.

One evening Brother Dave and I went out to gather some fruit from the garbage piles in front of the many fruit stands along Fourth Avenue and in Greenwich Village. He was very pleasant, singing to himself, seeming lost in space. After we had filled our packs he remarked, "It sure is a blessing when a trial is over."

Brother Dave had trials like me? I couldn't believe it. I had never seen him shout at the top of his lungs at God, fast for three days, walk in circles or bang his fists on the prayer room floor. He had trials, too?

The next morning we all gathered before breakfast for an announcement. Brother Alan began, "Lord willing, we have a special announcement this morning." He nodded and said quietly, "Brother Dave…"

Brother Dave stood with his arms folded across his chest and smiled, looking down at the floor as he spoke. "Lord willing, I am getting married today." We were all stupefied, but glad. Different brothers had different reactions. I looked across at Sister Esther and thought, I hope he's not marrying her. I wish I were an older brother, then maybe I could get married. But I've only been with the church for a few months. They would want to prove me first. I wonder who he's marrying. How does one work out a marriage anyway?

Brothers and sisters began clapping and praising God. Sisters began guessing to themselves who the lucky sister might be. Others groaned within themselves, having comforted themselves with the thought that they could endure celibacy as long as no one else got married. As long as celibacy was universal, it was tolerable, like death. But if some were allowed to marry, and others not, then celibacy seemed more like a joker in the cruel card game of life. Some were getting older, growing lonelier, their ability to bear children slowly draining away, their hope of marriage growing faint. They could not approach Brother Evangelist and request a certain brother for a husband like a brother could ask for a sister. Nor could they request a husband in general. Sisters had to wait and pray that a certain brother would find them attractive and godly and would select them. Although they had the right to refuse, they did not have the right to choose. "God's order" seemed stacked against their happiness, seeing they had lost the right to pursue in the feminine manner the man of their choice.

Brother Dave made preparations for his honeymoon cottage. On the fifth floor, he had been assigned his own room to prepare for the wedding night. With some two-by-fours that he had salvaged from a construction site, and cardboard from dumpsters, Brother Dave constructed an elaborate marriage chamber in the bedroom for privacy from other brothers and sisters.

Other brothers spent the day trying to witness and forget the enviable blessedness that had come to Brother Dave. The whole issue of marriage depressed and grieved most brothers. It seemed only a select few in these "latter days before the end of the world were called to marriage. Celibacy, in Brother Evangelist's mind, was the spiritual option for those serious about the work of God, and he was going to have a spiritual church, the happiness of the brothers and sisters be damned!

That evening, a brother announced, "Come to the marriage feast! We're gathering now!" We filed into the large gathering room, about thirty brothers and sisters, waiting anxiously for the bride to be revealed. Brother Alan did the honors, his wife Sister Abi standing directly behind him with her eyes superglued to the floor, holding their young daughter, Humility: "Brothers and sisters, we are gathered here for a wedding and a wedding feast. Brother Evangelist and I, and some other brothers, have been praying for the Lord's will in this, and we agree that it is God's will for these two to be joined."

"As you all realize, we are living in a late hour and the Lord is coming soon to judge this wicked earth. We believe in this late hour that it really has to be the Lord's will for a brother and sister to get married. As Brother Evangelist has said, 'Marriage is not for everybody.' Marriage brings so many new responsibilities and burdens. Raising children, being the head of a family, and instructing the wife are great responsibilities. Brother Dave has been a blessing to all of us; he has lifted up the standard, and been a faithful brother. The sister has been a real blessing, too, and has shown many acts of charity toward the brothers and sisters. She has been faithful to the standards of the church and we agree it would be a blessing to the church if these two were joined." (Brothers and sisters listened carefully to the criteria behind the leaders' decision to permit the marriage.)

"Brother Dave, do you have anything to say?"

He did. He said a few encouraging words about being faithful to the Lord and the Church and finished. Brother Alan then instructed the brothers and sisters to form a large circle around Brother Dave, and to let the sister through. Our eyes riveted to the sisters standing behind the brothers. Was it Sister Esther? To my relief, Sister Elizabeth lumbered forward, weeping like a waterfall, while the brothers and sisters gasped and rejoiced in excitement. We formed a circle around them as they got on their knees side by side, and we prayed for them. No vows were made, no rings exchanged, no flowers or wedding dresses, just two young people on the floor surrounded by prayer. When the praying stopped, they arose as husband and wife.

"Brothers can greet the brother, and sisters greet the sister. Then we'll have the marriage feast…a spaghetti dinner!" Tears were flowing everywhere, Dave was "beaconing," and all of the brothers were congratulatory, although wondering to themselves when and if their turn would ever come. Some of us decided to make an opportunity to talk to Brother Dave about how he was able to get a wife.

The days passed by slowly, and I witnessed things I had never seen before. One night I was reading the Bible by candlelight near one of the fourth floor windows overlooking Tenth Street, when I heard six shots and a scream. I looked out and saw a man hightailing it toward Avenue D, wearing polyester pants and black dress shoes. Another man pursued him, shouting for help to stop the man he was chasing. A third man, about twenty-five years old, told the pursuer to let the murderer go, which he did. The third man then walked down the middle of the street laughing and saying, "Boy, he shot the s**t out of her!"

A few days later, a brother was standing in a fifth floor window reading the Bible when he accidentally knocked a small object off the ledge into a crowd of Puerto Ricans drinking and arguing below. One of the men was so incensed for having been willfully attacked that he got his shotgun and started walking up the stairs to the fifth floor. Brother Caleb met him on a lower floor and began pleading with him. "Sir, it was an accident. We didn't mean to do that. You need to understand that and have mercy. Please don't hurt anyone." He followed the man to the fifth floor, begging him all the way. When he got to the top, he turned around and walked back down to the street, not saying a word.

That summer, Brother Evangelist gathered us and gave us some instructions about our families. "Brothers and sisters, some of you are still holding to those old ties to flesh relations. I know that many of you don't understand the Church's standard regarding this, but you need to accept it by faith. You have older brothers who are more exercised than you in the Word of God who can see things you cannot see. Remember that Jesus always spoke the truth, even though it offended some of his disciples and they turned back. In the love of God I have not withheld the truth from you. Jesus said a man's foes would be they of his own household, and we've seen that in our midst. Brothers and sisters have been dragged away from the Lord by their flesh relations, and 'programmed' back into the world by some who thought their parents would never do that! Now they are back in Babylon, building bricks for Pharaoh, instead of building up the Kingdom of God. You need to forsake them completely in your hearts if you expect to endure to the end to be saved. Remember that some of the Jews couldn't enter into the Promised Land because of unbelief. Of the 600,000 that came out of Egypt, only two entered into the Promised Land. If you are unwilling to believe all that Christ said the easy things and the hard things then you, too, might fall because of unbelief." An arrow pierced my soul. I had been living with the hope that I could someday be rejoined to my family. I was denying the subtle hints that I had been getting all along from brothers and sisters that a total cutting-away from my family was required to be a member in Brother Evangelist's church. What a decision! What a choice! A non-choice! Love God or love my family and go to a blazing inferno for an eternity and a half? Why couldn't I love God and my family? Why the choice?

I crawled into a dusty closet to be alone with my torpedoed heart. I had no choice.

They would never "repent" and join the group. My mother was getting on in years and could never adapt to this lifestyle. Why was God so strict and demanding? An hour later I emerged, depressed, broken, cleaving to what little hope could fit between my fingers. This was just more of my cross to bear for Christ, I resigned. A cross is heavy and hard to bear; so must this real Christianity.

Later, I spoke to an older brother. "How did you get used to the idea of forsaking your family?" I asked.

"Well, it was difficult at first, but I learned not to think about it. The Lord has given me a lot of peace by just forgetting them."

"How long has it been since you have contacted them?" "About eight years," he said.

Great.

13

Jailed For The Lord

On my twentieth birthday in 1976, we decided to move from New York to go to a small farm owned by Harold Johnson in Sharon, Vermont. Our first stop, however, was Binghamton, New York, to meet up with Brother Michaiah. I traveled with Brother Chris, who was not feeling well. He asked me to do most of the hitchhiking because he needed to rest.

The journey was slow, with three-hour waits followed by ten-mile rides. The road soaked up the heat and then reflected it back at us. Hot, tired, and discouraged, I could bear no more. I prayed. Whether it was my imagination or not, the reader may judge. But the thought came to me very clearly, "Look behind you seven times."

"Get thee behind me, Satan," I replied. Then I stopped. Didn't God tell Elijah to go up seven times to look for rain that he was praying so desperately for? Shouldn't I try what the Lord says? As I stood there a thought came into my mind, "Look behind you."

I turned and saw nothing, no one stopping, nothing, "One."

Again, "Look behind you."

Nothing. "Two."

And so it went until the seventh time, when I turned around and saw a car pulling over, who took us all the way to Binghamton. We camped there a couple days, then left to go north.

Brother Chris gave us detailed instructions about where to get out of our rides and what to do. At a certain overpass, we were to ask the driver to let us out, and we were to scurry down the hill and hide in the bushes below. A brother would come by on the hour in a car to look for arriving brothers. Under no circumstances were we to be spotted by anyone driving on that road.

We did as we were told and arrived at the farm a couple days later. Harold owned about 500 acres in rural Vermont, and had invited the brothers to live on his land in exchange for some work. He owned an old sawmill which had a large, unprotected blade that ate wood like Jaws ate swimmers. On one end of his property he was building a large house which he hoped to rent some day. A large hill bordered his property on the east, and the cattle roamed as freely as convicted drug dealers in Washington, D.C.

Across the dirt road was a small trailer in which a couple of married couples resided with their children, and behind it a small wooden shack that Brother Dave was renovating and insulating with sawdust between the walls for his new bride. Farther down the road and across the street again was a large barn with hay and rats, in which most of the brothers slept at night.

We spent the days there reading the Bible, praying, building the house for Harold, working at the sawmill, and having Bible studies. We were too far from any town to witness daily; the nearest town of any size was Claremont, New Hampshire, just across the border from us. Every day, the car would go to the nearby towns, and brothers would check the local IGA markets for food. Every evening, they would return with the trunk filled with broccoli, green beans, bread, yogurt, milk, cookie dough, and every other item that supermarkets sell.

Things were tranquil there until one morning, when an older brother awakened us before dawn, and told us to go to the barn and pray. The house was nearing completion, and most of us were sleeping there, about a quarter mile from the barn. We shu ed out of bed and made the trek, not sure what was going on, but certain something had happened. Although Brother Evangelist told us to pray for God's mercy, he did not tell us what was happening.

We obeyed and hit the floor, wailing and saying, "Oh, please Lord, have mercy on us. Pleeeeasse!" We prayed that way for about an hour. When we were done, Brother Evangelist explained to us what was happening.

Brother Kraig's wife had awakened at dawn to feed the baby, only to discover that the baby had died in the night. There was no foul play; it just appeared to be Sudden Infant Death Syndrome. She became hysterical, and awakened her husband, who then summoned the Elder. He woke us to pray for the child, as if perhaps God would have mercy and raise the child from the dead.

Sadly, the child remained dead.

Brother Evangelist told us that in all congregations of people tragedies happen which cannot be explained.

After recounting the situation of the night, he comforted us saying, "I feel very badly for the brother and the sister that they have had to suffer such a thing. The brother can say as David said when God took his child, 'I shall go to him, and he shall not return thither to me.'" (2 Sam. 12:23) A few hours later, I saw Brother Joel putting his arm around Brother Kraig, trying to console him.

A few days later we were almost finished with the house. I saw Brother Abel struggling with a saw as he labored to put the finishing touches on an outhouse for the brothers to use until the plumbing was installed in the house we were building. I walked over to him and offered to help. He looked up, smiled, and asked me, "Do you know how to saw?"

"What an insulting question!" I thought. Of course I knew how to saw a board with a handsaw. I also knew how to tie my shoes! When Abel read the shocked look on my face he explained, "I didn't know how to saw wood until I joined the brothers."

The next day, six of us crammed into the Buick, and drove to Claremont, New Hampshire, to witness for the Lord Jesus Christ. After days of Bible study and prayer, we were ready and willing to share the Gospel as we knew it.

As Brother Caleb dropped us off, he left us with a final admonition. "Don't tell anyone where you are staying if the police stop you. If they throw you out of town, I'll look for you on this main road leading back to the camp." We agreed and split up in pairs, setting out to witness in the one block strip of town called "downtown."

We were a local gazing stock. We paraded up and down Main Street like a Labor Day parade. The shop owners became suspicious and felt the police ought to at least get our names. It looked like the Manson gang had moved into town and was desperately in search of nurses. After a half hour of traipsing back and forth and having trouble getting even the local newspaper reporter to talk to us, we were becoming discouraged. Suddenly an unmarked police car pulled over to the curb, and a portly detective jumped out, flashing his badge and acting quite intimidating.

"Stand still, gentlemen, and let me see some identification." I had some since I learned my lesson at State College when I had led the policemen back to where the group was camped. However, the brother with me, a Salvadoran refugee who felt it was wiser to say nothing in crisis than to risk saying something untrue, had little valid identification.

"Where are you from?" he asked.

"We're just traveling," I blurted, seeing Brother Herbert was not inclined to communicate at all.

"Where are you staying?"

I replied, "Jesus said, 'The foxes have holes, the birds of the air have nests, but the Son of Man hath not whereto lay his head.'" (Matt. 8:20)

Herbert looked at me like I was grossly out of my place as the younger brother for having answered the policeman.

"Why are you here in town?" "We're here to preach the Gospel."

After a few more questions, he searched us and took us into the station, where the captain attempted to question me. Whenever the captain would ask me a question, I would fire back a Bible verse, going so far as to explain my unwillingness to communicate as a desire to "avoid vain babbling," and labeling the captain's queries as "foolish and unlearned questions." Fortunately, the captain was far too mature to get angry.

After battling with the captain for ten minutes, he let me go and sent me back to the detective. He asked me where I was from.

"Upper Marlboro," I replied.

Then he asked me to describe it. "It's a one-horse town with a courthouse on Main Street."

"Very interesting. What's behind the courthouse?"

"The Board of Education and the Police Department," I replied.

"Excellent!" he smiled. "You see, I studied criminology at the University of Maryland, and quite often I had to go to Upper Marlboro to get information I needed for my case work.

I am quite familiar with the town. You have described it quite accurately."

Then I began to tremble. Did this man happen to know my mother, since she worked for the county government there? Would he call her and get me dragged from the Church?

When he was done with me, they booked all five of us. After confiscating all our belongings, we were led downstairs to the jail, and locked up for the night. A large police o cer came over to me and told me to give him my belt and shoelaces.

"Why is that?" I sneered. "Are you afraid I might hang myself?"

Containing his anger, all he could do was nod his head and wish there wasn't a Constitution defending smart asses like me.

After he left, the dam of excitement burst. I looked over to Brother Nathanael in the next cell and related to him how I handled the captain. Brother Nathanael approved and added a story of his own.

"One time the police took me and a brother in and wanted to question us about the brothers. We were polite but refused to give them a straight answer to their interrogations. After a few minutes of questioning, a policeman came in, and offered us an icy cold glass of lemonade in a frosty glass. We said sure and drank heartily until we were finished. The other brother put his glass down and seemed relaxed and refreshed. However, I took a handkerchief out of my pocket, wiped the glass clean, put it on a table in front of the captain, and thanked him for his hospitality."

"Aaah," I remarked. "They were just trying to get your fingerprints!"

"That's right. And boy, were they upset when I did that!"

This confirmed the exhilarating feeling that we were dealing with a crafty enemy who would like to trick us into becoming a part of their system. They just wanted our fingerprints on record so they might some later day force us to take the Mark of the Beast.

Brother Doug refused to be fingerprinted, so the police were especially upset with him. He felt it was an invasion of his privacy, and since he had done nothing wrong, these centurions of Satan had no right to fingerprint him.

The lights glaring into the cell made it almost impossible to sleep. I asked the guard if the lights were ever going to be turned off and he said no. I ended up taking off much of my clothing and weaving it between the bars to block the light.

The next morning, Brother Silas came sneaking down the steps into the cell block. I was relieved to see him, and we explained exactly what had happened. He seemed dismayed that we had been so crass and deceitful with the police and told us we should have "agreed with our adversaries while we were on the way to the magistrate."

Apparently we had really misunderstood what the Church taught about not denying the Lord. It would have been all right to tell the police where we were staying and who we were. The only faux pas would have been mentioning Brother Evangelist's name.

Shortly thereafter, Brother Silas left, assuring us that he and Brother Alan would be in court with us that day to help us. They had negotiated with the police captain and the detective who had arrested us, and they agreed that if we plead guilty to a misdemeanor charge of loitering, and promised to leave town and never return, they would drop the charges and release us.

At the hearing, Brother Alan stood up and explained to the judge that the whole matter was just a big misunderstanding, and that we would never trouble the town again. We each plead guilty (except Brother Doug, who was adamant that pleading guilty was lying under oath) and the judge released us. Brother Doug resolutely held his ground and refused to change his plea, until he realized he would have to come back to a hearing a few days later ,while the rest of us were getting off scot free. With great reluctance, he admitted his guilt, and drove back to the farm with us.

During this time, I grew more and more pressured about my Christian performance. I observed older brothers fasting at least once a week, while I squandered a large portion of the day thinking about food. Although I was reading the Bible about three or four hours a day, and praying in the interim, I still felt I was too proud to be accepted by God. I missed my family and thought about them often, but I continued to deny my emotions and to force them out of my thoughts whenever I realized I was thinking about them. I wondered if it was really wrong to contact them to relieve their fears.

One day, when I was sure I hadn't prayed enough, and wasn't feeling really accepted by God, Brother Evangelist came over to me and gently said, "I'm not saying this is true of you, brother, but remember that Martha was 'careful and troubled about many things,' and the Lord wanted her to trust Him and listen to His Word." (Luke 10:41)

When he said this, my heart leaped with comfort, realizing that I shouldn't worry about things, but that even with my salvation I should trust the Lord. At that point, the man who had burdened me with his doctrine released me for a moment to enjoy my faith. I told a younger brother what I had learned and then climbed the large hill on the east side of the property to worship God on the mount. I spent a day shouting at the top of my lungs. "Praise God!" and then came down feeling quite proud of my spirituality.

The next day, I was invited to go with Brother Silas in the car, to go witnessing at an Ivy League school nearby. As soon as we hit the campus, a feeling of nostalgia came over me, and I began to miss Harvard and the friends I made there.

Something in the walls, perhaps the scent of tradition and excellence, started tugging me back toward Cambridge: the Harvard Lampoon castle, the Hasty Pudding theater, the Adams House pool, the Charles River raft races, and the dignity and sophistication I absorbed when I was accepted as a member of the class of 1978. It was only a few months behind me, and it seemed so enticing from the distance.

Brother Silas immediately realized what was happening. He looked at me through his large, concerned eyes, and asked me if I was having a trial. I said I was, and rather than rebuking me, he assured me that we all faced trials every step of the way.

"Even older brothers?" I asked, still seeing them through the myopia of admiration.

"Even older brothers."

"Does Brother Evangelist go through trials, too?"

"Yes. He has to care for the Church, and we've had a lot of persecution over the last few years."

"Like what?"

"Some people have written some evil things against the brother. They have said that he owns airplanes and some property in California. He wouldn't even know how to fly a jet if he had one. Besides, what has he to gain by going through all the suffering he does? He doesn't get any money out of this!"

"They accuse him of being a cult leader. They say we're a cult.But if they knew him, they'd realize he's a humble man who really loves the truth. He owns less than most of the rest of us do. He's not interested in money or making a name for himself. If there is a good sweater in the 'extra things' box, and a younger brother needs a sweater, he'll let the brother have the sweater and take a lesser sweater. He's not into it for the glory. He doesn't even like to be called 'the Elder.' He refers to himself as the 'older brother.'"

From Dean's List to Dumpsters: Why I Left Harvard to Join a Cult

I reeled for a minute. "People say we're a cult? We're not a cult. We're built on the Word of God. We don't do this for money. We're scriptural in everything we do."

"That's true, but the devil has some counterfeit groups out there whose lifestyles are similar to ours but who do some evil things. The 'Children of God' forsake all and live communally, but they are into fornication and adultery. The hippies during the sixties were into communal living and wearing long dresses and not shaving their beards, but they also were fond of free love and drugs. Other groups like the Moonies, who are zealous to witness and to work together to bring about God's kingdom, unfortunately are confused about who God is. They think it's Reverend Moon himself. The trouble is, people tend to lump us into the same categories as these groups and assume we do the same things they do. Remember, Jesus was 'numbered with the transgressors,' (Isa. 53:12) put on a cross between two thieves, so that he would be judged guilty by association. We, too, the body of Christ, are numbered with the transgressors like the Unification Church, Hare Krishna, and the Children of God."

I looked at Silas' eyes and saw the compassion he had for me in this weak moment. He was telling me things about Brother Evangelist that no one had told me before. I knew he was a godly man but I had no idea some people considered him a cult leader. Jesus had prophesied, "Blessed are ye when men shall revile you, and persecute you, and say all manner of evil against you falsely for my sake. Rejoice and be exceedingly glad: for so persecuted they the prophets who were before you." This proved that Brother Evangelist was truly a man of God: He was being falsely accused.

As the days passed, I witnessed some interesting things. Brother Silas borrowed Harold Johnson's hunting rifle one day and set out to hunt deer. An hour later, he returned with a five point buck, which the brothers cleaned for the sisters to cook.

At a gathering soon thereafter, Brother Joseph humbly gave a testimony. "I was in the barn earlier today seeking the Lord about all the sin in my life," he began with his Tennessee drawl, his eyes squinting as he listened to the Holy Spirit, his finger wedged in his tattered Bible marking a verse he had meditated upon for hours. "While I was praying I heard a voice. It said 'May I share something with you?' At first I ignored it, and then it said again, 'May I share something with you?' I thought it might be the Adversary, but then the voice said, 'The Lord is good.'"

A shocked silence followed. Then Brother Joseph continued, "The Lord really is good."

We looked around at each other and smiled and then broke into shouts of "Praise God," and "Hallelujah, the Lord is good!" Brothers and sisters theorized among themselves that it must have been an angel who spoke to Brother Joseph.

The days grew crisper as winter crept into the state, and the brothers grew restless to move on. Brother Evangelist asked the brothers to tell him if they had a leading from God to move on to another location. He wrote down the names of those who volunteered to go and then approached me.

"Has the Lord shown you anything about going on from here?"

"I'm not sure. I really would like to go on the road soon, if that's all right." I was surprised that he valued my opinion. I was just a younger brother.

"Well, if you want to go on, we can take that as a leading from the Lord. Could you be ready to go tomorrow?"

"Lord willing."

The next morning I rose early, filled with anticipation about going on the road to places I had never been. Little did I realize I was about to go to Washington, D.C., and dwell for two months only a few miles from my beloved parents and brothers and sisters.

14

In The Land Of The Enemy

After a three-day journey, we arrived at Dupont Circle in Washington, D.C., to meet the brothers. Brother Chris, with whom I had traveled from Vermont, had left me stashed in some bushes in Rock Creek Park while he went to look for the brothers. That morning's meal, although late and desperately pined for, finally came in a greater measure than I expected: slightly bruised bananas, Red Delicious apples, Lucerne cottage cheese, yogurt, whole wheat bread, and chocolate chip cookies. It satisfied and relieved me, although my fingers were so icy I could hardly bring the food to my mouth. My bad habit of licking my fingers to clean them was a serious liability when eating outside in October.

We met the brothers and were transported to an old house at the corner of 10th Street and M Street NE. Brother Barry had spotted the house in stagnant renovation and contacted the owner, a rich middle-aged woman who lived in Potomac, Maryland who renovated houses as a hobby. She had heard of our need for housing, and trusting in our integrity as men and women of Christian character, offered to let us stay in the house, in exchange for watching it and doing some minor construction.

The three-story brick structure faced 10th Street, but had a path that led around to where the building was fairly open in the back. As one came around, one first saw a set of cement steps leading into the basement of the house on the right, and at the other end, an open porch that ran the length of the two houses. What appeared as one solid house from the front was really two separate houses divided in the back. We had access to both houses.

Brothers quickly set up in the city. After visiting the Chamber of Commerce, we had several good, free street maps of Washington and vicinity. With the help of the C & P Yellow pages, we plotted a store-checking map, and soon loaded up part of one floor of the house on the east. That was to become our "kitchen area." Inside were two large wooden tables, which served as cutting boards when the kitchen was only occupied by the sisters, and underneath we laid boxes upon boxes of produce, bread, and dairy products the brothers had gleaned from the dumpsters of the Connecticut Avenue Safeway, and pastry scraps gathered from Clement's Bakery dumpster about three blocks from the White House.

The older brother responsible for arranging who would "check stores" could be found in the kitchen after the morning meal, inspecting the food and deciding what things the brother checking stores should bring and what things he should leave behind. Some had gotten so acute at judging the alimentary needs of the group that they could just glance at the food, calculate how many could be fed with it, and whether a brother should check stores to add to the pile.

We feared the Lord when it came to checking stores. If someone went out when we had enough, all kinds of things could happen. A brother could check twenty dumpsters and not find anything. The Lord Himself would rebuke us for being greedy at the dumpsters. Sometimes brothers would get to a dumpster just as the trash truck arrived and would not be able to check it.

But the thing we dreaded most was having a "situation." It was the shame of shames. We would hang our heads and confess to the older brother later how the manager of a store came out just as we were filling our store-checking pack with granola cereal and Fig Newtons, and yelled at us, forced us to throw the food back, and threatened to call the police. It was especially shameful if the next day the manager had decided to eliminate the problem forever by putting a lock and chain on the dumpster. The offending brother would be rebuked for "not using wisdom," of "tarrying too long at the waste places," or "not being diligent when checking stores." It became a mark of your maturity if you were never caught at the dumpsters.

In Washington, I went through some of the most difficult internal struggles in my life. Daily, the older brothers would preach against pride, lust, and worldliness. Those who were newly in positions to exhort the flock felt it was their duty to be as harsh and strict as possible. It seemed the more demanding and less merciful they could portray God, the greater wisdom and fear of the Lord they displayed to the group.

"There were souls with us who became overcome with the lust for food, and eventually left the group to be closer to a refrigerator. Woe unto you if you let your belly destroy you in the same way that Esau let his belly destroy him for a morsel of meat!"

"Those of you who think you stand, take heed, lest you fall. There have been souls with us who said, 'If it gets down to just Brother Evangelist and me, I'll never forsake the Church.' Where are they now? The moment persecution hit they were the first to fall."

Preaching like this did nothing to encourage or strengthen my faith. If I had one problem that first year, it wasn't thinking I was spiritually invincible. I gradually expected to be "cut off" by the Lord for my pride. Why would he want someone like me, someone so obviously filled with pride and lust? I loved food. I liked women. I enjoyed a good laugh from time to time. These things the Lord hated were obvious in my life. I had tried to act more humble, to be obedient to eat less and control my belly, and to be sober, but I slipped occasionally and felt very guilty. I really didn't expect to survive in the group.

These fears began to increase daily, until I found myself every day for hours in the cold basement under the kitchen, crying aloud to God for mercy. I assumed He hated me. I would wrap myself in my sleeping bag, hang my head, and walk in circles pleading with God, "Please, Lord, deliver me from my pride!" Thinking I wasn't being fervent enough, I would get more desperate, and walk around more and more, pleading and wailing and shouting and crying, certain that God hated me and would not tolerate any imperfection in me. I took to fasting, and felt filled with guilt whenever I ate. Eating was "lust," and I wasn't "pressing in" enough. I saw other older brothers eating only one meal a day and spending hours on their knees in quiet prayer, and wondered why I didn't have their strength. God wasn't answering my prayers, and so He seemed bent on destroying me. If God was against me, who could be for me?

This went on for weeks. The house was icy cold, and I got the idea that if I didn't wear a coat I would be "suffering in the flesh," and thus ceasing from sin. We believed that suffering helped us become more holy. However, as I was to learn later, only the most unstable in the group (like me) actually thought God wanted us to a ict ourselves by not wearing proper clothing in the winter. Most realized that suffering came in many forms, and that if handled correctly, could develop lifelong character in the sufferer.

One day, I had been shouting at God for about an hour, accusing Him of wanting to kill me, and weeping in despair and depression at the impossibility of pleasing Him. I had tried so hard, yet it seemed one mistake wiped out all the good I had done. Who could please this God? As I laid there on the cold cement floor, an understanding came over me, a revelation from the God I was so bitterly accusing.

Deep in my spirit, I felt the warmth and love of the Holy Spirit come over me, and a Voice asking me very kindly, "Who do you think I am?" My soul was shocked but gladdened by His presence.

I responded, "You're the Spirit of love, and joy, and peace! You're so good to be around!" I was so relieved to find that God loved me and that He personally cared about my welfare.

In the days to come, I learned some of the basics of the Christian faith for the first time. One of the things I learned is that we cannot please God in our own power. When the believer has a problem, a sin greater than him, he is to pray to God, confess the sin, and trust in the goodness and power of God to gradually remove that sin from his or her life. We are not to attempt to please God in our own goodness. It's impossible. I also grew to realize that some sins were going to take time to overcome, and that God had plans to save me, not destroy me.

Things were not so great for us physically, though. The thirty of us shared one bathroom, one water spigot, and no heat. As a younger brother, it was my job to carry water from the basement of one building to the kitchen stairs in the second building. We had accumulated about two dozen empty carton milk jugs, and washed them out to bring water over to the kitchen. We could fill four at a time, getting our hands wet, and would have to warm our hands inside our pants before we could carry the jugs over.

I remember one day carrying water outside through the snow, up the steps of the kitchen, and turning the empty jugs for more. I had no time that day for myself, to pray, read the Bible, or rest. I wondered if anyone noticed how hard I had worked, and if so, did they care? I must have looked pretty puppy-dogged, because toward the end of the day, some of the older brothers began thanking me for my labors. However, I wanted to know if Brother Evangelist cared. A little later I saw him standing in the backyard, deep in thought, obviously meditating on Scripture, or silently praying for direction to lead the group.

He looked up, as if God had told him my desire, and said, "Thank you, brother, for your labors today. You have been very diligent in your service for the brethren. The Lord bless you."

I almost fainted! Could this man read minds, too?

A few days later, we had a surprise that almost drove us out of town. I was standing in the living room near a window when a man on the street called out to me. "Hey, is everything all right in there?"

I waved and said yes, looking guilty because I knew I wasn't supposed to be standing near the windows. He replied, "There's an awful lot of smoke coming out of your roof. You got a chimney or something?" By then I knew I was in trouble. I replied, "We have a fireplace in here and we're burning wood to keep warm. And yes, we have a chimney." The chimney at that time was only a few feet above the roof and couldn't be seen from the ground. It made it look like the house was on fire whenever we burned wood in the fireplace.

The next thing I knew, sirens wailed and fire trucks began encircling the house. A concerned neighbor had alerted the fire department and they had come to the rescue. An alert older brother told us all to go upstairs and be very quiet so they couldn't determine how many people were in the house. I wanted to stay and watch, but orders were orders.

As soon as we fled up the steps, the first firemen came into our living room, astonished to find inhabitants in the building. A few older brothers remained downstairs to meet the firemen and explained the chimney situation to them. One of them seemed irate that we were flaunting the health codes by living in a house without heat and su cient plumbing, but others were more understanding when they learned we were a traveling Christian ministry temporarily in Washington. They called the owner to verify that we had permission to stay there, and then left, admonishing us not to use the fireplace until the chimney was lengthened, according to the strict D.C. building codes.

That night we gathered, and the testimonies flew. Some saw the sudden unexpected arrival of the firemen as a symbol of Christ's sudden and unexpected return for which we must be ready.

Others viewed it in the context of persecution, that we must be ready when the enemy strikes, willing to lay down our lives for the sake of the brethren and the Gospel. An older brother reminded us that we needed to tear the heartstrings we may have for our former families, because Christ is coming soon, and would be leaving our unbelieving families behind. If we loved them more than Christ (or loved them at all), we would be passed over at Christ's coming. Another brother took advantage of the situation to remind us to "use wisdom" and stay away from the windows. No doubt the events of that evening were talked about for months to come.

15

A Visit To Richmond

"We're getting up now, Lord willing," the brother chimed to us mummies on the floor.

"Brother Jim, pack up…You're going on the road today."

Finally! I was ready for a change. After a hot breakfast of vegetable stew and pastries, Brother David, Sister Joanna, and I took the metro to southern Virginia and got off at the last stop. We walked over to an on-ramp and hitched south toward Richmond, Virginia.

It was a crisp autumn morning. The frost-etched grass broke under the weight of our Vibram-soled army boots as we trudged with our backpacks to where cars could see us and have plenty of room to stop. We got a few short rides, taking us south about fifty miles, and seemed stranded for the night near a rocky and windy creek that laced along the interstate. The creek was shallow and frozen, and scattered here and there were colorful pebbles and broken sticks that had broken off the frozen trees that edged the creek. We found dry spots down the creek bed where we laid out our ground cloths for the night. Brother David was in good spirits, singing Psalms to the Lord, smiling as he shared a new song that made all our hearts leap for joy. Sister Joanna smiled, but avoided eye contact with the brothers, connecting only long enough to kiss our spirits goodnight. A physical kiss would have been out of the question.

The next morning we rose to the sound of eighteen- wheelers storming past trying to submerge the sweet primeval sanctity of our virgin resting places. We were closer to nature and God than those abominable post-industrial freight haulers, whose only merit was that they sometimes stopped to pick us up hitchhiking. But something special within us castrated the truck's power to spoil our peace. We were separate, holy, and chosen for the great task of enlightening a darkened world. We had hope, faith in a God that was present and intimately interested in every detail of our lives.

Beyond that, we were delivered from the responsibilities and pressures that full participation in the economic system of America creates. We had no mortgage, because we turtled our homes on our backs; no medical insurance, because God was our Healer; no fear of being fired from our jobs and suffering financial ruin, because we had no jobs and were already financially ruined; no fear of hunger, because the supermarket dumpsters were abundantly fruitful; no stress of working for an oppressive and power-crazed boss, because we awoke daily to do God's work; no loneliness, because we traveled in groups, and were a large extended family. We didn't worry about inflation, recession, stock market plunges, or depressions. We were learning to live on two dollars per day. However, what we did fear was drifting away from God, and being eternally cut off from His church.

After a spartan meal, we walked back up to the on-ramp, and got a ride with a truck the remaining fifty miles to Richmond. At the local park, we spied Brother Justus verbally contending with some young men who were apparently Christians, and trying to defeat Brother Justus' version of the Gospel. A few minutes later, after watching Brother Justus from a distance, a couple of other young men came up to Brother David, Sister Joanna, and me, and began to spar theologically.

"Why do you say I am not a Christian simply because I don't wear a backpack and travel like you?"

Brother David replied, "I have never seen you, and I don't even know who you are. I never said you weren't a Christian." After a few minutes, with Brother David being slow to speak and cutting in his replies, the two men backed off. But before leaving they asked, "Have you seen our brother Paul Simpson? He was with us last night, but disappeared after speaking with several guys who looked like you."

Brother David truthfully replied, "I have no idea what you are talking about." However, we all were gladdened to hear we had snatched a new brother from the clutches of this other false ministry.

A few minutes later, Brother Justus got away from his young sparring partners, and came over to tell us what had happened. The night before, he and another brother had arrived in Richmond, needing a place to stay out of the cold. The Forever Family, later known as "The Church of Bible Understanding" (C.O.B.U.), lodged them that night.

At dinner, Brother Justus had begun to witness to Paul. Paul was a young man, about twenty years old, with a real zeal to be obedient to God. With C.O.B.U., he had to get up very early to make his lunch (the sisters didn't want to help in this). He spent the day at a tree nursery, and donated all his earnings to this Christian commune in exchange for room and board. Paul was fed up with the way C.O.B.U. oppressed him. He was constantly so tired after work that he had no energy for the mandatory street witnessing at night. Brother Justus' message of quitting work to serve the Lord was especially appealing that night. Paul took the bait, and told Brother Justus he wanted to leave with him.

Of course, this did not sit well with some of the older members of C.O.B.U., who felt that Brother Justus and the brothers were really wolves in sheep's clothing. They began to scrutinize his words and his appearance.

"Where do you live?" they queried.

"The foxes have holes, the birds of the air have nests, but the Son of Man has not where to lay his head." (Matt. 8:20)

"But don't you have a home? Even the early Christians had homes."

"We just travel and live by faith. Our kingdom is not of this world."

"Why do you wear sandals in the winter? Don't your feet get cold?"

"Jesus said if we don't forsake everything we have we cannot be his disciple. (Luke 14:33) I wear sandals because Jesus said to forsake all."

He winced inside himself after saying this, because even he didn't believe that forsaking all meant wearing sandals, and that forsaking Reebok sneakers for open-soled sandals was a divine commandment. Of course, Brother Justus didn't want to correct himself, because it might mean losing his credibility with them. He instead chose to be quietly angry with himself. After they leaped on this statement, Brother Justus opted to remove himself from the ring and go to his corner for another round the next day in the park. That's what we observed when we got to the park.

Brother Justus was still disgusted with himself for preaching a false gospel, but he was thrilled that he had met a new brother. After giving us directions to a house where the brothers were going to stay, he split up from us, and went to another part of the park. It was understood that we were not to congregate in public, because too many people dressed alike and wearing backpacks were likely to draw attention, especially in conservative cities like Richmond. We got our backpacks on, walked a few blocks in the direction that Brother Justus told us, and came to the house where we met Brother Alan.

After the customary greeting, we had a hot meal and bedded down, waiting until morning to find out if we were going to stay in Richmond or not. Brother Alan went to the phone to speak with Brother Evangelist, and after he returned he told us it was prudent for us to flee the city immediately, and return to D.C. with the new brother. We all packed up and went to the on-ramp.

This time I was paired up with Brother Abel, a gifted tenor who often led the brothers in songs during our evening gathering. He was my older brother, having joined the group about two years before I did. At the on-ramp we met Brother Daniel, who at five feet, two inches, was the smallest man I had ever submitted to. But I reminded myself that it wasn't physical stature that mattered to Christ, it was spiritual stature. I was a babe; he was an older brother and more experienced than I was. I was commanded by the Scriptures to be subject to him.

Brother Daniel was traveling with the new Brother Paul, soon to be known as "Younger Brother Paul" (since we had a Brother Paul already in the group.) We sat there in two separate groups,

Brother Daniel and Brother Paul farther up the on-ramp and closer to the freeway, and Brother Abel and me nearer the head of the ramp. We sat there for hours, and I began to joke with myself that if this was "fleeing", we weren't doing a very good job of it.

Brother Daniel came over and tried to encourage us. "When we was hitchin' one time an' trying to gets away from some fowls in a city once, we waited for a ride and cried out, 'Lord, get us a ride!' There was another group hitchin' with us now and it didn't look very good for the Lord to get us a ride. So we waited a little longer and then the Lord had two cars stop at once and they took both groups! Hallelujah!" He smiled, revealing the gap between his top incisors and his canine teeth.

We laughed with him, and the next thing we knew, two cars were pulling over for us: one on the freeway for Brother Daniel and Brother Paul; one on the ramp for Brother Abel and me. We rejoiced and praised God, certain that He was aiding our escape from the false Christians who were trying to drag Brother Paul back to spiritual bondage in Babylon.

16

The Road To San Antonio

After we arrived in Washington, Brother Evangelist informed Brother Bruce and me that we would be going on the road the next day. Three days later, after numerous disappointments, we got word to leave. As we walked past the Washington Monument on our way to Interstate 295, I kept my eyes open so I wouldn't run into my mother, who often spent time at the Smithsonian Institute hearing lectures and going on field trips to historical sites. I told Brother Bruce of the danger, and he watched with me.

As we passed the monument, I began to share my opinion that they were nothing but massive chunks of rock, and that people were stupid to come from all over just to see a rock. They were just dumb idols, phallic symbols, monuments to frail and dead people who probably were sitting in hell and wishing they had it all to do over again. Brother Bruce wagged his head and hissed along agreeably, making me feel like I was really getting insight.

Five days later, we arrived in San Antonio, and waited at the Alamo for some brother to meet us. Soon, Brother Alan appeared, and gave us directions and a bus map to where he and Brother Joel were staying. We caught a bus on Broadway and rode it out to Brackenridge Park, and disembarked where they were building a new freeway behind Trinity College. Along a fence, the brothers had set up their camp: Brother Joel with his Quonset hut-shaped tent, and Brother Alan with his massive two-pole nylon tent. Humility, Alan's infant daughter, smiled at us and pointed. Fatigued by the long journey, we set up our tent and tried to catch up on our sleep.

A few minutes later, a police helicopter patrolling the area swooped over our campsite about 100 feet over our tents, stirring me to take cover from the persecutors. We took that as a sign from the Lord to leave that campsite and look for a house in which to dwell. The next day, Brother Abel, armed with the confidence found in prayer, went out to look for housing while some of us hid in the woods. A few hours later, he came back, his quarry bagged a house being renovated that needed someone to watch it. We moved in, and rejoiced that God had met our needs.

While in the house, I was sent out to check stores for the brothers several times. I was going through some fierce trials, since there was so much preaching about getting rooted in the Bible and in our faith. Brothers related stories to me about souls who hadn't gotten a strong foundation in the faith and had been swept away by persecution; parents using deprogrammers; and others falling prey to the police and their warrants. I knew I had some serious faults, and felt I was not strong enough to endure whatever the Lord had for me. Consequently, I slummed around in great anguish and fear I would not be among the few who would endure.

One afternoon, I asked Brother Asher to pray with me in the attic of the house. He agreed and I confessed, "Brother, I have to confess that I am far too self-centered. I need to die to myself. Will you pray for me that the Lord delivers me from myself?"

He agreed, looking at me with compassion and a little fear, wondering what was really going on in my head. We shouted to the Lord together, me pleading and contorting, panting out a prayer with all my breath, leaving me a little winded and dizzy. I felt no noticeable difference at the time, but felt I had done my part.

Later that night, the owner of the building came over, complaining that the house was lit up like a Christmas tree. The older brothers had a few words with the man, and decided to leave the next day to go to Dallas, Texas. We packed up and headed north the next morning, planning to meet at the main Post Oce. Not much later, persecution hit the Church.

In our camp, about three hundred feet into the woods, off the Santa Fe train tracks in Dallas, we prepared to bed down. Our tents were set up randomly, with the married brothers' tents a modest distance from the single brothers' and sisters' tents. All week, the older brothers had been exhorting and warning us about impending persecution. I didn't know where they got their information, but it seemed like God was trying to warn us to prepare. As I was resting in my tent, a helicopter suddenly swooped over and its floodlights danced around our camp. Brother Joel shouted, "Freeze!" and I hit the tent floor praying it wasn't my time. After a couple of minutes, the helicopter flitted off, and I lay on the floor in total panic. Were deprogrammers and parents going to sweep through the forest, led by the helicopter's search beam, and drag us away to deprogram us? As it turned out, nothing happened there.

But meanwhile, in St. Louis, some family members posing as police took Sister Joanna from the group, and led her away to deprogram her. The brothers were right. We were going to be persecuted. She would be away from us for many months, and we would give her up for dead.

II
Section Two: Into The Wilderness

17

The New Standards

As the days passed, the church began to change in several ways. New standards were instituted by Brother Evangelist to "protect the Church from the enemy coming in like a flood." Several sisters had been dragged away by parents, deprogrammers, and spouses, and the Church seemed to be "everywhere spoken against." Consequently, he decided it would be safer if the church were scattered more throughout the country with fewer brothers congregating in any one city for any length of time. Having once flocked as ten in a city, we now huddled as four, painfully longing for more of the brothers and sisters to be with us.

During this time, Brother Evangelist announced two new standards pertaining to our travels and about marriage. It would be a new standard, he announced, that we would no longer tell anyone in the group what city we had just hitchhiked from, nor what city we were heading toward. Neither were we to make any references to the general part of the country, or any other details that might indicate where any present or past camps were located. The purpose of this, we were told, was to protect the entire church in time of persecution. If the police struck one camp and grilled us for information about where other members might be in other cities, we could honestly say that we did not know. We shouldn't have to lie. Only Brother Evangelist was privileged to know the whereabouts of all the members. The other members were not to be trusted.

In Detroit in 1978, after an exodus of several married members and their families from the group, Brother Evangelist gathered all the single members, and announced that he didn't foresee any more marriages in the church.

"This may cause some of you to leave the Church, I know, but I need to be faithful to your souls. You can easily find some carnal preacher in the world who is willing to tickle your ears and speak smooth things to please your flesh, but as Paul said, 'I am free of the blood of all men because I have not shunned to declare unto you all the counsel of God.'" (Acts 20:26-27)

"Some of you are still carnal and young and will not like what I have to say, but I do it out of love for your souls. I have seen over the years that marriage is not a good thing in these days in which we're living. Remember it said that the last days would be like the days of Noah, how men would be marrying and giving in marriage until the day Noah entered the ark (Matt. 24:38) and the flood came and destroyed them all. We're living in those days, and we can't be like the world, marrying and giving in marriage. We must be ready for Christ's coming and be counted worthy to sit at the marriage feast of the Lamb. I believe marriage is a very serious thing and should not be entered into lightly. Unless the Lord really shows me something different, and I don't think he would go around me in a matter this important, I foresee no marriages in this Church."

The brothers and sisters groaned within themselves at this announcement. A cloud of depression fell and dampened our spirits.

Then came the knockout punch: "This may cause some to fall away, but the Bible does prophesy that in the last days there would be a great falling away. Some have left this Church and the great truth because they weren't willing to be subject to every Word of God. Remember we must live by every Word of God, not just those that are easy to bear."

We left the gathering severely depressed and discouraged, any hope of future intimacy and affection forever banished from our heart. But we knew we could not leave. Our choice was to stay celibate, or marry and go to hell.

A few months later in Everett, Washington, I noticed Brother Evangelist was no longer wearing a shirt only to his crotch. He was wearing an unusual-looking garment that went below his knees, looking every bit like a dark polyester lab coat. A few days later, he sent out a couple of brothers to find material for shirts in a local sporting goods manufacturer's dumpster. They found many yards of gray 60/40 cloth, consisting of sixty-percent cotton and forty- percent polyester. Then, he announced we were going to be wearing our shirts down to the knees now, and no longer just to the crotch. He felt it would be more modest and more of a testimony to the world to take a stand like this. It was not as long as a robe, so we wouldn't be too noticeable on the street, but long enough to be modest. The church was growing in modesty.

I felt like a gazingstock when I first put the garment on, but I gradually got used to the idea. Soon, friendly neighbors in Louisville, Kentucky, referred to us as "the raincoat people," saying, "If you can't trust the raincoat people, who can you trust?"

My role in the Church gradually began to change shortly after the most trying journey of my life. In November of 1978, I was sent on the road with Brother Barry to go from Everett, Washington, to New York City. I didn't know our destination when we left, but I trusted the wisdom and guidance of Brother Barry who knew the plan.

After our first day on the road we were in Sacramento, California, where we spent the night with some kind people in the Shiloh Ministry. The next morning Barry had us dump out all our food and travel in faith that God would provide a meal that night. I began to doubt his sanity at this point, but then changed my mind and decided he just had more faith than me.

From Dean's List to Dumpsters: Why I Left Harvard to Join a Cult

During the day Barry got a revelation that we were supposed to go to New York via Austin, Texas, the town he had lived in and where his estranged wife still resided. I was thrilled about the prospect of a little spiritual sidetrack and about hitchhiking the warmer southern route. We left the eastbound on-ramp for Interstate 80 and shifted to the southbound on-ramp for Interstate 5, pointing ourselves in the direction of Los Angeles. We got nowhere that day and in desperation hopped a freight train that came by and rode all night. When we awoke in the morning we were in San Bernardino, headed west toward L.A. We got out at the train yard and walked to an eastbound I-10 on-ramp and hitchhiked east toward Texas. After being searched by undercover cops pretending to be plumbers in a pickup truck, we got about fifteen miles out of town and no farther.

In the next five days we got about ten miles. No one would stop for us, and our food supply ran out. Barry checked a Taco Bell and found a few scraps of food which he offered to another man hitchhiking in front of us on the on-ramp. He thanked us and Barry told me later that he gave our food away because he thought the Lord would honor our generosity and provide more food for us. I was not thrilled.

Perhaps Barry's hitchhiking strategy had something to do with our lack of rides. As we were walking down the freeway one day I asked him why he didn't stick out his thumb when he hitchhiked. "It would be a lack of faith," he replied. "The Lord knows we need a ride, and He can put it on someone's heart to stop for us if He wants to. I'm learning more about what it really means to walk by faith."

I found that a little hard to swallow, but I trusted Barry's wisdom enough to accept it with a grain of salt. As we stood along the side of the freeway with our arms folded, a curious group of bystanders gathered near the freeway fence bordering their neighborhood. One of them mocked us saying, "If you stick out your thumb you may have a better chance of getting a ride!"

"How carnal," I thought. "How carnal! They just don't understand the things of God." We didn't get a ride that night either and we bedded down along the freeway in some high bushes.

After about five days I gave up believing we were going to get a ride. I drew a zero in my Bible each day we didn't get anywhere, and after a few days I had a string of them. To survive emotionally and not become bitter I had to stop expecting a ride and set out to spend the day studying the Bible with no hopes, no disappointments.

We finally got a ride and found ourselves let out on Interstate 10 in Arizona, between the little towns of Bowie and Wilcox. As state highway intersected the freeway there and wound north through the town of Eden, Arizona. Barry thought it was edifying that we were at the intersection leading to Eden but I felt the route number was a little more ominous. "ARIZONA666."

Around sunset, after a grueling afternoon of waiting, Barry decided he would hitchhike west back to Wilcox to get dinner for us. As soon as he crossed the interstate to hitch west he got a ride, only the second ride we had gotten all day. I set up the tent about 100 yards off the road and prepared to wait for Barry. The shadows lengthened, the desert darkened, and Barry had not returned. We had no water so Barry promised to bring some back with him.

We had not had water since about noon that day and I was extremely thirsty that night. I couldn't get the thought of water out of my mind all night as I wriggled and moaned and prayed for water. Had I known my cactus species I would have put a spigot in one and drank, but I had only seen Roadrunner do it in the cartoons. In desperation I put my empty water jug outside the tent and begged God to fill it. After a while I realized that wasn't going to happen, so I changed my prayer: "God, deliver me from my thirst." After praying this wholeheartedly, I felt myself strengthened and the desire to drink water went away for the rest of the night.

The next morning I got up and went out looking for Barry.

That evening about sunset Barry came walking down the freeway with a box of food, and I rushed to greet him. "Did you bring any water?" I asked.

"No, I couldn't carry everything with me. Weren't you able to get some water?" I was stunned.

"What did you bring?"

"Well, some of this food does have some moisture in it. I found some egg scraps from a restaurant, and while I was leaving town I found a one dollar bill on the ground, so I went back to the store and bought this…"

My mouth dropped open with shock as he pulled an eight- ounce jar of peanut butter. He seemed surprised when I turned down his kind offer of a Ritz cracker smeared with peanut butter.

"The Lord really tried me on my trip to town," he explained. "I got a ride immediately that night all the way to town but couldn't find anything that night. The next morning, I checked a restaurant and found a bunch of spaghetti and bread, but the owner caught me and invited me into the restaurant for a meal."

"What did you do with the food?"

"Well, since the man invited me in, I had no choice but to throw the food back into the dumpster. When I went in you'll never guess what he served me."

"I have no idea."

"Well, I believe the Lord is really trying us on this journey," he chuckled. "He brought me a sausage sandwich and a Coke!" Pork and caffeine were Barry's two greatest gastronomical enemies, and neither were kosher for our group. "So I poured the Coke on the plant when the owner wasn't looking, and flushed the sausage down the toilet!"

I wondered if that was the right thing to do, and if it was necessary to carry one's convictions that far. "Did you go back to the dumpster to get the food?" I asked, already knowing the answer. Of course he didn't. It wouldn't have been appropriate.

After another tormenting night, we got up early to travel. I began to curse the Winnebagos in my heart as they sped benignly and neglectfully by.

Finally, I looked down the interstate and saw a sign. We walked up to the sign and it said "REST AREA 5 MILES." Barry and I immediately got our packs together and walked there after I first begged God for strength. About an hour and a half later we arrived and flooded our mouths at the water fountain. It was too good to be true.

We eventually got to Austin and found a place to camp near the train tracks, about a mile from the University of Texas. Nineteen days later, after waiting patiently in the woods and waiting for a sign, Barry decided it was God's will to go on to New York City. It had taken us nineteen days to hitchhike from Everett, Washington, to Austin, Texas, so shortly after Christmas Barry heard God's call to move on. Everything had gone wrong for him that day, including his shoelace breaking three times, so he knew it was God showing him to move on.

Three days later we were in Alexandria, Virginia, making tremendous progress and practically going from one ride to the next that entire time. In Alexandria, after the forty first day of our journey, we were imprisoned for two days for hitchhiking on the freeway, and released. On the forty fourth day of our journey we arrived in New York City and spent the night in the waiting room of a shelter to get a bed. The next morning we were given a bed next to an African-American who told me gravely, "The only thing I like that's white is biscuits."

We eventually found the brothers and spent two nights in the city before being sent to Immokalee, Florida, to meet some brothers. After spending the night there, I was sent back to California to meet some brothers camped along the Pacific Ocean near Santa Barbara.

18

An Enemy Among Us

In Everett, Washington, in the spring of 1978, I began to get some more authority in the Church. I could spell out in detail to the sisters what food to use in meals and what proportions to use. I got to "do camp" and announce the portions on the table before each meal. It was truly an honor trying to be wise and discerning enough to determine just how much food to put on the table. Too much food would tempt the brothers and sisters to gluttony and not enough would leave them hungry. It was better, however, to err on the light side than to put out too much food.

When I was told I would be promoted to doing camp the next day, I went into the kitchen, and like the experienced older brothers began to look through the food to figure out what to serve the next day. I must have been too joyful because Brother Evangelist felt I needed to be humbled. He came in, sized up my apparent arrogance, took over and decided the menu for me, and told the sister. I was both embarrassed and piqued that he felt he had to humiliate me this way. However, he saw it his duty to keep me in my humble place so the Lord's wrath wouldn't fall on me.

Before going on the road himself, Brother Evangelist gathered me and a sister, took out a sheet of notebook paper, and read a short statement he had prepared concerning Brother Alan: "Because Alan has not been faithful in raising his child properly and has been unable to lift up the standard as an older brother, he will no longer be serving in the capacity of pastor of the church."

A few months later I traveled from Everett, Washington, to Cincinnati, Ohio where we were greeted by Brother Evangelist who had gone there a few weeks earlier.

"Did you see anyone on your way when you came across the country?" he asked nervously.

"Like who?" I asked. It's difficult to travel 2,000 miles and not see anyone at all.

"Former members, or brothers, or anyone who might know the Church?"

"No. We didn't see anyone at all that we knew."

"You didn't happen to see Brother Alan or the sister, did you?"

"Or his wife? No." I was perplexed that he would ask that question, but he seemed relieved that no one had seen us. He relaxed after asking those questions.

"Praise God. Thank you," he replied, and pleasantly dismissed us without explanation. A couple of days later he called a solemn assembly where he began to explain some things we had to know.

"Let's turn to Galatians 4:16 and read: 'Have I therefore become your enemy because I tell you the truth?'

"It seems there has been a falling away in our midst. I know some of you were very close to the couple about whom I am speaking. Brother Alan and Sister Abi have served very preciously with us for many years. But in the last couple of years some things have been happening that most of you do not know anything about.

"I remember Alan when he first met the ministry, how joyful he was to meet the brothers and sisters and how he was baptized there in the river in Missoula. Let's read Galatians 4:14: 'And my trial which was in my flesh you did not despise or reject, but you received me as an angel of God, even Christ Jesus.'

That's how he received us. But it seems he has become offended at rebuke and has turned bitter against the ministry. I spoke to him about a year ago about his gluttony and about his lack of disciplining his child. He wasn't able to receive it and has gone around privately slandering his soul and saying all kinds of unsound things to other older brothers. Let's look at another verse: Proverbs 22:10 'Cast out the scorner, and contention will leave, Yes, strife and reproach will cease.'

I have been very burdened about what to do with this couple. When it was reported to me that they were slandering me I took them aside and spoke to them about it. Alan seemed broken and willing to repent for a while, but he fell right back into it. Some of it was envy, desiring to be in the high places. Remember that the angels who were not content with their first estate were cast down from heaven. No one is too big for God to abase. Well, there seemed nothing else to do, so I did what Scripture commands, 'Cast out the scorner…, lest the scorning and bitterness spread to the whole assembly.'" (Prov. 22:10)

At this point several of the members were saddened and shocked at the news of Alan and Abi being cast out of the church. So many years of faithful service down the drain! Another casualty in the war for our souls! How have the mighty fallen!

I was devastated, but clearly on the eider's side. He wouldn't lie to us. If Alan had become carnal and rebellious what else could God do but remove him from the fellowship? In my mind's eye I imagined a demon on Alan's shoulder and Alan's eyes darkened and his countenance soured. He was now an enemy to be avoided and not spoken to.

The gathering ended with stern warnings not to become prideful and rebellious, and to avoid Alan if we should see him or his wife. We met the next night, too, and Brother Evangelist continued to reveal his allegations against Alan and his wife, quoting from a number of older brothers' reports of the things Alan was saying and doing.

"It is not the custom of the Church to follow brothers around to see if they are riding Greyhound buses from city to city," he cryptically commented.

It wasn't until a few years later that I learned from Alan that Brother Evangelist often took the Church's funds to ride buses instead of hitchhiking like the rest of us. Alan asked an older brother to follow Brother Evangelist to see if that was the case. Alan had no problem with the Elder riding buses if he wanted to. The problem was that he did it secretly and didn't tell anyone what he was doing. The sisters also suspected it because he would come in off the road in clean clothing and all his shirts would be pressed and clean, hardly the attire of someone who had spent four or five days hitchhiking on a scorching freeway. Alan's spy discovered just what he had suspected.

Life returned to normal for a few months, and we found ourselves sharing a two floor apartment about a mile from downtown Buffalo, New York. It was a large camp of about twenty brothers and sisters, and we had access to another house about two blocks away. However, the second house was so hush hush that almost none of us knew there was a house there. Little did we suspect we would soon be moving to the house to protect us from persecution.

One day we were scattered around the house doing various services, when I heard a brother shout, "Oh, my God!" and another brother shout, "Everyone upstairs! Everyone upstairs!" Over that voice was a woman's voice crying loudly in deep pain and sorrow, "Innocent blood! Innocent blood! Have mercy on us, Lord Jesus! Have mercy on us!" A baby began to wail uncontrollably, and the brothers and sisters rushed up the stairs and bolted themselves in their quarters. The older brothers remained downstairs to deal with the intrusion.

A brother looked at me and said, "Brother Alan has found us." I learned that his wife had jumped through a low window in the living room area and had tried to rush up to the sisters' room to explain her side of why they had been thrown out of the group. A couple of older brothers hastily blocked passage to the sisters' room and Abi sat down on the steps to protest. We hid terror-stricken in our rooms, awaiting orders from our commanders.

The older brothers planned our escape. The sisters were let out a window onto a smaller roof and then helped down a drain spout to escape. We couldn't help comparing it with St. Paul's escape from Damascus in Acts 9:23-25: "Now after many days were past, Jews plotted to kill him. But their plot became known to Saul. And they watched the gates day and night, to kill him. Then the disciples took him by night and let him down through the wall in a large basket."

The sisters were rushed to the other house around the block. Neither Alan nor Abi knew we had moved the sisters.

Next, the brothers filed past Alan and Abi sitting on the upstairs steps and moved out of the house. Brother Evangelist warned us before we went down not to listen to anything they had to say because it was just a bunch of deceit. We obediently agreed, feeling it was an honor to suffer persecution for Christ. I put my fingers in my ears for an extra measure of safety. We strode past them without a word and were led by an older brother to the house around the corner where we had our evening meal.

The Elder decided it was expedient that we leave that next morning from the city. We made our preparations and gathered for one last gathering before fleeing the city. Brother Evangelist looked worn out and tired, similar to the Man who spent the night in a garden in prayer before being crucified. I loved him so much and appreciated all the flack he was bearing as our leader and Elder. He was truly suffering and did not complain. Now was his time to put the events of the night into perspective and address us one last time before we went out to war against future persecutions for the Gospel's sake.

"Brethren, it's a late hour and Christ promised persecutions would come. All those who live godly in Christ Jesus will suffer persecution. Remember what Christ said in the Book of Revelation: 'Hold fast that which you have and let no man take your crown.'

A brother came up to me after the sister came through the window and shared a dream he had last night before all this happened. Brother Jeremy, would you like to share your dream with us?"

A tall and lanky brother who had joined the group a few months earlier humbly shared that he had dreamed that two serpents had come through the window of the house and were striking at the heels of the Church. We were amazed and sure that the dream was of God, condemning both Alan and Abi, and justifying the Church. This embellished the eider's reputation in our eyes as the leader of our Church.

"I might add," Brother Evangelist commented, "That after a while the serpents stopped striking the Church and eventually went away. I believe that's what the brother shared with me, isn't it brother?"

Brother Jeremy hastily agreed. He had left out that part.

"I also want to exhort you to share your dreams with me. Had we known about that dream beforehand we might have been able to avoid this persecution. But take it as a warning that we are in warfare and souls get puffed up and fall away and become enemies of the truth. I remember that one soul said if it came down to just Brother Evangelist and himself, he would never forsake the Church. A few months later the soul left and was found somewhere lying on a street, with just a few bubbles of air in his lungs. Take heed ye who stand, lest you fall."

We were shaken by this story and discouraged. How could anyone with such zeal lose it so suddenly? How wrathful God is to those who leave the Church! I was becoming more and more aware of how trapped I was in the Church. There was no leaving or living once you committed yourself to this group.

19

Falling In Love

Perhaps one of the most difficult aspects of living in the church was the lack of companionship with the opposite sex. I joined when I was nineteen and had plans to marry sometime in my mid twenties. After joining the group I realized how reluctant the Elder was to approve marriage, and no one in the group dated. This policy offended many fine people who didn't feel God was calling them to a life of celibacy. To protect himself, Brother Evangelist was careful to point out that these brothers and sisters were not offended at him, but at the Lord.

I had feared asking Brother Evangelist about marrying a sister because I didn't feel I had a right to ask him until I had been in the group for several years and had proven myself worthy. We were worthy if we obeyed and humbly submitted ourselves to the older brothers. There was an unspoken assumption that if you wanted to marry that meant you weren't spiritual enough to be married. To express desire for a wife made you spiritually suspect. Several brothers were accused of "lusting after a wife" when they could not endure the loneliness and sexual frustration of being single and celibate. To be worthy, you had to conquer your desires and love God exclusively.

Isaac Asimov wrote: "Death is only tolerable because it is universal." Being single would not have been as great a struggle if everyone was single, but there were married and unmarried in our group; two castes with two sets of privileges. The married couples could have sex and children, private rooms, and certain priority to the finances. The single brothers shared a large room, had no privacy, had to endure sexual temptation, and were denied any contact with the sisters. Against this backdrop I fell in love.

I was selected to travel alone with the sisters quite frequently. For me this was an honor and a privilege. It meant behaving in a comely and mature manner with the sister, limiting our conversation on the road, finding discreet places for us to sleep at night, and keeping our minds fixed upon the Lord as we hitchhiked.

I admittedly had trouble keeping my mouth shut when I was alone with a sister on the road. I would ask them for things, make comments about people who gave us rides, ask them to sew things for me, and just about every excuse I could think of to communicate with them. Some sisters seemed to enjoy talking to brothers, others responded like they had just been spiritually raped. There was always the danger that too much conversation could lead to other things.

Sister Noahh was a dedicated sister from Ferndale, Washington, who joined the group a couple of years after I did. I was immediately attracted to her when I saw her, and quickly repented and got my mind on spiritual things. A few weeks later I was selected to take her from Everett, Washington, to Portland, Maine a journey of about 3,000 miles. I was delighted because I knew this would mean about ten days alone with her with no other brothers around. Since she was a new sister, it would also be my responsibility to instruct her in godly ways, which at the time was ridiculously narrow.

As we sat on Interstate 90 hitching east, I noticed several men driving by and turning around to stare at the sister. This would not do. I instructed her to sit on her backpack with her back to tra c facing away from the men who were lusting after her. Later she asked if she could walk around a little and I told her she could for just a short distance. I wouldn't want anyone making a move for the sister. Noahh patiently agreed, and I prided myself for being a faithful watchman over the sister. During a journey with her she mentioned that she wanted a pair of surgical scissors to use for sewing. She had a pair before and knew they stayed sharp much longer than regular scissors.

In the next four months I proceeded to travel with her frequently and I subsequently fell victim to her charms. Who wouldn't fall in love with someone who never argued with you and always did your bidding? I decided I could not hold it in any longer, so I decided to ask Brother Evangelist the next time I saw him if I could marry her.

It was a few months later in Tacoma, Washington, that I got the opportunity to approach the Elder. He warmly took me aside when I asked him if I could speak with him about a trial I was having. We went into a spare bedroom and I made known my desire to marry.

He was warm and gentle all over. "Is there a specific sister you have in mind?" he compassionately asked with a glow in his heart.

"I was thinking, Lord willing, of Sister Noahh."

He looked down approvingly and smiled. "That's a good choice, brother. She has been a real humble sister ever since she met the brothers."

I interrupted and enthusiastically added, "She's been a real blessing to travel with. She always lifts up the standard on the road."

"Not that I think you would do such a thing," he continued, "but have you spoken to the sister about this at all?"

I was horrified. I wouldn't drop the standard like that. I didn't think anyone who was a Christian in our group would disobey and go around the Elder in a decision like that. "No, sir."

He looked relieved and explained that several brothers in times past had gone around him and spoken to sisters about marriage without his permission, leading to all kinds of trials for the sisters. Some, he said, paced around and around the sisters' room wondering if it was God's will that they marry, when it was just the brother acting "in his flesh."

He smiled, "Is there anything else you want to add, brother?" as he gently cut off the conversation.

There were a thousand things I wanted to ask, "Could I talk to the sister about it?" and, "what's the next step?" but I recognized the dismissal in his voice. I understood from another brother later that Brother Evangelist would be quietly pondering whether this marriage was of God, and would let me know in due time perhaps a month, perhaps a year, perhaps ten years. I didn't want to wait, but I knew Brother Evangelist wasn't going to be rushed. He would consider my faithfulness and devotion to the group and to God, and decide whether I was good for the sister or not.

I left the conversation feeling very positive about my chances. He had not tried to discourage me and seemed even favorably disposed toward the marriage. At the evening gathering I subtly tried to get a glimpse of my beloved without being too obvious about it. I was going on the road the next day to Salt Lake City and I wanted to look upon her one last time before I left.

The next morning, Brother Steven was appointed to travel with Sister Noahh, and I was appointed to travel with Sister Cassia. Brother Evangelist warned me to keep my heart and not allow myself to get offended concerning marriage like so many other brothers and sisters had in the past.

In Salt Lake City we stayed in a row of townhouses that were being renovated. Brother Chris was in charge of the camp and greeted us warmly at the door. I was in an emotional tizzy, dreaming and imagining how agreeable it would be to marry Noahh and travel with her for the rest of my life. For the next month and a half, I built up my hopes and lived in a fantasy world of love and expectant marriage. I wrote her name in Hebrew letters on my hitchhiking signs. I thought about her and wrote poems that she would never see. I hugged my makeshift pillow, a bag full of my dirty foundry that would get washed when I got into camp. I opened my Bible hoping it would land on a verse that would indicate that I should marry her. Her name went through and through my mind, and with it the terror that Brother Evangelist would somehow miss the will of God and forbid us to marry.

While camping on a kind Christian's property in Durango,

Colorado, I could endure the suspense of waiting no longer. I had to know something. I told my dilemma to Brother Chris and he passed the word on the phone to Brother Evangelist about how I was feeling. He sent for me to come to Salt Lake City where he could speak with me about my request.

Two days later I arrived and Brother Evangelist met me at the door. He greeted me with indifference and seemed a little piqued that he had to deal with me about marriage. "I'll speak with you tomorrow, brother." If I had been keeping my heart I wouldn't have to burden him with these things. Instead, I was setting my heart on things below and making his job as Elder that much more difficult.

The next morning he found me praying and silently begging God to give me grace in speaking with the Elder about marriage. I knew I was in for a great disappointment and I didn't want to become offended at the Lord about not getting a wife. But I couldn't live in limbo. Something had to be decided. I couldn't live my life all the time in the future wondering if I was going to win the celestial marriage lottery. I dreaded what he was going to say and hoped God would steel me to endure the disappointment.

"I'll talk to you later," he said. I was in great anguish and paralysis, desperately wanting to talk to him to know what his thoughts about Noahh and me were, but he decided to put the conversation off until the evening. I spent the whole day in grief and anguish, praying fervently that I would be able to do God's will in the matter and accept "no" for an answer. When I had no power or hope, Brother Evangelist told me he was ready to speak to me.

"Brother, I want you to keep your heart in this. Some souls have fallen away because they got offended in the Lord in this matter. Remember, we are living in the last days and in a time of a great falling away."

I nodded. I had heard these things many times.

"I only want to do what's best for you and the sister. That's why God has given us watchmen and shepherds, to keep the sheep from always doing what they want. Sometimes the sheep don't know what's really good for them."

I could feel it coming. He was setting me up by demonstrating the goodness of his intentions, and reminding me that I was not capable of caring for myself, but he was. It was believable. I knew I wasn't an objective participant in the decision. I was infatuated and in love, that temporary insanity that God gives to young couples to draw them into marriage. Perhaps he, as an "objective" participant, could see more clearly than I.

He proceeded to give his speech about the dangers of marriage, about what happened to souls who rebelled against him and got married and about how sure we must be before committing ourselves to another who might just lead us away from the Lord. I agreed, but didn't think it applied to everyone who asked to be married. Nevertheless, I got the message.

"The Lord hasn't shown me anything, so I assume it's not his will until he shows me something different."

"But I believe the Lord showed me it was his will," I protested. (In Salt Lake City a few months earlier, I had a wonderful experience, where I felt the Holy Spirit was poured out on me. I was so overwhelmed with joy that I began to cry as I was walking down a city street. I quickly found a park bench alone and proceeded to cry for joy for another hour. I took it as a sign from the Lord that I was going to marry Noahh.)

I described the experience, but it only made him raise an eyebrow in interest. Nevertheless, until he himself heard from the Lord, he wasn't going to approve the marriage.

"Does this mean I won't be seeing sister Noahh anymore?" I was concerned because I was afraid he would send us to separate cities and never allow us to see each other again so that we wouldn't be tempted to marry again.

He smiled patiently. "No, brother. I wouldn't do that." I was relieved and resigned myself to giving up the pursuit. If God wanted me to marry, he'd alert Brother Evangelist. I was just in my flesh, I concluded, as I walked out the door and across the bridge into downtown. I needed to keep my heart in the future to assure that I wouldn't fall into this love trap again.

Nevertheless, I kept the hope alive in my heart. I knew I couldn't go through life single. All the prayer and fasting in the world, all the cloistering and Bible reading I could do, could in no way create the calling of celibacy. It was a straight and narrow path I was called to, and now I had to bear the cross and endure it. It couldn't be any more unbearable than the plague of mites that was to come on the Church.

20

The Plague Of Mites

They bite you. They seem to be born pregnant. They dig into your skin and create a biting itch that feels great to scratch but only destroys the skin and leaves oozing sores the size of your thighs. At two in the morning they start moving up your legs to nestle in your crotch area. Changes of temperature stir them up when you get out of your sleeping bag and when you get into your sleeping bag. It was rumored that cold weather slowed down their activity and granted you a peaceful night's sleep. These are the most tormenting beasts on the face of the earth. They are highly contagious and willing to dwell on anyone's skin, and you can't see the mites.

I was in Philadelphia in November of 1980 when Ronald

Reagan won his first term as President. It was there that I got a taste of the most physically trying time in my life. It began when I discovered my towel was packed away in my backpack and I had to borrow a brother's.

"Sorry brother, I can't. I have that a iction." "What a iction?" "Mites."

I understood. The brother didn't want me to get infected by any mites that might be lingering in his towel. So he went into voluntary quarantine and adopted the behavior of those with mites.

1. Wipe the toilet seat thoroughly when you are finished.

2. Keep your own set of spoons and bowls.

3. Do your own laundry separately from the rest of the brothers and sisters.

4. Scrub the tub out with cleanser when you are done bathing.

5. Sleep on the mattress designated for brothers who already have the a iction.

6. Do not share possessions with anyone who is not a icted nor your comb, nor your towel, nor anything else on which the mites could be spread.

From Dean's List to Dumpsters: Why I Left Harvard to Join a Cult

There was a whole set of war stories from brothers and sisters who had gone through the plague of mites before I joined the group. The whole thing sounded so romantic being chastened by the Lord to become more faithful and disciplined disciples. I wanted to suffer with the Church in the chastening so that I could have my stories of endurance, too. I had no idea what I was asking.

The house in Philadelphia was a ramshackle building with no heat. The owner planned to renovate the building, and let us stay there to guard the building from vandals. As the days grew colder, sanitation became a problem. A cold shower in thirty-two degree temperatures is not even easy for a polar bear.

As we went about our daily routines, it became apparent that the plague of mites was spreading. Some brothers and sisters were up at night crying out, "Please Jesus, help us endure!" Others kept a bucket of cold water by their bedside and dipped a towel into the water to place over the spots where the mites were feeding and mating in their skin. They seemed to get some relief and even fell asleep sometimes, awakening in the morning looking no more rested than Richard Nixon on the evening of his resignation.

To try to contain the plague, Brother Evangelist issued the quarantine measures and encouraged us that the key to overcoming the mites was "prayer and restraint."

By "restraint" he meant no scratching. Consequently, several of the members felt guilty whenever they scratched because they knew it wasn't right and only spread the mites to other parts of their bodies. Some brothers were even taken aside and mildly rebuked if they scratched.

One morning, as I climbed out of my down sleeping bag, the lower parts of my legs began to itch. I rolled up my pant leg and scratched fervently for about five minutes. It felt wonderful, so relieving, so pleasant to the skin.

When I was done the itch ceased, and my legs were red from the knees to the shins. I thought nothing of it since my legs had itched before from perspiration and going several days at a time without a bath when there were no bathing facilities available.

Several days later, after repeating the scratching whenever I got up in the morning, I decided that perhaps I had the a iction, too. I didn't see any of the red spots that indicate infection, but I did have the itch and cold water did relieve it. Brother Barnabas, who had the a iction himself, had taken me upstairs and encouraged me to shower in the cold water one night before I went to bed so that I wouldn't itch during the night. It was difficult, but it did seem to help.

After a few weeks there I was sent to Kansas City, Missouri, to meet the brothers there. Again they were staying in a renovated house and Sergeant Louis and Brother Chris were the older brothers in charge. There was some friction because Brother Wayne and Brother John had gone before and found the house for the brothers. They worked out an agreement to work for the owner, but Sergeant Louis didn't like to share his power with anyone.

The a iction worsened there as the skin began to open up wherever I scratched. The inside of my thighs was one oozing, open sore, and I wore bandages cut from sheets to soak up the bodily fluids. When they dried, I was left with large scabs on each thigh that stretched from my knee to my crotch. Each day the sisters would cut new bandages for me that would cover my wounds and I would remove the old. At night I would sleep in a wet t-shirt to try to contain the itching, and when that didn't work I would scratch, and pray, and cry myself to sleep every night by about 2:00 am.

We began to develop theories about how to treat the mites. I felt I should let the scabs form, and when they would heal I would be free from the mites. We continued to pray more for healing and thoroughly examined ourselves to see why we were being a icted by God. Brothers began confessing sins in hopes that confession would bring healing. We adopted new practices of cleanliness. I showed my scabs to an older brother who told me to bathe immediately and keep the wounded areas clean. Others found immediate relief in hot showers. They discovered they felt much better after a shower, only to discover that the hot water opened the pores of the skin and helped spread the mites to other locations.

I found out later that physicians have a cream that you spread on your body after a hot shower that kills all the mites within twenty-four hours. Had I done that I would have missed out on God's purpose in the trial: to learn to trust God for healing, and to become more patient in a iction. Although these were two byproducts of my experience (God being able to use even our stupidity to His glory), had I had the freedom of conscience to see a physician, I would have. We knew our faith wouldn't allow us to turn to man to get help. It would have been a denial of God to get help from a hospital, though I was certainly in need of some serious medical attention.

To add to my woes, I stepped on a finishing nail protruding from a scrap of wood behind the house in a woodpile. After a day, the puncture got infected, and my foot swelled up to about twice its regular size. Sergeant Louis didn't want the owner of the house to know I had hurt my foot, so he hid me in a back room every time the owner came over. Right before we were to leave on the road, the owner told me he was glad my foot was better.

To relieve the swelling in my foot, we decided that puncturing the wound would release some of the fluid and alleviate the pressure on my toes. Sometimes it felt like a balloon ready to explode. The brothers sharpened a finishing nail, sterilized it under a flame, and shoved it into the wound with a pair of pliers. I did it willingly, but it was terrifying waiting for the nail to go into my foot. It gave me a greater appreciation for what Christ must have gone through in anticipation of his own crucifixion: sheer terror! The swelling subsided somewhat, but it didn't fully heal until about a month later. As soon as I was able to walk, I went to Miami, Florida, with Sister Hannah. She helped carry my pack and lovingly took care of me as we hobbled toward Miami. I wanted to stay in the cold weather because it kept the mites at bay when the skin was cold. I was afraid they would get more out of hand in the warm Florida sun.

From Dean's List to Dumpsters: Why I Left Harvard to Join a Cult

In Miami, Brother Evangelist greeted us warmly and confessed that he was insensitive to rebuke brothers and sisters for scratching their mites. He himself was not a icted, so he couldn't relate to the torment of those who were. There were several brothers and sisters there who were a icted by the mites and the camp was designated to take care of them.

Brother Evangelist took a spiritual approach to the healing process, trying to understand why God was a icting the church. In an act of repentance, he began a series of Bible studies on the sin of gluttony and started limiting us to one meal a day. Since we were stuck at the camp because of our sores, we couldn't go out and get food for ourselves. At first it was very difficult, but in time we got used to it, spending our days counting the hours until dinner hoping not to appear too eager to eat. When dinner finally did come, we would all pig out, the portions offered were so generous that we ate too much after all.

He also decided we were straying as a group and wanted to bring us back to some of our purity. The group originally didn't hold any jobs and just lived off dumpster diving and the wealth of new converts. They spent a lot of time in campgrounds, parks, and patches of woods near major cities. They rarely stayed in houses and suffered a lot from the elements. In Waco, Texas, in 1973 they were flooded out and had to endure scorpions and rattlesnakes. They had slept outside in winter storms and washed dishes in icy streams. They spent the majority of their time witnessing.

After I joined the group, some subtle changes began occurring. We were indoors more and started doing some minor remodeling in exchange for rent. Brothers and sisters stayed back in the houses more and went out to witness less, preferring to focus on their own spiritual growth than on the needs of others. Our group stopped growing in number.

Brother Evangelist decided we were headed in the wrong direction and gathered us to announce some new things. We were not going to be staying in houses anymore and would not be working either. We were going to go back to our former way of life and focus on spreading the Gospel. Some of us rejoiced at the announcement since that was the original vision of the group that attracted us. Others, like married brothers and sisters with children, weren't too excited about being out in the woods with their children again.

After a few weeks there, I wasn't getting any better, and the a iction seemed to be spreading to new areas of my body. Some sisters were developing staph infections and had to wash them out daily. There were rumors that God had healed a sister who was at the point of death from staph. Nevertheless, I was convinced that I needed to be in colder weather if I was going to halt the spread of the mites. Brother Evangelist decided to send Sergeant Louis and me to Raleigh, North Carolina, in January to give me the cold weather I requested.

At the bus stop to ride out to the freeway, my legs began to itch uncontrollably. We were standing around several dozen people waiting for the bus and the itching became unbearable. I started to scratch as discreetly as possible, putting my hands through the slits in the sides of my long brown garment, and rubbing in a way that no one would notice. Unfortunately for me, the bandages wrapped around my thighs came undone and fell down my pant leg to the sidewalk. Several young women glanced my way and looked horrified when they saw the bandages on the ground. I, of course, felt stupid.

On the second day of the journey, I decided I didn't have the heart to continue north. I desperately needed someone to take care of me and I was alone on the road. As I thought about Miami, I remembered the hot baths, the abundant fellowship, and the sisters who washed my bandages and cooked my meals, and I decided that I needed to be there instead of alone in a tent in the dead of winter with Sergeant Louis.

I reversed course and headed back, unbeknownst to Sergeant Louis, who had gotten a long ride ahead of me. The next night I shu ed ashamedly into camp and explained my motives to a bewildered Brother Evangelist. "This has never happened before," he said, mildly reproving me.

After a while his tone changed and he welcomed me, but I knew I was there on borrowed time. It was like leaving a friend's house after spending the weekend with him and coming back to stay an hour later after you have said your goodbyes.

A day later he came to me and asked how I was doing. He was genuinely concerned. As a final word of encouragement he noted, "I pray Yahweh heals you of whatever is causing that itch. The brothers are calling them 'mites,' but we don't know for sure what they are. We need to be careful we don't lean on our own carnal understanding. You know, no one has really even seen one." He smiled wisely and I played along, saying "Amen" to this insight.

Inside, my "carnal" mind was reeling. We have never seen God and yet we believe in him! If you just get a microscope, you can see these bugs at work, and even see other viruses that make us ill. There are photographs and libraries of documented evidence that these things exist. Why is it carnality to believe in microscopic parasites that cause skin rashes and red spots? I really questioned his wisdom when he shared that one with me.

Brother Evangelist gave me some time to reconsider my decision and then a couple days later sent me up I-195 to Savannah, Georgia, until he could decide what to do with me. The brothers were camped about a quarter mile from downtown, in a patch of woods circumscribed by railroad tracks. From the adjacent dump the brothers had salvaged some plywood and two by fours and had built a little shack village in the woods, replete with wooden pathways connecting the shacks. Because the campsite was easily flooded, the buildings were on wooden lifts to keep the floors dry. I marveled at the craftsmanship of the homes, and noted that the brothers had even made a wood stove to heat one of the buildings. Such resourcefulness and jerry-rigging made me very proud to be with the brothers.

Brother Barnabas took me inside one of the shacks to demonstrate the quality of the work. The floors were solid and there were no cracks in the walls. The doorway was hinged and had a small lock cut from a #10 can and some screws. The door sprang shut when I let go. Against the back window was a platform bed large enough for the longer brothers. A small window cut in the wall and covered with plastic let in some light. A small desk and hutch, both handmade by the brothers, sat perpendicular to the bed and contained a small oil lamp for light. An inverted plastic five gallon pickle bucket with a board on it served as a chair and sat close enough to the wood stove for someone to feed the fire when necessary. The whole thing seemed terribly cozy, an ancient's dream. I could envision myself cloistered in the hut, staying up late at night studying my Bible while it rained or snowed outside, bathing myself in warmth and security, growing wise and old and safe. Did Robinson Crusoe have it this splendid?

My heart dropped a day later when I was told to move on to Raleigh, North Carolina, by myself. Sergeant Louis would be there and not too thrilled to see me. I said goodbye to Savannah and ended up walking with a full backpack from downtown to Interstate 95, about ten miles away. At the end of the day I got a good ride and ended up somewhere in South Carolina that night and in Raleigh the next day. Sergeant Louis greeted me with feigned enthusiasm and then let me know how he really felt. He could not understand why I had turned back to Florida since I obviously wanted the colder weather to be healed of the mites. He wasn't in the mood for anything but a humble apology and an acknowledgment that I was wrong to have turned back.

We headed off to some woods he found about a mile from the University of North Carolina. Being winter, the barren trees gave us little cover from being discovered, so we had to camp quite deep in the woods. A frozen stream went through the middle of the camp and the ground everywhere was sharp and icy. I stepped on what appeared to be solid ground several times only to have it break up under my feet and reveal an underground rivulet that splashed up and soaked my army boots. Ahhh, the abundant life.

Sergeant Louis was paranoid of "having a situation" and so the comfort and well being of his underlings were his last priority. If there were the least chance we would be discovered camping in those woods, Sergeant Louis would do all he could to avoid that, regardless of what it may cost us personally.

Several brothers met us there a couple days later and Sergeant Louis went out to find a better place to camp. He came back that afternoon with great joy and told us to make preparations to leave. It was a frigid afternoon and the woods had taken a toll on all my winter clothing. As I put on my backpack to leave with Sergeant Louis, he looked at my raincoat and decided it was too dirty for me to wear on the bus and ordered me to take it off. I submitted, and replaced it with a sweater which he also didn't like and ordered me to take off.

Having just washed my hair in the icy stream and having a wet head, I felt I needed something to keep me warm so I wouldn't get sick. But Sergeant Louis felt that my choice of clothes would only bring attention to our moving to the woods and would spoil our chances of being there unnoticed.

I then asked him if I could put on my orange down jacket and again he said I couldn't. The color would stand out too much and we might have a situation. 'Well then, what could I wear?

I asked. He then explained that he always kept his clothes clean and that I should try to be like him. In other words, I had to travel for two hours in the cold with only a shirt and flimsy down vest to keep me warm. I was furious.

However, not wanting to let my anger make me sin, I shut my mouth and began praying fervently for grace to submit and say nothing. I knew if I opened my mouth I would get in trouble, and I was in enough trouble with the mites. Sergeant Louis noticed I had an attitude, but did not notice I was praying with all my might not to let it cause me to rebel. I followed him obediently out to the bus stop and said nothing, all the while warring against the rage I was feeling.

At the bus stop, Sergeant Louis tried to make amends, smiling and pointing at the digital thermometer of the bank clock. "Twenty-eight degrees!" he said. "What a blessing!" I smiled weakly and Sergeant Louis became upset.

"Isn't this why you wanted to come to Raleigh? To get into the cold weather? You wanted to leave Florida because it was too warm and now you're angry because it's cold here! You can't have it both ways. It's the flesh that never wants to be content."

I desperately tried to hold my cool and not explode at Sergeant Louis as we got on the bus. I had a long history of being abused by him, and didn't want to make matters worse by talking back. Sergeant Louis accepted no back talk. He wanted to be as unquestioned as the Elder. Unfortunately for the disciples under him, he had none of Brother Evangelist's kindness and patience when others disappointed him. For the remainder of the bus ride, Sergeant Louis beat upon me with his mouth, complaining about my character and behavior, and slandering me without mercy to my face. When we got off the bus, the tirade continued as we walked to the woods.

"Brother, this is what I want you to do. Follow behind me about three steps and do exactly what I tell you to do. There are helicopters that circle this area, and if we see one we need to duck into these woods as quickly as possible. Do you follow?"

I nodded. As we walked, he kept looking back to make sure I was in formation, and not making myself too obvious. I was freezing and angry and wrestling to submit myself to God. Sergeant Louis barked out orders as we walked, incessantly scolded me for not turning quickly enough, and suddenly ducked into the woods when he heard the helicopter. My reflexes, frozen by the weather and the spiritual exhaustion I was feeling as I was dragged down by this arrogant older brother, were too slow to suit Sergeant Louis. I followed as quickly as I could, but nothing I did pleased Sergeant Louis and he began ripping into me again with his "Christian" tongue.

"Please brother, have patience with me. I am trying to do what you say!" I broke into tears. Sergeant Louis scorned my tears and began to upbraid me more about how proudly I had been walking and how I needed to submit and seek God for more humility.

From Dean's List to Dumpsters: Why I Left Harvard to Join a Cult

Then a strange thing began to happen. I accepted his assessment of me and vowed to myself to seek God more to change. I was grateful for the rebuke and blamed the whole incident on myself. Sergeant Louis was right; I needed to change. That night I wrote in my diary that I had received some much needed rebuke and that Sergeant Louis was the one faithful to give it to me. For some perverse reason I loved my tormentor.

Perhaps by then I had learned to trust others' assessments of me above my own. Since we assumed that others could see us more clearly than we could see ourselves, we were more inclined to receive criticism than praise. Being guilt-driven anyway, I was more accustomed to accepting blame than being exonerated when an older brother accused me of some spiritual offense. How could I be right? I was just a younger brother, and my heart was too deceitful for me to discern. But the older brothers could see me in ways that were hidden from me.

During the stay in Raleigh, my legs healed up and the mites spread to other parts of my body. I maintained a large sore on my knee that stubbornly refused to heal for about a year and which was a constant source of discouragement and discomfort. Sergeant Louis did his best to rule the camp with an iron fist and succeeded in making life miserable for those of us who had the misfortune of being submitted to him. Nevertheless, I committed myself to the Lord and obeyed Sergeant Louis without question for the entire time I was there.

When word came that we were going on the road, I jumped for joy. My Redeemer lives who delivers me out of all tribulation and oppression! When Sergeant Louis got the phone call he took me aside and began to preach to me. "Lord willing, you'll be going on the road tomorrow," he said. He seemed a little glum that he wasn't going to be in charge anymore. "You've been making an attempt to be subject in the last couple of weeks, and I wanted to exhort you to remain in your place. Not that you would do it, but some souls, as soon as they hear they're going on the road, suddenly start having trials about submitting to the older brother. That's not to say that you would do it, I just wanted to make sure you're watchful in this matter. Remember, 'The heart is deceitful above all things and desperately wicked.' as the Elder has said, 'We must be watchful, because sometimes we don't know our own hearts.'" (Jer. 17:9)

I took this "vote of confidence" patiently, but felt it was entirely unnecessary and manifested the heart of a man who loved to rule over people, just the opposite of the kind of man Christ wants in authority in his church.

Gradually the church recovered from the mites. Over twenty brothers and sisters had been a icted, but fortunately no one died. Brother Evangelist and a few others never contacted them because of their careful behavior around those who were a icted. At the end of the mite infestation, Brother Evangelist found a scapegoat.

"Brothers and sisters, we have often mentioned that you cannot break one of God's commandments without reaping judgment. This includes submitting yourself to those who rule over you. We have gone through an a iction that might have been avoided if a sister had been

127

heeding the instruction concerning children that we have preached for years. It is shameful to see the way carnal men treat young babies. They make carnal faces at them, lift them up, and throw them in the air which makes them foolish and exalts their little hearts, when they should be trying to make them sober. I have seen the look on some of these children's faces, like they're grieved to be around their parents. We have taught that in the Church we are not to be handling someone else's children and acting carnal around them. It seems a sister was handling someone's baby and the baby had the a iction. That's how it got into the Church. Perhaps it seemed like a small thing to the sister to not submit to the good instruction you have heard in the Church. But if she had been faithful, we could have avoided this a iction."

It only took a few whispers to select older brothers to find out who the transgressor was. It was the first time I remember hearing that we weren't even supposed to pick up children outside the group. I felt badly for the sister because she had only been with the group for a short time and didn't know any better. Having finally fixed blame, the matter was o cially over.

21

Descent Into Insanity

One should never underestimate the power of religious error to corrupt even the most well-intentioned. During the winter of 1980 I entered a phase of religious insanity in which I temporarily lost control of my mind. It was propelled by the necessity to become perfect in a very short time.

Hanging over my head was the legacy of hundreds of souls falling away from the Church, and I didn't want to add my name to the legacy. I wrote a poem describing my feelings:

I want to be known as a brother I want to be perfectly whole
Lest I fall by the wayside as others
And my name is then changed to "that soul."

Rather than being "Brother Jim," I would be known as "that soul Jim."

I feared falling away from the Church more than a decade of mites.

Occasionally an older brother would make a remark about certain people and why they had fallen away from the Lord. Ultimately there was some sin in their lives that they had failed to conquer and God had become disgusted and removed his Holy Spirit from them. No matter if they had served Him for two years or fifteen; sin eventually eliminated everyone who participated in it.

One evening Brother Abel ambled over to me as I prepared to bed down and offhandedly remarked how crucial it was to get the victory over all sin. Naming a former group member, he concluded there must have been some sin in his life that he didn't conquer, leading God to hurl him back to the world. "God gave him a chance to get the victory and he didn't." We all knew that meant the unfortunate soul was damned forever, and there was no hope of repentance. He hadn't prayed or fasted enough and his sin eventually caught up with him.

I trembled. Dozens already had fallen away, some of whom I thought were too established to fall. There was no security. It was possible that after all our suffering we still wouldn't be considered worthy of eternal life because of a fondness for food or reading newspapers.

Food! I feared that my love of food offended God deeply. That was the sin that was going to eventually eliminate me! The hourglass was rapidly draining, and I had just a little time to change.

In Boise, I decided to win God's favor by fasting as much as I could. I begged God one night to give me the grace to fast for a week and not to let me eat, even if I wanted to. He answered that prayer to teach me a lesson. When dinnertime came around, and I changed my mind and decided to eat, a wave of tormenting guilt and condemnation flooded over me and I had to retreat into the prayer room for relief. I opened the Bible and saw a verse about denying myself and decided I couldn't run from my conscience. The guilt subsided when I decided not to eat. I wearily prayed for grace and waited out the cravings.

This process repeated itself every day and night for a week. I grew feeble and could barely lift my arms. When I sat up briskly I got dizzy and had to grab a chair to avoid fainting on the floor. At night when I slept, my pelvic bone ground against the wooden floor because there was no longer any cushioning fat there. I still drank water and urinated, but after a couple of days my bowels dried up. I counted the hours for the week to end so that I could eat again.

At week's end I ate some applesauce and yogurt. Although I was ready to eat more solid food, Brother Daniel advised me to eat food that would be gentle on my digestive system since it had not been operating for a week. My conscience was better for a short while, but I still felt I needed to fast more to save my soul.

It was December of 1980 when I was sent from Boise, Idaho, to Eureka, California, with Brother Asher. With a crippled conscience and a sewing machine in our backpacks, we hitched rides in the snow and icy rain for three days. I was still obsessed, thinking that God was scrutinizing me, trying to discover me enjoying food so He could eliminate me from His kingdom. So many Bible verses were coming to mind about self denial and cross bearing and the need to suffer in the flesh to become perfect. I could not eat meat even when I was eating for strength without a guilty conscience.

Eureka is a small town in northern California pleasantly set on Humboldt Bay near the massive California redwoods. Primarily a middle class town, it is about eight miles from Arcata, a college town which is a throwback to the sixties. Both towns were pleasant to witness in, although our destination was to be farther south.

The brothers had arranged to stay on a ranch just south of Orrick, California, wedged in a canyon surrounded by redwoods and sequoias. I gasped for breath when I saw the beautiful, Edenlike surroundings of this camp. A cold mountain spring ambled through the backyard and into the woods behind the house. The house itself was a one story farmhouse, about 3,000 square feet, heated with a wood stove. It had a rustic look that made it blend perfectly with the primeval surroundings. About a hundred yards from the house was a large wooden shack where brothers had gathered and chopped firewood for the stove in the house. Just to the south, about 100 feet from the kitchen, was a large pond about 400 yards across, stocked with trout and a mischievous otter. As I scanned the paradise, I decided that God was very good, and that I could live there forever.

Brother Evangelist was outside as I walked up the driveway to the house. I smiled and told him I was going through some serious trials and was going to get the victory. He was pleasant and encouraging, but I could tell he looked frightened, partly from a pastor's concern for his sheep, and partly from paranoia that I might soon join the ranks of those persecuting the Church. Perhaps he noticed a look in my eye that indicated I was not entirely stable.

I determined my crusade to overcome my lust for food by fasting regularly every evening. At first I did it out of guilt, but soon I started taking pride in my spiritual superiority, comparing myself to other brothers and sisters who were not fasting as much as me. When brothers were called to eat, I would slip out the side door and sit next to the pond praying and meditating on Bible verses that commended my diligence. Soon I began to keep a tally of how much fasting I was doing and how little others were. I flattered myself to no end, beginning to despise even Brother Evangelist for his eating almost every meal. But I was not without competition. Sister Hannah, as always, devoted herself to fasting fastidiously. I entered into secret competition with her, gaining a new respect for her self sacrifice and diligence. In prior years I had harshly judged her as being "caught up" in fasting, going overboard exceedingly. Now I realized just the opposite was true. We were the only ones in the Church really "pressing in.

Part of the deception was that as I took these actions, Bible verses would come to mind, as if the Holy Spirit were directly speaking to me, when I fasted, I would hear, "Well done, thou good and faithful servant." When I was tempted to eat I was reminded not to eat: "Lest there be any fornicator, or profane person like Esau, who for one morsel of food sold his birthright." (Heb. 12:16)

When I began to feel famished I remembered Matthew 4:4: "But He answered and said, It is written, Man shall not live by bread alone, but by every word that proceeds from the mouth of God."

If that didn't suffice, I was reminded that Philippians 3:19 said: "Whose end is destruction, whose god is their belly, and whose glory is in their shame; who set their mind on earthly things." I certainly didn't want my belly to be my god, the thing that controlled me, lest my end be destruction.

After a while I became accustomed to this voice quoting scriptures to me and eventually I lost all confidence in eating. Every time I would approach a meal, I would be driven back to some Scripture. One night I went ahead and ate anyway, fearing the consequences of my decision.

As I prepared to bed down in the woodshed with several other brothers, an inaudible voice came to me telling me that because I had eaten, I had to stand outside and stay awake all night. I was reminded how Jesus fasted forty days and forty nights and stayed up all night on one occasion praying. "A disciple is not above his teacher, nor a servant above his master," (Matt. 10:24) the voice reminded me. "If you are a disciple of Jesus, you are not above suffering as he suffered. Remember what Peter wrote, Therefore, since Christ suffered for us in the flesh, arm yourselves also with the same mind, for he who has suffered in the flesh has ceased from sin.' This is to help you cease from sin." (1 Pet. 4:1)

I was convinced that God was calling me to stay up all night and watch. After all, didn't Jesus ask his disciples, "Then He came to the disciples and found them asleep, and said to Peter, 'What? Could you not watch with Me one hour?'" (Matt. 26:40)

Perhaps we were going to be persecuted that night, and I would be awake to save the camp. I was alert and ready, albeit greatly distressed at how hard I had to work to please God.

I went outside and sat upon a fallen tree, and watched the stars move in their orbits toward the horizon. It was a chilly night and "the Lord" had told me not to wear a coat because I would be more perfect if I suffered in the flesh. I waited for the morning when this verse popped into mind. "My soul waits for the Lord more than those who watch for the morning; Yes, more than those who watch for the morning. (Ps. 130:6) Again it confirmed that I was doing the right thing. I began to have my doubts after I spent three nights in a row awake outside the woodshed. Why did I have to work so hard and others didn't? I remember going to prayer and perceiving the god I was praying to as a furious ball of fire, very angry and wrathful. I wrote in my diary that day, "Drawing close to God is like drawing near to a consuming fire," thanks to the verse that came to mind, "For our God is a consuming fire." (Heb. 12:29)

A little later, as I warmed myself by the wood stove, a voice said, "Go stick your head into the pond and keep it under for awhile. He that suffers in the flesh has ceased from sin." I laughed that one off, but it made me suspect that the voice I was hearing was not from God.

Through all of this Brother Evangelist was very worried about my mental and spiritual state. One morning before breakfast he came to me and asked me if I was going to be eating that morning. I said I wasn't sure, so he kindly looked to the ground and humbly told me he thought I ought to eat. I was thrilled to have permission to eat and grateful that he had approached me. "Yeah, I have been having some trials about eating recently, and felt the Lord wanted me to fast to get the victory."

He listened very carefully and told me he had been very burdened for me and had been praying for me. "Not to do my alms before men," he said, "but I have been very concerned about your trial. I would recommend you eat so you don't get sick."

I thanked him and went to the morning meal, feeling relieved to be able to eat with a good conscience. If Brother Evangelist determined it was okay to eat, then it must be. He was my Elder and I was subject to him.

A little later that morning, I noticed Sergeant Louis and Brother Evangelist go off for a walk. Brother Evangelist was deeply troubled and downcast, looking more serious and sad than I had ever seen him. I could only guess what had happened, but even the best guess would not have been tragic enough to be correct.

Later that day, Brother Evangelist gathered everyone together. He was inordinately somber and seemed to have very little spirit. We waited and then he sternly announced that when we were going outside we should dress accordingly and not allow ourselves to get chilled. He underscored the need to wear hats and gloves when it was cold, and to dry our hair when it was wet before we left the house. "If any of you needs a warmer sleeping bag, or if you are sleeping cold at night, please let me know. Lord willing, we can try to get some better sleeping gear for you."

Then he began to mildly scold us. "We should use wisdom and take care of our bodies. We are not much use to the Church if we get sick and have to have someone take care of us because we didn't use a little wisdom and dress warmly enough before going out. You become a burden to the Church and someone has to do the duties that you would normally perform. So please use wisdom in the way you dress and take care of yourselves."

We were dismissed and began to wonder why Brother Evangelist suddenly exhorted about taking care of ourselves. Perhaps too many brothers and sisters were getting sick and he felt we needed to take better care of ourselves. I was growing more and more bitter at God as the demands for self sacrifice increased. I sat outside in the cold instead of by the fireplace because I didn't want to pamper the flesh. I still ate rarely and very little when I did. The camel's back finally broke. One night the voice told me to go outside and spend the night awake, and I got disgusted. I told Sergeant Louis what "the Lord" was saying to me and he lovingly took me aside and began to straighten me out.

"That was not the Lord, brother," he said. "Jesus said that his yoke is easy and his burden is light. (Matt. 11:30) You aren't putting your faith in God, you're just trusting in yourself. Let God make you righteous, and stop trusting in all your fasting and prayers to save you."

"That's not the Lord, huh?" I asked. I desperately wanted to believe him. I was tired of hearing voices. I was sick of buffeting and beating my body into submission. I was sick and insane, seeing no end to my efforts to please God. I may have been pleasing God, but He sure wasn't pleasing me.

"Nay, brother," he replied. "Remember that the devil can quote Scriptures, but he twists them to his own advantage. He quoted Scriptures to Jesus when Jesus was fasting in the wilderness. Besides, God doesn't make us do those things. His yoke is easy and his burden is light."

How sweet were those words to me! Jesus did say the truth would make me free. I thanked him for his counsel and prepared to go back to sleep. As I fell asleep a strong spirit came to me telling me to go outside. It was the same voice I had been hearing all along. I awoke and began to pray, rebuking it in the name of Jesus. To my surprise, the spirit left me alone and I quickly fell asleep without any guilt. Then I was sure the voices I was hearing were not of God, but were of the evil one.

I did not heal all at once. It took several months before I could shake off the effects of my misguided search for God. I repeated some of the same errors for months, only to discover again and again that they were not getting me any closer to God.

Finally I came out of the woods when I realized that prayer was a means of appropriating help from God, but the act of prayer itself accomplished nothing. Going to a restaurant and ordering a meal doesn't get you food if the waiter doesn't deliver it. Saying the proper words and bending your knees doesn't change anything; God hearing your prayer and answering it does. I was caught up in the mechanics of seeking God, but not trusting in God to help me. There's a big difference.

A few weeks later, in Cincinnati, Ohio, Brother Evangelist revealed why he had been so somber that day he had spoken to us about dressing warmly.

As we gathered, he began: "Brothers and sisters, what I am sharing tonight is not to go outside this room. You shouldn't even discuss it among yourselves. I spoke on the phone a while ago with Brother Silas and he told me a brother had fallen asleep in the Lord. I didn't ask any questions, and neither should you. It doesn't really matter how it happened.

If anyone was ready to go to be with the Lord, this brother surely was. I remember when we first met him in Boulder, Colorado, at a Rainbow gathering. He swam across the pond there and asked the brothers what they believed, and when he heard the truth he left immediately with them. He was a very edifying brother who labored hard to be in his place and to walk humbly before the Lord."

We all wondered which brother had died, shocked that such a thing could happen to one of our own.

"Brother Vic was a generous brother."

A gasp went out and several sisters started crying. "Recently he was traveling with a brother and came across a man who had no shoes. The brother took off his own shoes and gave them to the man and walked down the highway without any shoes. A little farther down the road he found another pair of shoes that fit him. They were his exact size. Praise God.

Let's remember this brother who has gone on before us, and pray for Brother Silas as he deals with the camp where this brother was. I would appreciate it if you didn't share this with any brother or sister who might not know about this. I believe it is my place to inform the Church about this matter." Shocked, we walked off and said nothing. Our faces said it all. Several years later I learned from eyewitnesses what had happened. A small contingent of the Church was staying in a drafty, barely-heated house in the winter, and Brother Vic had contracted pneumonia.

Although the brothers and sisters did what they could for him, he gradually grew weaker and weaker. The night of his death, Brother Steven was in the room with him listening to his breathing. When Vic stopped breathing, he went and told Brother Silas that Brother Vic had gone to be with the Lord. Brother Silas evacuated the house the next day, and contacted the authorities. When they came, they were enraged that Vic had died without any medical treatment to save his life. Vic's death was needless, since a shot of penicillin and some hospital care would have brought him through the crisis. The authorities took Silas' children from him and tried to charge him with neglect, but returned the children a couple of days later. I do not know why they released the children.

22

"E.T. Phone Home"

From 1980 until 1984 the church changed in ways that made it more difficult to endure. Brother Evangelist was becoming markedly more paranoid, announcing new standards of secrecy that were designed to protect "the church." A code of total silence developed between brothers concerning where they had witnessed or where they were going to travel to witness.

Brothers and sisters were kept in separate houses in cities, many times not knowing there were other brothers in the same city. In 1981-1982 a man permitted the brothers to stay in a house near the corner of Nevins and Atlantic, near downtown Brooklyn, New York. A four-story upscale town house being renovated, it served our large number well for many months. The brothers fashioned a wood stove out of a fifty gallon steel drum, complete with a door on the side to put the wood. It was attached to the chimney with a series of #10 cans riveted together as a stovepipe. Nails were put in the walls at opposite points of the room, and nylon cord was stretched across to serve as an indoor clothesline. The wet clothes were hung over the wood stove to dry shirts, pants, skirts, and socks, but no underwear. Such private garments were hung in closets or under wash cloths so that no brother or sister would see them and be tempted to think lustful thoughts or, God forbid, about marriage.

This served as a major meeting point for two years. Brothers and sisters were continually coming and going. Some took large amounts of food with them and seemed destined for long trips; others quickly scampered out the door with subway fare and a secretive look, hiding their real intentions from fellow believers. One day Brother Evangelist told me to pack up to leave after the morning meal. I asked him if it would be a long journey, and he indicated it would not. He would tell me more when I was ready to leave.

He brought me a few "road things," canned food set aside for those times when dumpsters were not immediately accessible, like when we were on the freeway.

"You're not going far, Lord willing," he said. "The brothers would probably appreciate leaving a few of these things where they are.

He took me aside and very quietly stressed that no one should know about the place I was heading.

"We're in warfare and we must be as wise as serpents and as harmless as doves. We need a place for brothers to flee to in case the fowls should find us here. I don't want the other brothers to know about this because if they are pressed by the fowls they might tell them about the camp. It's much safer if only those who need to know were aware it exists."

After explaining all this he gave me a subway token and told me to ride the L train to Coney Island and get off at the last stop. A brother would meet me there and walk me to the camp. When I got to Coney Island I met several brothers there whom I assumed had left New York City altogether. It was then I suspected there were things going on that I knew nothing about. It made sense when I was told we were actually going to witness in Coney Island and not go to uptown Manhattan. Brother Evangelist would coordinate where we would witness so no one would discover there were other brethren in town. When traveling, brothers were told to bypass certain cities lest they discover other brothers were there. When brothers and sisters traveled, if they had to pass through a town where other members were, the brothers in town would be told not to go witnessing that day to avoid being seen by brethren passing through. When arriving in a town, brethren knew to dispose of any maps that might indicate their origin, any bus schedules, subway maps, or maps with routes marked on them.

Meanwhile, Brother Evangelist was scattering the group and segregating the brothers and sisters more before brothers were sent out in groups of two to cities to witness. Although there was strength in being around dozens of like minded people at one time, the Church was decimated and sent everywhere. Consequently, brothers and sisters grew increasingly lonely and frustrated at not having suficient human contact to meet their emotional needs.

Brother Evangelist used depriving members of fellowship as a means of punishing those whom he distrusted. One afternoon he phoned me: "Brother, there has been word that Brother Refesh has not lifted up the standard concerning keeping locations of camps quiet. I don't think he's quickened to the warfare we're fighting. He told a brother he hitched on an interstate coming out of a certain city. Tell him if he wants to enjoy fellowship, he needs to lift up the standard and not talk about other camps.

"Yes sir," I replied

"Also, share with the brothers that when I hear of brothers asking around about where camps were in the past, it creates mistrust in the older brother."

"Yes sir," I replied. I thought about that and it made me realize how paranoid Brother Evangelist was getting. He blamed others for creating mistrust in him.

Another change that occurred around this time was the introduction of Hebrew into the church. Several brothers started studying it on their own, using Hebrew grammar books they had acquired at used book stores. They convinced Brother Evangelist that Jesus' name was really "Yeshua" and that we should use the Hebrew titles when speaking about or addressing God. Soon it became a commandment in our group to call God "Elohim," Jesus "Yeshua," the Lord "Adonai," and the proper name of God in the Old Testament "Yahveh." Brother Evangelist got so fired up about this revelation, that he even refused to say the English titles anymore, preferring to spell them as if he were referring to a dirty word.

Soon other brothers and sisters followed in the act, and

many of our worship songs began to be sung in Hebrew. Then Brother Evangelist decided we should use the Hebrew whenever we said "yes" and "no." So we went from the Elizabethan "yea" and "nay" to the Hebrew "ken" and "lo." Several discerning brothers felt this was getting out of hand, but no one dared approach the Elder on this fad.

Brother Evangelist got more revelations. He told this story. "One evening I was out and the brothers needed one of those buckets you get at bakeries. I asked a man for one of them and he went inside and got me one.

When I received it, I said, 'Thank you, Lord,' and the man looked at me and said, 'Why did you thank Him? I got you the bucket!"

"I knew that only Elohim should get our praise and thanksgiving. We shouldn't try to steal God's glory. The man didn't know it, but he was being used by Yeshua to provide for his people. From now on, we aren't going to thank anyone for things they do, for the service the sisters do for the brothers. We should say, 'Thank you, Elohim.'

It was quite awkward not thanking one another for deeds of service and kindness done. When a sister spent five days and nights making you a new sleeping bag, it was difficult to look her in the hair and say, 'Thank you, Elohim,' and hear her respond "Praise Elohim." How much more awkward and rude to apply it to the people who daily helped us out! Not only did we not shake their hands, we didn't even thank them anymore.

That lasted for a little while and quietly faded out of use in the group. Nevertheless, it was one more commandment to hound us and condemn us if we didn't obey.

Brother Evangelist got more revelations. The group have long held that in the last days "the mark of the beast" will appear. In the Book of Revelations it speaks of all unbelievers receiving a mark in their right hand or their forehead, without which they could not buy or sell. Originally the brethren got rid of their Social Security cards because it is a number you must have to work in the United States, and therefore related to buying and selling. But to further eliminate dependence on the "world's system".

Brother Evangelist decided we would limit our purchasing of certain items from stores. He gathered us one day and explained that because the mark of the beast would soon be upon us, we would no longer be purchasing toilet paper, laundry detergent, or salt, those three items exclusively.

This led to some creative scrounging. Brothers decided it would be sanitary to take the paper towels from public restrooms that other customers had used to dry their hands and dry them and reuse them as toilet paper. Other brothers took the tissues that pears are wrapped in and brought them from the produce dumpster and used them. Sisters went to restaurants and begged for salt and to hotels and begged for the used bars of soap they normally throw away after they clean the rooms. They were quite successful, although Brother Evangelist probably didn't know what measures the brethren were taking to make up for this new restriction on spending.

Meanwhile, no one questioned why we were still buying shirt material but not salt. Most of us were probably afraid that if we brought that to the Elder's attention he would add that to the list of no-no's and we wouldn't be allowed to buy material for clothes anymore.

In the winter of 1981, I grew curious about how my family was doing and what they thought about my being in the Church. I was also overwhelmingly burdened to speak to them and assure them of my safety and free will in following Brother Evangelist. I felt I was finally strong enough to call them and face their questions and pleas to leave the group. In Salt Lake City, Utah, that March, I got permission from Brother Evangelist to call them. However, there were two stipulations: one I could not call collect, lest they trace the call and find out where we were, and two; I was not to mention Brother Evangelist's name to them. I agreed and was given some extra change to make the call from a phone booth anywhere in Nevada that I could find one. The next day I was sent on the road to Stockton, California.

Sister Esther was chosen to travel with me, and this was a tremendous comfort to me. She had matured into a beautiful twenty year old woman, and I was very attracted to her. My hopes of marrying her were quite slim because I assumed she must be interested in another brother. I told her when we got on the on-ramp that I was glad she was traveling with me because she was a comfort to me. She seemed surprised but not displeased that I had said that to her. I then explained the upcoming phone call.

We got rides all that day and as the evening approached we were in a ride in the midst of Nevada on Interstate 80. As I looked out the car window I saw great darkening clouds in front of us as we approached a storm front. It looked like we were approaching a major thunderstorm that would flood the road and cause much damage. As we approached the storm, the black clouds appeared grayer and less ominous. In the midst of the storm, the clouds were lighter still until we passed through without any harm. I took this as a parable. Although I was apprehensive about calling my mother, I knew it wouldn't be as bad as it seemed from a distance.

That evening we were let out near a gas station that had a phone booth. We took off our backpacks and I dialed my mother. My younger brother John answered.

"Hi. This is Jim. Is Mom there?

"Oh my God! Mooooommm! It's Jim!" he shouted to her.

She rushed in and grabbed the phone and began to vent some of the anger she felt for my not calling. "Jim? Is it really you? It doesn't sound like you." she nervously answered

"Yes, Mom. It's me. I just want you to know I'm fine. What do you mean it doesn't sound like me?"

"Your voice sounds different. It doesn't have any of the life in it that it used to have. Why haven't you called? Don't you know how worried we have been about you?" She was crying uncontrollably.

"I'm fine. Please don't worry about me. I'm happy doing what I'm doing and I'm doing it of my own free will. I have plenty to eat and I'm safe."

"Where are you?" she asked.

"I can't really say except to say that I'm about 2,500 miles away."

"Jim, you know we've always allowed you to do whatever you wanted to do. We'd never tell you that you couldn't do that. All we ask is that you contact us once in a while and let us know how you're doing."

"Has anyone contacted you about what I'm doing?" I asked, trying to figure out how much she knew about the group and whether she would be a threat or not.

"I don't know anything!" she remarked, exasperated. "I haven't heard from you since 1976. Why are you so damn secretive?"

"Well, we've been persecuted in the past by parents who were worried about their children and who didn't believe in following the Lord. Remember, Jesus said a man's foes would be those of his own household." (Matt. 10:36)

"Well, you've got your Scriptures and I've got mine. What about, 'Honor thy father and thy mother?'" she asked. She was getting really frustrated then.

"Honor your mother and father in the Lord," (Eph. 6:1) I corrected. The conversation continued on in this manner for several minutes as she caught me up on what had been happening in the family, including my sister's wedding. I was glad to hear the news since I really did want to know what had happened to my family in my absence.

"Jim," she proceeded cautiously, "Do you remember a doll you had as a child that you really loved a lot?"

"Yes," I replied, annoyed that she was bringing up something so trivial as that.

"What was that doll?" she asked.

"It was a clown," I said, feeling stupid and belittled.

"And do you remember the name of that clown?" she pried.

"Yes, Mom," I replied, my eyes doing circles in my head as I answered her silly question. "Gogi Clown."

"That's right," she said, sounding relieved and triumphant. She then knew she was speaking to me. I wanted to go on to more substantial things, like the Gospel. I knew the Lord didn't want me fraternizing with the enemy lest I threaten my own soul. When it was apparent she wasn't interested in discussing the Truth, I knew it was time to cut the conversation short.

"Mom, I love you. I have to go now."

"Oh, Jim, I'm scared. If you hang up, will I ever hear from you again?" She panicked.

"Yes, Mom, I'll keep in touch. "Promise?"

"Yes." I didn't know if I'd be able to keep the promise because I still needed permission to call home.

When I hung up I was relieved the call was over and I had taken the time to relieve my burden of not communicating with her for all those years. I also became quite scornful. After describing some of the disgust I felt about my mother's carnal attitude, we went back out to the freeway to hitchhike.

We arrived in Reno, Nevada, later that night and set out to find a place to sleep. We were about to bed down under a freeway bridge when a police patrol spied us getting out our gear to sleep. Shining their bright lights upon us, they ordered us to come down and speak with them. We obeyed. They checked our identification and told us to move on. "Prostitution is legal but sleeping under bridges is not?" I commented.

"That's right," they agreed, and warned us that we would be put in jail if they caught us camping anywhere in Reno. "Yes sir," I replied, wondering if they realized how strange their laws really were. Transients don't build the tax base or attract tourism, and the great state of Nevada had little else to offer.

After a fruitless search for a discreet place to bed down, we saw a taxi driver pulling over to help us. Esther was pleasant and didn't seem to mind whatever I decided to do, and we accepted the offer for a ride out of town. He turned off his meter and ran it from time to time just to cover his tracks in case his dispatcher questioned him. At the end of a two mile ride we owed about $1.25, and he let us out exactly where we had left the ramp.

About five minutes later we got a ride going to Truckee, Nevada, at the top of the mountain pass.

We were greeted by an all night snowstorm, and decided to bed down under the freeway bridge in Truckee. Esther insisted on sleeping in the chamber a little more exposed to the elements than I was, and when she awoke in the morning her sleeping bag had small patches of snow on the lower ba es.

She smiled and prepared herself for the day, praying a little and packing up her damp down sleeping bag and nylon ground cloth. I was so glad to be with her and thankful we had gotten out of Reno without going to jail.

The next day we arrived in Stockton where Esther was thrilled to see her mother Eunice. Eunice and Esther had traveled together for years since Esther was only twelve when she joined the Church. They were extremely close, and spent hours serving the Church and each other together. When Esther turned eighteen and was of legal age to travel without a parent, Brother Evangelist decided to split them up.

They went months at a time without seeing each other, and when one would request to go to a camp to see the other Evangelist would reply, "It may not work out for awhile." A little later Brother Evangelist said to Esther, "We cannot have families within this family. We are all one family." Later, when Eunice's grandson called her "Grandma," Brother Evangelist instructed the child not to call her that. "She is Sister Eunice," he said.

The homecoming was brief, unfortunately. Eunice and I went on the road a couple days later to go to San Diego, with plans to go to the interior of Mexico. Esther and Abel traveled together and met us in San Diego. We were to hitchhike to Cabo San Lucas at the tip of Baja, California, and take a ferry across to Puerto Vallarta. We were then going to meet Keith and his family in Mexico City and stay with them for a while. I dreamed about making this journey and of being together with Keith, Elaine, and their seven children. I also liked the prospect of being with Esther for a long time.

Instinctively I knew it wouldn't work for us to go to Mexico. I had long ago learned that if I wanted something really badly, I wouldn't get it. The trick to getting something from God was not to really want it. If you had strong desires for anything outside the work of the Gospel, you were "setting your heart on things below" and in danger of becoming self willed. I really wanted to go witness in Mexico, so much so that I expected a change in plans.

After two weeks of preparing ourselves to go to Mexico, we got a call to go to Spokane, Washington with no explanation, just a call. At the time I was sorely disappointed and wanted to cry, but after suffering so many disappointments over the years, I learned to not set my hopes on anything. To do so was to set oneself up for disappointment because we had no power to make our own decisions. About a year later, in June of 1982, I would no longer be disappointed about not seeing my family. It was to be a traumatic and awkward time.

23

Visiting Home

It had been six-and-one half years since I called my mom that night in April of 1976, telling her I wouldn't be coming home. At that time I had no idea I would have to wait so long before seeing my family again. I had proven myself faithful many times not to call when I had the opportunity, not to leave when I could have, and not to write when I should have. I had passed through my hometown of Washington, D.C., several times, including being thrown in jail in Alexandria where a phone call home would have spared me seventy two hours in custody. The Word of God said to forsake all, and that included my family, those closest to me who had the greatest influence on me. I had done that amidst great anguish of soul and sense of personal loss. Deep down I wanted to explain myself, my life, my doctrine, and to part with their blessing and understanding. At night I dreamed they accepted what I said and even came along, city to city, hopping the freights, spreading the Gospel.

But I didn't want to visit them too soon. Because they were emotionally close, they could sway me, that is my flesh, to renounce the path I was on. They would remember the "old man," the creature with the jovial, witty personality who had left Harvard several years ago and had been transformed into a "sober," godly follower of Jesus Christ. The old was dead and I didn't want to resurrect it. I had a new nature and I battled daily to keep it holy, unspotted from the lust and pride of this world. My parents and brothers and sisters were the ones most likely to draw out the old man and lead him into sin and possibly to renounce the truth.

I began to sense that the time was coming when I would face my family. The dozens of pages of letters I wrote but never sent, the explanations of my severe and austere lifestyle, the pleading, and the comforts I tried to impart…at last I could do these face to face and clear my conscience of the guilt I felt for abandoning my family.

The summer of 1982 found me in Brooklyn, New York, again at the house we had on Nevins Street. I had spent much of the Winter going from South Carolina to Georgia, and then to New York. In New York Brother Evangelist told me there was a house in D.C., and asked if it would be a trial for me to go there for a while. I told him it would be a blessing, and I set out the next day. While I was hitching a ride by the Holland Tunnel the next day, a pickup truck going to D.C. stopped and let me ride in the open back. It was about thirty degrees outside and all I had to roll up in was a stiff tarp which he used to cover gravel. By the time we got to D.C. I was shivering uncontrollably all over, chattering like a skeleton in the wind. I walked to a house in repair on 18th Street between "S" Street and Swan, just a few blocks from Dupont Circle.

We greeted the brothers and sat in front of a fire to warm the shivers out of me. We were staying in a fire damaged townhouse that still had no roof, but did have a door to keep people out. Brother Shor was the older brother and explained to me that the house and the one next door were being renovated and it was our duty to watch them and protect the workmen's tools. Fair enough, no roof, no rent.

After I finally warmed up, I took out a map to see how close my sister's house was. My mom had given me her address when I spoke to her the year before, and to my surprise we were three blocks from her house.

I hit the prayer room floor and began to pray. "Does this mean this is the time for me to visit? Is the Lord finally letting this happen?" I braced myself for another disappointment. I knew if I wanted to visit too badly I wouldn't get my way. Like the rest of God's will, it was permitted only if it wouldn't make me too happy.

A couple days later Brother Evangelist arrived and became the older brother. I cautiously approached him and asked if I could talk to him. He smiled very kindly and asked me what about, and I told him about visiting my "flesh relations."

He seemed open to it and didn't say much, I continued: "Please pray with me that Yahveh's will be done because I wouldn't want to go if it weren't His will. I wouldn't want those things to happen to me that happened to other brothers that went home to visit their flesh relations. I really fear the Lord in this and wouldn't want to be given a strong delusion and fall away. I don't want to be in myself about this. I fear the Lord."

Well, my speech must have impressed him because he smiled and assured me my heart was in the right place, and that he would pray with me about it. Three months later he came to me and said, "Has the Lord shown you anything about going to see 'those people?'" (He was referring to my family.) I didn't know, so I said I was ready to go if it was God's will. He smiled and told me to be ready to go the next day.

The next morning he came to me and asked me to wait another day. He wanted to be sure the Lord was in my visit.

Severely disappointed, I held back my depression and submitted myself. This was no time to act rebellious. The following morning he asked me again if I had received anything from the Lord, and I explained that the Lord rarely gave me dreams about leadings. "Do you feel led?" he asked. I wasn't sure. I'd wait another day.

Finally, on the third clay, he again asked me the same question. This time I had dreamed about my family, probably because I was thinking about them all the time. I told him I dreamed I had gone to see them and he smiled and said, "Pack up." A half hour later he came to me with specific instructions about what to say and not say to my family.

"Brother, you don't need to mention that we're staying in this house. You may want to tell them you're passing through. Or you could tell them that as Yeshua didn't have a home, neither do you; that we're not above our master who didn't have a place to lay his head."

I agreed, although I felt he was acting a little paranoid. "Also, you don't need to mention this soul's name. We

need to be as wise as serpents and as harmless as doves and awake to the warfare we're in. There are parents who have threatened to kill this soul."

In each case, "this soul" referred to himself. I knew my parents wouldn't do anything violent to Brother Evangelist, but I agreed to protect him by not saying anything.

"What should I say if they ask me who our leader is?" I queried.

"Just say you have many older brothers and that Christ is the leader of the Church." I agreed to answer that way and then requested some support. "Could Brother Shor and Brother Barnabas come with me?"

He smiled and seemed relieved. "Of course. When we're facing our flesh relations, it really helps to have some fellowship with you. You know, you aren't going to find much fellowship out there in the world." I agreed, made facial gestures that indicated total agreement and submission, and asked a final question. "Would it be okay to call them before I get on the Metro so they can meet us at the station?"

"Do you think that would be wisdom, brother? It may be more wise to call them from the last station so that they wouldn't have the time to gather police or deprogrammers. If they know you're cornered, it gives them more time to get the fowls together."

I felt he was being too cautious but I didn't want to risk the opportunity by questioning him at this late date. I spoke to Brother Shor and Brother Barnabas and they agreed to come with me. We prayed for safety and left to face my flesh relations for the first time in six and a half years.

At the last stop on the blue line I called my mother and told her where I was. Shocked, she replied, "I'll be right there." About thirty minutes later my younger brother John, whom I had not seen since he was seventeen drove up, looking so different I hardly recognized him. He choked back tears and hugged me, telling me that a lot of people were very upset at me for having disappeared for so long without contacting them. We piled into the car and set out for the thirty minute drive to Upper Marlboro, Maryland, to our nineteenth century tobacco farmhouse on Route 4.

John was obviously glad to see me and tried a little humor with me to lighten the tension. True to my Gospel, I remained sober and didn't laugh.

When I explained my conviction against humor he looked at me with disgust and disbelief. I must really have been brainwashed; all I did was joke around when I was in the world. That was my personality. John could see I was radically different and he didn't like the change. My personality must have been submerged under the influences and teachings of the group, and I ceased to be the bubbly, fun-loving guy he had known for years.

A short while before getting home, John alluded to how badly I had hurt my mother by not contacting her.

"Jim," he began, "losing you was worse than death. For years we haven't known if you were alive or dead. If we knew you were dead, we would have buried you, grieved, and gone on with our lives. If we knew you were alive, we would not have worried as much. But you left us in limbo, not knowing if you were alive or dead, and it was too hard for us to handle. Mom walked around like a zombie, blaming herself for you leaving the family. Do you know how much you hurt her?"

I knew deep in my heart that he was right, but the party line spewed forth instead. "John, I know this is hard for you to understand, but I did this to follow the Lord. He said if anyone did not forsake all that he had, including his family, he could not be his disciple. I had no choice. It was either forsake you or go to hell."

This did not sit well with John. It was still a heartless thing to do. I was beginning to dislike my own doctrine.

As we drove up the circular driveway of Old Marlboro Pike, I saw the two towering tobacco barns a few hundred feet off to the right, and remembered how, as a child, I had hit baseballs off its wooden sides and sheet metal roof. The farm looked about the same as I had remembered it, shaded by an ancient maple tree that now had hypodermics in the roots feeding it nutrients to keep it alive. I was anxious to see my mother, but didn't know what kind of reception I would receive. I quickly got out of the car and walked into the kitchen with John. The wood cook stove was still there, but the ten foot ceiling now had a rotary fan. The table against the wall was overgrown with plants, like usual, leaving little seating space unencumbered by the hanging leaves of some exotic plant hanging in your face. Mom still loved her plants.

Out of the living room a fearful, tearful woman emerged fixing her reddened eyes on my eyes, quietly welcoming me back. Mom was a bundle of contrasting emotions: hatred and love, fear and relief, anger and joy. She was glad I was home, but wanted to see if it was really me. What kind of person had he become? she wondered. When should I speak my mind, or will this only drive him further away? How do I welcome him and make him feel that I care without letting on that I feel he is brainwashed and following a cult leader?

From Dean's List to Dumpsters: Why I Left Harvard to Join a Cult

She took my hands and rubbed them, examining them front and back. "Yes," she choked, "These are your hands. The same ones I used to rub when you were a child. They are bigger now, but they haven't changed...same lines, same folds, same stumpy fingers."

I wanted to scorn and pull away because I thought she was being silly. "Of course they're my hands," I sort of joked. "I haven't been able to purchase another pair."

Not being familiar with how to deal with another person's strong emotions, I drew back into my shell, hoping not to feel what she was feeling. After this, she let my hands go, and John took Barnabas, Shor, and me up to the bedrooms where we would be staying. When John left, I turned to them and said, "Do you see the worldly sorrow the devil is trying to put on me? Looking at my hands and comparing them to when I was a baby? This is too much!"

Shor shared how he had a hard time when he went to visit his parents a few months earlier. "I love them very much," he said, "It was really hard to see them." That was comforting, and I decided to hold my ground and be faithful to the Lord.

The next morning my mother cornered me in the kitchen and with a burst of boldness asked, "Who is your leader?" The gloves had come off at last. "We have many older brothers, but Jesus is the head of our Church," I replied. (Polly want a cracker? Awk!)

She clarified the question, but clearly she could see I was stonewalling her. "So you don't want to tell me, huh? That's what I don't like about this whole thing: too much secrecy! You can't give me an honest answer, you hide from the family for years, you won't tell us the name of the group. Need I remind you the Bible says 'They which do the truth come to the light, that they don't hide and run around secretly?' (John 3:21) Aren't we supposed to let our lights shine before men and all that stuff?"

Here was a chance for me to get back at her years of feminist leanings. "Mom, haven't you read it's not a woman's place to teach? I know what the Scripture says about those things."

She was exasperated. "Well, what about the verse, 'Honor thy father and thy mother?'" (Eph. 6:1)

"Obey your parents in the Lord," (Eph. 6:2) I retorted.

"I can see you have your verses and I have mine. But what I don't understand, Jim, is why you did this to us."

"Mom, you wouldn't understand, You're carnally-minded and don't understand the things of the Spirit of God. Only God can open your eyes and show you the truth." That finished the conversation.

Later I saw her on the porch looking through her binoculars at the varieties of birds that frequented the garden behind the woodshed. She had her Audubon Society bird books out trying to identify some new species that she had never seen before. Brother Shor sat with her and participated in the bird watching, enjoying the exercise with her, subtly looking for opportunities to witness to her.

I came up to her as she sat there trying to get her mind off the monster I had become. "Jim," she invited, "come and look at these birds with us." Not being thrilled with birds since my childhood, I certainly didn't admire them in my adulthood. I reluctantly took a seat next to her on the porch and looked through the binoculars. It was great to see focus for once as I saw the clear outlines of the barn, the highway behind it, and the electric wires that ran from the shed to the well. Nevertheless, this gave us an opportunity to speak.

"Do you see that one with the pretty yellow tail and the red stripe on its wing?" she asked.

"Naw," I said, hoping the subject would change. "I remember one time I was camped in California and found a pretty shell. When I showed it to the older brother he reminded me that we should be careful not to worship the creation more than the Creator."

Again I had alienated her by misusing a Scripture. She was then convinced I didn't have both oars in the water and she didn't like the person I had become.

That night, immediately after I called my father who lived about forty-five minutes away, he came over to see me. He was gentle and very loving, not condemning me at all. He had grayed considerably and was slightly bent over with age, not the robust man I had remembered from 1976. He gave me a long hug and we sat down on the steps to talk.

"So, how are you doing, son?" "Fine, Dad."

"Are you happy with what you're doing?" "Yes."

"Really? Are you really happy, son?"

I thought back on the time I had spent in the group and, except for the pain of leaving the family and being celibate, life was all right. "Yes, Dad. I am happy."

"Do you miss us?" "Yes, I do."

"Are you allowed to write?"

"Yes." It was a half-truth. I could write if I didn't mind the stigma of being suspected of being unfaithful.

"I have been worried about you, son. Did you ever break into my house in Rockville one summer when I wasn't there?"

I was shocked by the question. "Why would you ask that?" "Well, when you don't hear from someone for a long time, you begin to imagine funny things. While you were gone, someone broke into the house in Rockville, climbed through the basement window, ate some food, watched some TV, and then left without taking anything. It has haunted me for years. We thought maybe you had come and dropped in and left."

"No," I said. "That wasn't me."

"I told myself if I ever saw you alive again I would ask you that question. I'm just so glad to see you that you can't imagine. Your sister, Catherine, thought she saw you on an on-ramp in Connecticut or somewhere when she went on vacation. When she turned around to come and get you, the person was no longer there. She cried for a long time after that."

By now I was getting the message. My disappearance and silence over the years had hurt them deeply, and they couldn't imagine why I was behaving this way. "I used to come down to Dupont Circle every weekend for about two years to look for you. I think I met some of your buddies, but I didn't bother asking them about you because I knew they wouldn't tell me anything," he chuckled. "Would they?" he asked.

"No," I agreed. "They wouldn't have told you anything." "That's what I thought," he replied. "Well, son, are you sure you are doing what you want to be doing with a free will?"

"Yes, Dad. I'm doing what I want to be doing with my own free will." At the time I didn't realize the way I was being manipulated and how trapped I was to the group's doctrine and fear tactics. I believed that leaving the group would destroy me spiritually forever.

"Can you write from time to time to let us know how you are doing?"

"I'll try. We aren't allowed to send mail from any cities that we are in, but I can write to you when I am on the road."

"Why is that? Is it a security precaution?" I was amazed at how insightful my father was. He seemed to see through the group better than I did.

"Yes. We have had problems in the past with parents of members of the group persecuting us."

"Don't you think maybe you brought this on yourself by disappearing and not contacting the families? Perhaps if you kept in contact with the families you wouldn't have so much persecution!"

That made perfect sense to me, and I remember having thought it when I first learned about the secrecy of the group.

He asked me a few more questions about how I lived and how we provided for ourselves, and he was mildly amused at the ingenuity and the survival skills I had acquired. Then he hit me below the belt.

"Do you think you'll ever get married?" "I'd like to."

"Does the leader permit marriages?" "Yes, some."

"Isn't it hard for you to be alone and not have a mate?"

"It is difficult, but God gives me the grace." That answer satisfied my doctrinal side, but did nothing for my testosterone level.

"I want grandkids!" he bellowed in jest, with a big smile. "I'd love to make you some," I thought to myself. I was really troubled about the strictness of Brother Evangelist's marriage policy, allowing only one marriage in six-and-a- half years, but I didn't want to let on that there was anything wrong with the Church. I was there to convert them as much as I was there to appease my own conscience.

We parted on good terms and he invited me over to see his new family the next day. I told him I would like to, and when Brother Evangelist called the next day he told me to be careful.

On the drive over, my father began to vent his real frustration and anger about my leaving the family and not contacting them. I was surprised and became very defensive. I felt like getting out of the car and almost asked him to let me out on Interstate 95. He finally settled down as we arrived in Rockville, and we avoided any further conflict that day.

On the final day of the visit, Brother Evangelist called and told me to pack up and return to the house on Nevins Street in New York City. I was ready to go. Emotionally, I was drained and could take no more confrontation. Brother Barnabas accompanied me as I walked around the farm one last time before leaving it. Behind the toolshed I began to weep openly for them, consciously telling myself I was weeping for their lost, sinful state, but really weeping because I was ashamed and sorry for how much I had hurt them and how much they loved me.

I hadn't realized how much I had hurt them until this visit, nor did I realize how much they loved me. But instead of facing these realities, the religious beast within me swallowed up the pain and renamed it "Godly sorrow for sinking sinners." Shor tried to comfort me, relating to me his visit home.

"It does strange things to you," he said. "You think you're going to be strong, but you are never really ready for what emotions you meet when you go to visit your family." That was so true.

24

The Bermuda Love Triangle

My father intuitively knew I would never be truly complete without a spouse. I knew it too, but because the Elder was so dead set against marriage I didn't want to set myself up for more disappointment than I could handle. As long as I didn't ask, there was always room to hope that someday I would be married If I asked and he said no, there was no more hope. I felt this loneliness and fervent desire for intimacy would be a permanent part of my existence as long as I dwelt in this corrupt flesh. If I argued with him about marriage, I could kiss any chance goodbye. It would only prove how rebellious and unprepared I was for marriage.

When I returned to the house on Nevins Street in Brooklyn, New York, the Elder greeted me at the door. He had arrived from D.C. just a day earlier. Because there were so many brothers and sisters, it became apparent that some of us would have to move on soon.

We spent several weeks in Coney Island with a pocket of brothers there in the house near the boardwalk. When I would go out during the day to witness, my testosterone was stirred by the bikinis parading around everywhere. Then I would see Sister Esther walking past on the other side, smiling with her eyes while avoiding eye contact. I knew she loved me as a brother, but doubted it went any deeper.

One day I asked her again if she had had any dreams pertaining to me. "What about?" she asked nervously.

"Oh, I don't know. Any dreams about marriage?"

"Yes, but Brother Evangelist asked me not to speak about the subject with brothers."

"Can you give me some idea, whether it was positive or negative?"

She wanted to answer, but was afraid to say anything. She repeated her charge and frustrated as I was, I let her be true to her command. She had gotten in trouble before by speaking with brothers who had approached her about marriage without the Elder's permission.

Nevertheless, I had to know what the dream was. I wrote a letter to Brother Evangelist describing the conversation and how faithful the sister was not to tell me anything. I requested to speak with him, since she had shared the dream with him. Since God had revealed His will concerning me on a subject quite important to me, I felt I had a right to know.

During this time I had changed my name to "Ariel," a Hebrew name that means "Lion of God." I liked both the sound and the meaning of the name, since I had never felt I was strong and uncompromising. Perhaps a name change would help a character change.

When I spoke to Brother Evangelist on the phone, he angrily told me he had told the sister never to talk to brothers about "that subject" (marriage).

When I told him I had approached her, he still felt the blame belonged to her since she knew better and I didn't. He told me she had a history of talking about marriage with brothers and that this alone indicated she wasn't ready to marry. If she could not obey those over her, how could she be ready to submit to a husband?

I tried to explain that she didn't tell me anything and that she was trying to be faithful. He still didn't buy it; it was like he was personally offended by her disobedience. He also told me he would talk to me later about the dream. Meanwhile, Sister Esther was to be sent to the house on Nevins Street immediately.

That day, the day known as "Black September," was my birthday. Internationally, the Jews had entered a Palestinian camp and slaughtered about 1,000 refugees in the middle of the night. The tabloids were filled with grotesque descriptions of slit throats, machine gunnings, and other unspeakable atrocities. I was going through a storm, desperately wanting to know what God had for me since I realized I needed a wife. What was the dream? How could I go on until I knew something? I moaned and slithered through the streets of Coney Island, sat on the boardwalk, and waited for the sunset, desperately waiting for the Elder to come to speak to me. The headlines spoke to me: "Ariel Sharon Weathers Storm." The Israeli defense minister had his storm to weather, too, and his name was Ariel. At last, some comfort from God!

Looking back, I believe Brother Evangelist was incredibly insensitive to the struggle I was going through. A phone call and a discussion of the dream would have saved me two weeks of agony. Instead, he chose to wait and let me twist and turn like a washing machine with a broken spin cycle.

After two weeks he called me to come to Nevins Street to talk about the dream. We went to the cool, secluded basement with the bare light bulb where we stored the food in boxes. He reminded me that brothers weren't supposed to talk to sisters about marriage, and then he revealed the dream.

"I haven't talked with the sister for awhile about this, so I may not have it exactly like she told me, but the gist of the dream was like this: She was standing in the sisters' room when a man walked in with a lion on a leash. The man said, 'This brother is seeking a wife.' When Sister Esther saw the lion, she ran out the room shouting, 'Not me! Not me!' and then the lion turned into you."

That wasn't a hard dream to interpret. I was a lion (Ariel) and it wasn't the Lord's will for us to many. I was carnally seeking a wife, and it wasn't the Lord's will. Case closed. Although I didn't like the dream or the interpretation, I had no doubt it was divinely inspired and that was the end of marriage for me. I was both relieved and depressed; relieved that I was no longer in limbo, depressed that it wasn't the solution I was seeking. I felt sheepish in front of my shepherd. I thanked him for telling me and went away to go on with life, firmly resolved that I would bear the iron cross of celibacy.

Several months later Brother Evangelist told me to pack up and take Sister Esther and Sister Phebe to a house in Waite, Maine, where we could encourage and refresh some of the brothers. The road to Waite took us through Boston, Massachusetts, north through Bangor, Maine, east to Calais, Maine, and about twenty miles north to Waite. It was located on the edge of an Indian reservation in the far northeast of Maine.

In one ride in Massachusetts, a man asked me if I ever planned to get married. I knew Sister Esther was listening as I spoke. "No, I won't. The Lord has made it very clear to me that he doesn't want me to get married." Sister Esther squirmed in her seat. Something was troubling her conscience.

Later I lost my small Bible by leaving it in a ride. When I discovered it was gone, Sister Esther offered me hers, saying she had had a dream the night before that I had lost mine and she had given me hers. I smiled and praised God, feeling all warm inside and sensing that perhaps God had a reason for this sister being with me and my losing the Bible. When I finally got the nerve up, I asked her, "Have you had any dreams concerning me?" I wasn't really looking for a dream about marriage, but I thought that since she frequently had dreams of things that came to pass, perhaps I could know a little of my future.

She froze and said nothing. I didn't push it any further. I didn't want to get her in trouble again.

After arriving in Waite, we got a call from Brother Evangelist saying that Esther and I were to come back to New York. I thought that was strange since we had just arrived there the night before. I did, however, look forward to traveling with this sister alone, since I was so fond of her and enjoyed her company.

The journey to New York was too quick for me. I fell deeply in love with this beautiful, warm, loving sister. She was consistently pleasant, very unselfish, gentle, kind, and a joy to be around. I wished I could marry her and that her feelings were the same toward me, but the Lord had ruled out marriage and I had to endure it.

When we arrived in Brooklyn, Brother Evangelist told Sister Esther that her brother Silas, her mother Eunice, and she were going to visit her father in Bradenton, Florida. Esther was glad to bear this since she missed her father and was worried because his health was so bad. That night she had a dream that I had accompanied her to Florida. She shared it with the Elder and he okayed the trip after asking her if it was a trial for her to travel with me. "Not at all," she emphatically replied.

We left New York the next morning and arrived in D.C. that night. We went to the house near Dupont Circle where Brother Chris was the older brother. Esther wanted to hitch on since she was afraid Brother Evangelist would call Chris and cancel the trip, and we would stay in D.C. Instead, we were told to go on the next morning after the phone call from the Elder. That night we got twenty five miles past Richmond, Virginia and were sitting down on our backpacks along Interstate 95. The day had been pleasant, and we had enjoyed each other's company, when I felt like broaching the topic of "The Dream."

She became very uncomfortable. Her conscience smote her. I began, "I appreciate your bearing with me when I got you in trouble concerning the dream you had. I was really out of order when I asked you about it. I'm sorry."

She squirmed some more, knowing God was listening.

"It was really convicting to me how I was in the flesh in seeking a wife. I really believe it was of God.

She put her head down and prayed. She was really troubled now and wanted to set something straight. "I don't think it was of God," she quietly said.

My heart leaped into my esophagus. "Why don't you think it was of God?" And thus began a cryptic conversation, a conversation in which she would drop a clue or a hint and a rm me whenever I drew the right conclusion. She was desperately trying to avoid coming right out and saying what was on her mind, but she had no problem leading me into the conclusion she wanted me to find.

Soon after beginning the conversation a truck stopped, going all the way to Atlanta. Perfect! We were supposed to meet Silas in Atlanta prior to going on to Bradenton. (Later Esther told me she had a dream that we would get a truck ride at sunset that would take us to Atlanta.) In the truck the puzzle began to fall into place. The Elder had not told me the correct dream, only what Esther had told him. She had been in love with another brother and this dream messed things up for her, so she changed the dream slightly.

"What? You told him a false dream?" I was both upset and relieved.

"What was the real dream?"

She knew she couldn't get into any deeper trouble than she was in but she had to confess only what was wrong. "What did Brother Evangelist tell you about the dream?"

"You were in the sisters' room and a man came in with a lion on a leash. The man represented the 'old man,' the sinful part of our nature. The man said that 'This brother is seeking a wife,' and you ran out of the room screaming, 'Not me, not me!' Then the lion turned into me."

She put her finger on her brows and looked down in shame. "That's not how the dream really went." She would volunteer nothing. I had to sleuth it out of her.

"What was different?" I asked.

"The man wasn't a carnal man leading the lion. It was a king, and the lion was the king's son."

I was shocked. "You mean I was being led of God to ask you to marry me?"

She nodded, avoiding eye contact.

"And you told the Elder another dream?" Nod.

"And your fleeing meant you were running from God's will?"

"Yes."

During the rest of the trip I was in ecstasy. Eventually we were able to express our mutual feelings of love, and I was thrilled to find she cared so deeply for me. I was dizzy with love as we arrived in Atlanta. We took a bus to College Park where the brothers were staying with Brother Ezekiel, a married brother who had left the church several years before. As we got off the bus we found a baby bottle at the bus stop with Esther's name on it. I was sure it was a sign from heaven that our marriage was meant to be.

Ezekiel had lost an arm several years earlier in some construction mishap and now supported his wife and daughter whom they named Glory to God, by rebuilding Volkswagen engines and selling them. When Brother Evangelist received news several years earlier that Ezekiel had lost his arm, he had latched on to that misfortune to warn the flock to walk in the fear of God. Ezekiel was given as an example of someone who didn't fear God enough.

I didn't know how to process Ezekiel's spiritual state since he was obviously not a part of the Church and yet was trying to live for God. We were even having fellowship with him while we ate his food and lived in his house. He obviously loved the brothers and was more than hospitable to them. He drove them around to check dumpsters and his wife cleaned up and prepared the food for us.

During the month that Esther and I stayed with her father and her brother in Bradenton, Florida, we grew extremely close and decided we wanted to marry. We showed each other the proper affections that young couples do who wish to marry, but did none of those things that were reserved for marriage. Although we convinced ourselves that we would marry if we had the unfettered choice, we knew we would have to convince Brother Evangelist to let us, and that wouldn't be easy.

The month spent in Bradenton was my happiest month in the Church. It was also the guiltiest. I knew the Elder wouldn't approve of my love for Esther, especially since we didn't consult him first. But I couldn't deny that I felt God was bringing us together. She had loved me from afar for a long time, as I had her. When I prayed to God about it He seemed pleased to bless me with her; I felt peace and joy approaching Him. I told her one time that we ought to tell Brother Evangelist everything, and that God would bless our honesty if we confessed all. She, seeing through Brother Evangelist more clearly than I, told me not to mention anything to him about anything. He would surely forbid it if he knew she had spoken to me about marriage.

The month ended, and we were sent back to Nevins Street in Brooklyn to meet up with the brothers. It was bittersweet, since our time alone together was ending, but we needed to see Brother Evangelist to get his permission to marry. As we walked to the house from the subway stop, Esther dropped back behind me as an obedient sister and I muttered my final words, "Please don't give up on me. I will never break my vow to marry you."

We entered and greeted the brothers. Brother Evangelist was bedded down, and Esther went upstairs as she was accustomed to doing. When Brother Evangelist heard us come in, he told me to come into the living room adjacent to the stairway and asked me where the sister was. "She's gone upstairs already," I said, which upset him. "Tell her to come down here. Sisters should know not to be working things out themselves without going through the older brother first."

Esther came back down as commanded, and when Brother Evangelist saw her, he rebuked her for going up and not waiting for him to dismiss her. She took it very meekly and apologized and went back upstairs at his command. I bit my tongue since I knew she hadn't done anything wrong. Sisters always went right upstairs unless they were told to wait. Esther did what she was supposed to.

The next evening the trouble began. Brother Evangelist took me aside and asked me, "Brother, I don't mean to doubt you or anything, but did you lift up the standard on this journey?"

I gulped. Trembling, I said, "No, sir. The sister and I did too much talking."

He looked both shocked and disappointed. Then he got a disturbed look on his face, "You didn't talk about that subject, did you?"

I knew I couldn't lie and that I couldn't hide anything from Brother Evangelist. God had surely revealed our entire trip to him, including the displays of affection that were so contrary to his standards. "Yes sir," I admitted.

"Brother, I'm shocked at you that you would do such a thing!" he raged. "I'll talk to you after the meal."

I ran upstairs to inform them that I wouldn't be eating (my appetite had suddenly left), and went down to the basement to pray for God's mercies. I pleaded with God for about ten minutes, and then Brother Evangelist came down and said he wanted to discuss this with me.

Alone in the dark basement, he had obviously cooled off some. Since this was the first time I had done this, he would forgive me, but not the sister. She knew better. She had spoken too many times with brothers and couldn't be trusted around them. Not only that, but her continual resistance of the Elder in this matter indicated she wasn't ready for marriage. "There are a lot of things you don't know about that sister that I'm trying to save you from."

I couldn't let that stand. "I really believe it's God's will for us to marry. I believe God showed it to me in prayer and other circumstances. We even found a baby bottle with her name on it when we got off the bus in Atlanta. And her dream was different than what she shared with you. It wasn't a carnal man that was leading the lion, it was a king!"

He seemed unmoved by all this. He dismissed my reasoning by saying, "You said it was the Lord's will to marry Noahh several years ago." I couldn't argue with him about that. I had said it, but he had forbidden it. Perhaps it was okay with God if I married either of them, and Brother Evangelist had been standing in the way, hindering God's will. I was confused.

"Do you realize she has spoken with several brothers about marriage already?" he asked. I did. She had told me how several brothers had randomly approached her and spoken to her. Brother Evangelist made it seem like she was drawing brothers aside and proposing.

After saying several more negative things about her, he agreed he would consider the marriage. He also promised not to tell Esther that he knew about the trip, and that he would speak to me in a while when he knew what to do. The next day I left for Buffalo, New York, extremely depressed and confused, desperately clinging to the hope that I would someday marry Esther. In a ride I heard the "Wedding Song" by Paul Stookey, and felt it was a message from God to wait on him and he would work it out.

After a week in Buffalo, Brother Evangelist called me and invited me to come to Detroit where the brothers had a house near downtown.

"When you get here, we'll talk again about that matter."

His voice was warm and congenial. He had gotten over the shock, and he seemed ready to forgive me and accept me back into favor. I thanked him and was glad I had again found favor in his sight. In Buffalo, Brother Evangelist took me to another house where we were doing some yard work and spoke to me inside. He was calm and friendly, ready to discuss the issue without anger. I had decided that I needed to come clean before God in confessing the physical aspects of Esther's and my relationship in Bradenton. Before I confessed these things, though, he reiterated his belief that he didn't think Esther was ready for marriage. If she couldn't be subject in the church, how would she be subject in marriage? He had seen it too many times: Sisters were meek and obedient until they got their husbands, and then they became horses of a different color. Esther wasn't even obedient as a single sister!

I disregarded his opinion in this, feeling he was being too strict. She had always been the most agreeable and pleasant sister I had ever traveled with (except for Noahh) and I had never had any trouble with her.

"Some brothers think I wanted her for myself," he smiled, assuming I would see the absurdity in that statement. "But that's not the case."

"I can see why so many brothers approached her," I said. "She really is like Esther in the Scriptures, fair and exceedingly beautiful."

He looked puzzled after I made that comment. "Perhaps it's just the grace of God, but I don't see her that way," he said. He seemed pleased that God had kept him from his biological side. When it seemed we were finished, I added, "I need to share something else with you about our trip."

"Okay, brother."

"I'm ashamed to tell you…but we got physically involved when we were together."

He was shocked and began to tremble. "The Lord bless you for confessing this," he panted quietly. "Did you…"

"Thank God, no," I sighed. "It was mostly kissing and hugging."

"I don't know what to say, brother. This has never happened before. You realize you may have kissed the lips of another man's wife?"

"Yes," I admitted, although at the time I had no doubt she was going to be my wife. I still felt ashamed.

He hurriedly left the house and said he would talk to me again in the near future. That evening he took me aside, and said. "I don't want to suggest anything here, but you know that Sister Noahh has been doing real well recently."

I was shocked and mumbled out the response, "Really? In what way?" "She's really been pressing in and lifting up the standard. One older brother says that she has been praying a lot and walking very meekly."

I knew what he was getting at. He wanted me to consider Noahh for a wife after having blitzed the idea years before. Perhaps he realized I was serious about needing a wife and he wanted me to have the best one possible. Or possibly, as was the case, he was trying to divert me away from Esther and create confusion until I gave up on marriage completely.

I was a little angered at the suggestion that I should consider Noahh after so many years, especially since I knew I wanted Esther. But in the situation I was in, any wife was better than no wife, and I saw a glimmer of hope that if one sister didn't work out, he would allow me to marry the other. So I said, "Could I pray about both of them and let you know my decision?" He agreed.

I didn't want Esther to know I was praying about another sister after I had told her I would never leave her. That was still my intention. I just didn't want to pray for three years for Esther and be told it wasn't God's will, and then have to pray for another three years for Noahh. There were limits to my patience. The best policy would be to pray for God's will and wait for Him to bless me.

I did realize this could cause problems with Esther if she knew I was praying about marrying Noahh. I didn't want Noahh to know I was considering marrying her either, if it turned out I was going to marry Esther. I therefore requested that Brother Evangelist say nothing to Noahh about my praying about marrying her. He agreed. Several weeks later he told Noahh (I discovered much later), and word got back to Esther through the other sisters who saw Noahh suffering emotional turmoil, wanting to know why I had not spoken to her about marriage.

He seemed pleased that his ruse had worked, and decided that his best ploy to hinder my marrying anyone would be to cause a love triangle which I had no intention of forming. Over the next several months, whenever he would approach me about the issue of marriage, he would smother me in good reports about Noahh and bad reports about Esther's reprobate behavior.

"Esther was coveting an $8.00 towel while Noahh was humbly washing dishes in a frozen stream," or "Esther was forsaking modest dress and trying on a pair of pants while Noahh was meekly laboring faithfully for the Church." During this time they were a continent away so I had to trust Brother Evangelist's word.

Months of confusion followed as I thought of the two sisters. What did the Lord really want? Whenever I thought the Lord was showing me to marry Esther, Brother Evangelist would come to me, appearing perfectly neutral and open to God's leading, and encourage me away from Esther. Taking his time to decide was critical to the salvation of my soul, he explained. If we married out of God's will we could be destroyed. (I learned many years later that Brother Evangelist created many love triangles to confuse and hinder brothers and sisters from marrying. One time a brother asked him for a sister, and Brother Evangelist went to another sister and told her to pray about marrying this brother. Since leaving the Church I have learned more than one brother has been hoodwinked by this strategy.)

Over the next several months I was obsessed with marriage. It was hard to pray not knowing if something I desired so much would come to pass. Several months after speaking with him about Esther, Brother Evangelist called me to come meet him in Portland, Oregon.

He had arranged a special task for me to take Sister Noahh to her parents' house in Ferndale, Washington, thirty miles south of the Canadian border on Interstate 5, just south of Bellingham, Washington. We were going north to witness to her older sister. We packed up to leave the next morning, me being totally unaware of Noahh's thoughts and desires. In the next few days things would radically change.

25

I Don't Remember Saying That

We traveled the 350 miles in over a day, and were picked up at the freeway by Noahh's brother Hans. He took us to a modest brick farmhouse on the edge of a rural route. Behind her house was a larger wooden barn where the hay was kept in the winter, and where she had played and jumped as a little girl. There were a handful of cows on the farm and some beehives where they had gotten honey and a few bee stings many years earlier. Noahh's mother was a strong German immigrant who had worked hard all her life and avoided conflict whenever possible with her husband. Her father was also an immigrant who worked hard and honestly all the days of his life and practiced his Catholic faith with the same integrity he brought to his work.

They were ecstatic to see her and were hospitable to the hilt. Noahh brought me some hot tea, sweetened with honey from their hives, and smiled graciously as she did so. I began to remember why I had wanted to marry Noahh in the first place. At this time I did not know Brother Evangelist had spoken to her or that she was hoping I would take advantage of this trip to approach her about marriage. I ignorantly assumed that Brother Evangelist would keep his word and help me not to hurt anyone.

The three days we spent on that farm, nestled in the house, taking walks around the farm in the snow, getting to know her family, and being served hand and foot, had an impact on me. Brother Evangelist knew it would. I headed back to Portland more confused than ever about whom to marry.

Brother Evangelist met us at the door and welcomed us back. Later I told him how edifying the sister was and that I thought she might be a good choice for a wife. I asked him again if she knew anything about my praying about marrying her and he assured me he had not told her anything. Several days later he left me in charge of the house and left town.

The morning after he left, Sister Noahh came to me in tears and said she had to talk to me privately. I wanted to keep the standard about brothers and sisters not talking too long in private, so I had her come with me and a brother into the basement and speak to me while the brother observed with his fingers in his ears. She was in torment, tears flowing like rivers from her eyes, her body seeming emaciated and weak. She had to ask me something very personal.

"Brother Ariel, I don't know if this is out of order or not, but I have to know something. Brother Evangelist told me several months ago you were praying about marrying me and you would be approaching me about marriage soon. I have waited and waited for months now, and I need to know. Have you found some uncleanness in me that you have decided you haven't found me worthy to be your wife?"

I was taken aback at the question and totally unprepared. Brother Evangelist had told her I was praying about marrying her? He told me he wouldn't say anything! Now this poor girl had her hopes up and I would have to disappoint someone, either her or Esther! I was trying to avoid this very thing that happened!

Not only that, but lack of open communication and honesty among the brothers and sisters led to months of trials and emotional suffering for this sister. She told me she had been so troubled by this she had been unable to eat much for weeks, she was crying for hours, and she had to keep herself busy to avoid thinking about marriage. This was the fruit of Brother Evangelist's handling of marriages: confusion, anguish, and depression.

I told her it was out of order to speak to her about marriage, but I had indeed been praying about marrying her, and I had not decided against her. "There's a lot going on that I need to explain to you, but I need the Elder's permission to speak with you about it. No, I haven't rejected you. I will ask the Elder when he calls tonight if I might speak with you about it."

That night the Elder called and when I told him what Noahh had said he assured me he didn't remember saying that, and then he said she had come to him. I accepted that answer, although it still didn't make sense, but because I trusted him so strongly I knew it was just a misunderstanding and not a lie. Besides, if it meant I could talk to Noahh about marriage it was okay with me.

Over the few months that Brother Evangelist had been working to turn me away from Esther, I had no contact with her to verify or deny what Brother Evangelist had been telling me about her. But being with Noahh and seeing her virtue tipped the scales in her favor.

Please don't misunderstand me. I was not some hot piece of flesh who could choose from a harem the woman who pleased me the most. Most women would be insulted if they were dating a man who was considering marrying another woman. In the Church it was not like that. Marriage was dictated from above and was not really a matter of personal choice. Final approval resided with the Elder. It was an objective matter to decide who was more worthy, or if the man was worthy to have a wife at all. If the sister was worthy, but the man was not spiritual, there would be no marriage. If the man was worthy, but the sister was not, there would still be no marriage. During the waiting period the Elder decided whether the couple was worthy and if it was in the best interest of the Church.

The next morning Brother Evangelist called me again on the public phone next to the park about two blocks away from the house. He revealed to me that one of the sisters had told Esther I was praying about marrying Noahh, and he asked me if I would like to speak to her privately about it. I agreed, and he told me to take her to a park or some private place and we could speak freely about it. I was relieved because I wanted to clear the air and let her know what was going on.

We walked joyfully to a shopping mall and sat on benches facing each other. The first thing I wanted to know was how she knew I was praying about marrying her. She repeated her story about the Elder coming to her and telling her he didn't want to cause a trial, but to pray about marrying brother Ariel since he was praying about it, too.

"Did you approach him or did he approach you?" I inquired. Something was not adding up about Brother Evangelist's story, but I still wanted to give him the benefit of the doubt.

"He approached me. The only time I ever approached him about you was when we were in Tacoma several years ago, and somehow I knew you had approached him about marrying me. I don't know how I knew, but I felt the Lord was showing me that you had gone to him about me."

My mind flashed back three years to the time I had first asked Brother Evangelist about marrying Noahh. Although I had not spoken to her about marriage while on the journey, I had prayed fervently that the Lord would show her that I wanted to marry her. Brother Evangelist seemed open to the marriage at the time, but nixed it several months later in Salt Lake City. I had no idea Noahh had approached him about my desire to marry her and that God had answered my prayer.

"What did he say to you?" I asked.

"He said he didn't foresee any more marriages in the Church. This caused a great deal of confusion because I thought the Lord had shown me it was okay for us to pray about this. I went into a long trial afterward because I didn't know when I could trust the leading of God or if it was my own deceitful heart leading me."

Brother Evangelist had hidden this information from me for years! Here was a confirmation, a miraculous leading of God's Spirit, and he chose to ignore it because it wasn't what he wanted! I was intrigued. "What else has God shown you?"

We unburdened ourselves for the good part of the day, and when it was over I had completely changed my mind about marrying Esther. I knew the Elder didn't approve of Esther and me marrying, but since he seemed so open to me marrying Noahh, she was the logical choice. I forgave Brother Evangelist for his deception, rationalizing that God was using it to bring me back to the one I was supposed to have married all along.

Noahh didn't want to cause problems for Esther, so she asked me not to consider her until it was clear it wasn't God's will for me to marry Esther. Although it seemed like a sweet thing for her to do, I had made up my mind that she was the better choice. The compliment thrilled her and she smiled meekly to herself, apologizing for the multitude of words we had spoken that day. She smiled toward the ground while avoiding eye contact, not wanting to stir up lust in me.

I realized that day that had not Brother Evangelist been involved in the marriage process, I would have married several years earlier. My feelings and leanings were not of my flesh; God was trying to give me a wife. Years later, when I fell in love with Esther, God was again trying to bless me. If not for the meddling arm of the marriage discouraging Elder, Esther might have been my wife instead.

That night the Elder called and I told him of my decision to marry Noahh, and that we wanted to send him a note. Seeming pleased, he told me to check the phone on Friday, four days away, and to bring plenty of change. Meanwhile, Noahh sent him a note telling him she wouldn't want to marry any other man, and my note detailed our discussion and how Noahh had "lifted up the standard."

Friday seemed like a year away. Brother Chris showed up a couple days later and took over as the older brother in the house. He knew the next phone call was Friday, and I think he suspected something unusual was going on. I could barely eat that entire week as I waited for a decision from the Elder about marriage. I didn't want to hope too much, but I scrutinized his comments of the previous six months about Noahh's good character, and his request that we bring a lot of change to the phone with us. That meant it was going to be a long phone call to work out the details of the marriage, and I was sure he was going to approve it. However, experience had long taught me that whenever I really wanted something in the Church, it was usually snatched away from me at the last moment without explanation. I was sick with apprehension.

Friday dawned in spite of the mournful overhang of clouds and drizzle. Chris sent Noahh and me in different directions to the phone booth so we wouldn't be noticed, and had us stand behind separate trees until the call came. A knot formed in my stomach as I watched the time tick down. What if he didn't call? What if he said no?

Suddenly the phone chimed and Chris snatched the receiver. He began to scribble notes furiously in his notepad and "Yes sir" every five seconds. He was obviously rushing. Brother Evangelist must be rushing through his conversation with Chris to spend some more time talking with us. I fully expected him to hand us the receiver at any time, but he kept talking. My heart sank. I knew the phone calls rarely lasted more than four minutes and time was running out on this one. Finally Chris put his hand over the mouthpiece, turned to us, and said, "Does either of you have anything to say to the Elder?"

I was crushed. That was code for, "The Elder has nothing to share with you but since you are there you may as well not have wasted your time, so he'll pretend you were the ones initiating the contact." Never had I seen a man set a table and clear it so quickly. Nevertheless, Noahh took the phone and spoke privately with him and then gave the phone back to Chris. I was speechless.

I slouched back to the house that night, having suffered the 1400th disappointment of my life with the Church. This confirmed what I believed: If I really wanted something, I wouldn't get it. I could only hope to get what I wanted by tricking God into thinking I didn't really want it. But He would see through that. Perhaps I could only survive by learning not to want things.

The next day Noahh went on the road with a brother and I was sent to California by myself to meet Brother Paul in Eureka. I was glad to get out of dreary Oregon into sunny California because the constant rain, beside my bitter disappointment, was beginning to depress me.

26

My First Disciple

My trip to Eureka was uneventful, except for the unusual man who picked me up in O'Brien, Oregon, near the Oregon border and drove me into California. (I had opted to take U.S. Route 199 from Grants Pass over to Route 101 on the coast.)

He was a dapper but eccentric young man dressed in a derby hat and driving a Mercedes-Benz. We discussed a variety of issues until we were a few miles from the California border when he told me why he had to let me off at the first rest stop in California. In his trunk was a lead box filled with toxic wastes that he was driving into California to dispose of. A large company hired him to illegally transport the material across the state line where it could be disposed of secretly. A man in a pickup truck was waiting for him at the rest area just across the California border to pick up the wastes to transport further south. The rest area was immediately after Collier Tunnel at the border. No one would think of inspecting his automobile since he didn't look like he was transporting anything but other English butlers.

He dropped me off at the rest area and met his connection. I walked out to the highway to continue hitchhiking, and a few minutes later the dapper man sped past me heading back to Oregon. He honked and I contemplated how to make some money being a whistleblower to the government.

After several days in Eureka, I hitchhiked to Arcata, California, to witness at Humboldt State College, about eight miles south of Eureka on US-101. I noticed several students erecting a stage in the quad outside the student union, preparing for a traveling Christian acting troupe called "The Lamb's Players." They specialized in humorous theater based upon themes of the Middle Ages, knights, chivalry, dragons, and damsels in distress. The half dozen young people who constituted the troop wished to use their theater to attractively present the Gospel to the unbelieving students. The local college Christian fellowship had sponsored them.

I sat through the performance desperately trying not to laugh, self righteously despising what I saw going on. They were so foolish, not sober like Christ was. Could you imagine Christ behaving like this? I questioned, feeling secure in my spiritual superiority. The poor actors had a zeal for God, but not according to knowledge.

At the end of the performance, as the crowd dispersed, I sat there waiting for an opportunity to witness. A young man about six feet, seven inches, weighing about 150 pounds, came over and kindly asked me what I thought. I began to share my criticism and hard sayings to him, including the need to forsake all his belongings, and he listened with great interest. Four hours later he was converted and wanted to come with me to serve the Lord. He wanted to inform his parents of his decision, but the older brother thought it would be wiser for Kraig to get out of town first and then send a letter explaining his decision. I didn't like shocking parents the way the group did, and I knew his parents would worry, but I still had to go along with the program.

Kraig and I left Eureka the following day, taking a bus north to Crescent City and hitchhiking back to Portland, Oregon. He was an eager trooper, showing a real heart to suffer for Christ and to endure tribulation and hardship. We hitched in the rain for a good part of the way, but he was so convinced of the doctrine, and so happy to be sold out for Christ, it didn't bother him at all. He could only remark on the great peace he had found living for Jesus.

When we arrived in Portland, Brother Evangelist was at the house. I wanted to talk with him about Noahh. He made himself generally unavailable but did say if I had a letter to send to her he would be glad to deliver it for me. Fearing Noahh would be having fears that I would change my mind and marry Esther, I wrote a letter assuring her she was my choice. I encouraged her to wait upon the Lord and live righteously before him, and he would soon give us the "green light." I gave it to Brother Evangelist and he assured me she would get the letter.

Over the next eight months, Brother Evangelist put Noahh and Esther in camps together and even had them hitchhike with the same brother from city to city. They shared a tent together for several months, each knowing about the other, neither being allowed to talk to the other. One morning, while Noahh was fixing breakfast, Esther innocently asked her if she could borrow a pattern for a shirt. Noahh, forgetting that the letter I wrote her was among the patterns, told her to help herself. Esther found the note and went crazy with anger, wondering why she hadn't been informed of my decision and why the Elder kept coming to her and encouraging her about the chances of marrying me. When she spoke to Brother Evangelist on the phone he said he knew nothing about me and Noahh or the letter, nor had he orchestrated events so that I would choose Noahh over Esther.

Back in Portland, Brother Evangelist held one last gathering and left Brother Chris in charge of the camp. Brother Kraig was my charge since I had recruited him, and I spent a lot of my time discipling him in the Church's doctrine. Several brothers were coming and going frequently during those days including Brother Amos, a kind, dedicated brother from Ohio who had a bachelor's degree in psychology. A tall, handsome young man in his late twenties, he was a favorite of all. He was able to avoid legalism and walk in a non-judgmental and kind spirit toward all people. He was not motivated by pride to witness; he truly loved his fellow man and cared about their eternities.

Brother Amos had met a young Jewish believer several months earlier and had a wonderful time witnessing to him. Robert and his wife Gloria lived about 2500 miles away in the small town of Bandon, Oregon. He came and went several times, each time returning feeling refreshed and certain that Robert and Gloria would soon join us in Portland. We were happy the Lord was adding another family to the church and that our labors in the recent harvest were finally bearing some fruit.

One morning Brother Amos left early to go to Bandon and never arrived. Several days passed and we began to speculate about his disappearance. Maybe he got offended and left the Church? No, he wasn't that way. Maybe he got arrested for hitchhiking and was in jail somewhere? That was doubtful because he wouldn't have been kept that long. Maybe the deprogrammers picked him up and he was in some hotel room battling for his soul? That seemed unlikely because he had just gotten back from visiting his mother and she had no evil intentions against him at all. She had even bought the Church a crock pot.

One morning a letter appeared on our doorstep and Brother Chris whisked it away to a private spot and read it. He was ashen faced but wouldn't let on what the letter was about. That day he rifled through phone books, being careful not to let anyone see what categories he was looking at, writing down phone numbers, and checking for more. That night at the phone call he related his information to Brother Evangelist who told him to follow through with what he was doing.

The next day Chris held a solemn gathering in which he explained that he had received a letter from one of the parents explaining that Brother Amos had been hit by a car and was in a coma in a resting home in Beaverton, Oregon. As Brother Amos was walking down the dark and misty on-ramp to Interstate 5 at 6:00 in the morning, a woman driving a midsize car broadsided him and drove him 150 feet through the air where he landed on his head on the concrete. The impact was so sudden it knocked the shoe off his left foot. He would have died had an onlooker not seen the accident and called the paramedics immediately. He was rushed to a hospital several blocks away and heroic efforts spared his life. But then he was only in a vegetative state.

We were all shocked by the news and several of the sisters and brothers began crying. We all loved Brother Amos, and it was inconceivable that such a thing had happened to him. Why would God allow this to happen to him? He was such a loving, dedicated, sincere brother! He didn't deserve this.

Chris went through the phone books calling hospitals and finally tracked Brother Amos down to a nursing home in Beaverton, a suburb of Portland. With Brother Evangelist's permission, Brother Chris and I went out to see him a couple days later.

We could hardly recognize him. Laid up in bed with tubes and needles stuck in him, his face gaunt and shallow, he was a mess. We sat with him and his mother and read Bible verses to him and tried to answer his mother's questions about the group. She was bitter about the accident and about Chris's involvement in the Church, but nevertheless treated us very kindly.

After several weeks, Brother Evangelist came to town but was afraid to go see Brother Amos in the nursing home. I knew there was no danger and that a visit from Brother Evangelist might help Brother Amos' recovery, but Brother Evangelist was afraid of persecution. I approached him one night with a question that had been troubling me. Since God only did things like this to people to punish their sins, what were Brother Amos' sins that God had to punish him like that? I said it would help me understand so that I would know what behaviors to avoid lest the same thing happen to me. He seemed enlightened by my question and said he would get back to me on that.

A couple of days later, Brother Chris, who had left Portland for another city, sent a letter to Brother Evangelist which he had another brother read in the gathering. Brother Evangelist said these were not his words, but that another brother was reporting to him.

Dear Brother Evangelist,

I know that we were all saddened by what recently happened to Amos and we are all wondering why it happened to him. In the fear of God I want to share some things about him that most brothers and sisters don't know. Let me first say that if God were to punish me for my sins, I should probably be hit by a train for the wickedness in my life. I don't want to write this to be self righteous, but to warn others to beware of sin.

I went through Amos' backpack after we found out about the accident. In it I found a perversion of the Bible we read (a different version) with notes in it. Obviously he was reading it and comparing it to the King James Version. I then looked to where he had made notes in the King James Version, and he had written some question marks like he doubted the quality of the translation. I also found several tracts written by Keith Green for the Last Days Ministry. He had been reading and carrying literature from outside the Church. He obviously wasn't lifting up the standard with regard to not bringing false Christian literature into the camp.

Also, I have found Amos a difficult brother to work with. He would argue about little things that were not important. For example, when he came back from checking stores and had some fresh whole wheat bread, he didn't understand why we wouldn't use it immediately when we had other bread that needed to be used first. It's that old snare the god of the belly; he was really snared by food.

These things show that Amos was really losing his understanding. Again, if I were judged according to my sins, God should hit me with a train. I don't write these things to appear righteous, but to help warn the flock.

We listened in shocked disbelief as the charges were read. Brother Evangelist again took no responsibility for the charges, but seemed in agreement with them. It was obvious that some of the sisters and brothers were offended by the letter, but it nevertheless had its intended impact.

169

We all needed to fear the Lord more and lift up the standard lest the same or worse thing happen to us. As Jesus said to the crippled man at the Pool of Siloam in John 5:14, "Sin no more, lest a worse thing come upon you."

After several weeks Amos came out of his coma and was moved to Ohio where he is still in rehabilitation. He is wheelchair-bound and has a speech impediment to this day, but has not returned to the Church.

27

Solitary Confinement

After these happenings, Brother Evangelist took me aside and explained that I would be going out from the Church with Brother Kraig and wouldn't have much fellowship for awhile. "But, I want to assure you, brother," he said, "that you are not the only ones going out like this. Brother Chris and another brother have been witnessing in a city for awhile together; even Sergeant Louis was by himself for a while, and Brother Shor is with just a couple of brothers, so press on and trust the Lord to keep you in these times. These are times when he tries your love for the truth and sees how faithful you can be when there aren't other brothers and sisters around watching."

I didn't really like what I heard, although I felt he honored me by giving me more responsibility. I had no idea I would spend the majority of the next two years in camps alone with Kraig, desperately starved for fellowship.

We all need to communicate and enjoy the company of other people. Cult members are no different. When I joined the group in 1976, I was surrounded by fellowship. The smallest camps had at least twelve people in them. As the years passed and Brother Evangelist became more paranoid, the camps shrunk to six, then four, and finally two. Living such a radical life against the current of the world required a lot of support and community. By scattering the Church the way he did, individual members lost strength.

When he wanted to wear out a member he didn't trust, he would send that person to a camp with the minimum amount of fellowship possible, hoping that person would grow weary and leave the Church.

I found myself in San Antonio, Texas, later that year after being in several cities alone with Kraig. Through the kindness of a realtor, we obtained permission to stay in a house on the outskirts of the city. Months crept by as I gazed out the window daily yearning to see someone familiar walk up the driveway. Once Brother Evangelist called to tell me that Sister Noahh was no longer interested in marrying me. He was deliberately vague when I asked him why she changed her mind, appearing not to remember the details. Depression set in and I moped through the day wondering if Brother Evangelist knew how desperately lonely I was, not to say that Kraig wasn't good company. He listened politely as I shared things with him, thanked me, made a comment, and went back to reading the Bible. The isolation didn't seem to affect him as much as it did me.

After several months a brother arrived and I ran out and hugged him, lifting him off the ground. He couldn't understand why I was so affectionate until I explained how long it had been since we had seen any other brothers. He understood well. He had been marooned the entire winter with one other brother in Waite, Maine, hoping to see others. When the brethren finally arrived, he told Brother Evangelist he never wanted to be left alone for such a long time again.

A few days later Brother Evangelist and several sisters arrived, including Sister Noahh, whom I hadn't seen for many months. When I saw Noahh, I thought it would be a good opportunity for me to find out why she changed her mind. The look on Brother Evangelist's face told me that asking if I could speak to her wasn't a good idea. He very reluctantly agreed to my request, but ordered me to keep it short and impersonal. I was angered by the limitations he exerted on me, but powerless to go against them. If I rebelled at any point, I knew he would never permit me to get married.

Noahh stepped outside in the backyard and seemed happy to see me. I asked her why she changed her mind.

"Esther has been really going through some difficult trials about marriage and I want you to be sure that it's not God's will for you and her to marry before I come into the picture. I really love her and don't want to see her suffer on my account."

"Does that mean you would still consider marrying me if I'm convinced it's not God's will for me and Esther to marry?"

"Lord willing, I would. I just don't want to be the cause of Esther getting offended and leaving."

"Well, let me assure you I want you for my wife and not her, and you're not responsible for what has happened. I think it is a real loving thing that you just did, and it convinces me you are the better choice."

This made her very happy, and we parted with an understanding that we would wait on the Lord for his timing in marriage. When I told Brother Evangelist about this he didn't seem too happy.

"Coincidentally," Kraig and I were then sent to look for housing in Pittsburgh, Pennsylvania. Brother Evangelist didn't want me and Noahh to be in the same house together for too long. We spent almost three months in Pittsburgh in a house in the Hill District, not far from the university district, about a mile from downtown. After three months there, we were sent to Kansas City, Missouri, to meet the brothers in a house. This ended two years of long isolation from the group, and I felt that perhaps I had found favor again in Brother Evangelist's eyes.

From Dean's List to Dumpsters: Why I Left Harvard to Join a Cult

When we arrived together in Kansas City, we met Brother Larry at the door. The house was a warehouse that the brothers had laboriously renovated and converted into living quarters. The usual amenities were there: the fifty gallon steel drum converted into a wood stove, the curtains and ground cloths strung around to set up separate living quarters for families and sisters and brothers; the five gallon golden bakery can heating water on the stove, a room set aside for prayer with the foams and mats on the floor; the kitchen area where the food and "eating gear" were stashed and the sisters prepared the evening meal; the single seatless toilet with the plastic bucket to flush it; laundry hanging on nylon cords drying in the heat of the wood stove; and brothers lounging on mattresses reading the Bible and meditating.

Convinced that my isolation was due to my lack of effort in prayer and Bible study, I determined that I would work as hard as I could to be holy and would then be allowed by God to see the brothers and sisters. I confessed to Brother Chris how "proudly" I had been walking and told him I was really "pressing in" to be a better brother. He didn't seem too impressed, but after I prayed for several hours a day for about a week, he changed his mind. I wrestled hard to obey the things I had been taught: read the Bible constantly, pray without ceasing, be sober, limit my words, keep my mind on spiritual things, and don't read newspapers. I desperately wanted to be right with God.

One morning I went out to witness downtown. It was a quiet morning. Few people were out that bitter cold morning, so I decided to stop in a public building to warm up and read the Bible. On the television screen in the lobby was a breaking news story.

I struggled hard not to look at it, but I finally glimpsed at the trail of smoke disappearing into an explosion several miles in the air. Several onlookers seemed stunned as they listened to the reporter describe the explosion of the space shuttle Challenger. The next day I found some newspaper boxes and read the news. "Another judgment of God against those who exalt themselves against Him," I thought.

It seemed that God heard my prayers for more fellowship because the next day Brother Evangelist called and sent me on the road to El Paso, Texas, where I was to meet up with Brother Shalom and his family. Across the border in Juarez, Mexico, the brothers had a house and a wonderful ministry going. I had heard about the Mexican ministry and had longed to go there. Brother Shor was praying for sick people and they were getting healed. The brothers were witnessing on the buses and being royally treated by the hospitable Mexican faithful. This began one of the most interesting and fulfilling times I spent in the Church.

28

Ministry In Mexico

Brother Shor told me of the wonderful things God did through the brothers' ministry in Mexico. A young boy with a bloated stomach, probably caused by a parasitic infection, came to the brothers and asked for prayer. After several days the boy was completely cured. Other brothers were getting on buses, with the bus drivers' permission, to preach. The buses, mostly old refurbished American school buses, had broken windows and dust covered seats. When accelerating they would billow out noxious fumes and ozone destroying hydrocarbons. Passengers smoked cigarettes and no one complained. If the bus needed gas, it would stop at the local Pemex and fill up with government regulated gasoline while the passengers waited, never examining a bus schedule to see if the stop would keep them from making connections. Women with babies strapped to them, carrying quart containers of Leche Zaragoza, patiently accept the dust and fumes and cigarette smoke. It was all part of life in Mexico.

When the brothers boarded, they would ask the driver for permission to speak. The driver, usually a good Catholic, would cheerfully give permission and turn off his Mariachi music to allow the passengers to hear. Being a religious people, the older Mexicans would listen patiently and mumble, "Amen, Amen," at the brothers' preaching and thank them for the word of God. This frustrated the brothers a good deal because they felt the greater part of their message was not being understood, that God wanted them to sell their possessions and live by faith. When the brothers were done, they would hop off the bus and get on another one to continue preaching.

We stayed for awhile in El Paso and walked across the bridge over the Rio Grande daily to witness in Juarez. Some days we would stand in the main plaza downtown and preach to a crowd; other days near the bridge, waiting for someone to witness to. The brothers on the Mexico side were staying in a house about a half mile from downtown Juarez. We would move from El Paso over there as soon as it worked out.

The brothers had been proselytizing in Mexico for about two years and already a small church had formed. Brother Shor had initiated the work there and was very successful in adapting our lifestyle to the Mexican culture. Many of them were poorer than we were, so telling them to "forsake all" didn't make much sense. Already he had translated many of our songs into Spanish and taught them to the Mexican converts. He also translated the Bible study notebook we carried, including the studies named Forsaking Flesh Relations, The Woman's Place, and Flee Babylon.

The Mexican people were not as wasteful as Americans, so the brothers had to find another way to get food. Instead of inspecting their supermarket dumpsters, they would approach the open air produce markets and say, "Excuse me, sir; I am part of a traveling Christian ministry that travels from city to city preaching the Gospel and living by faith. Would you happen to have any things that are going bad that you don't want?"

Inevitably, they would give us the finest things they had on their shelves: bananas, avocados, tortillas, grapes, carrots, squash, corn, chili peppers, mangos, papayas…whatever. We didn't realize we were playing on the people's sympathies and just begging for food. Nevertheless, we always thanked them and God for providing.

After being in Mexico for several days, Brother Shor told me we were moving out to a ranch about five miles outside of Juarez. One of the local churches offered to let us stay there because we were laboring in the Gospel and they wished to support us. We rode the bus to the RCA plant and transferred to another bus that dropped us off at El Satelite, a company that sold natural gas. We walked the remaining mile on a dust road past fierce dogs, small houses with chickens in the road, speed ditches dug into the road to slow down traffic, a donkey, and a field of horses and sheep.

The one story concrete ranch house set on seventy-five acres seemed the perfect place of rest. The nearest neighbor was about 100 yards away, a middle-aged Catholic woman who regarded the brothers as if they were the original apostles. Each morning at about 7:00 am, she would stand on her side of the fence and beckon the brothers over to her, where she would hand us our breakfast tortillas and pozole, a vegetable stew of some sort. She expected no thanks and did it cheerfully.

One day it rained fiercely and the woman came to our door carrying a five gallon bucket of sand she had dug from her yard. She began to put it around our doorway to keep the water from seeping into our house. We admired her love and were glad she was our neighbor.

The stay in Juarez was fairly uneventful until a vehicle arrived from the Apostolic Church with some members who told us we had to vacate the building the next day. That put us on the spot until the neighbor heard about what was happening. She and her husband and two children moved into one bedroom and they gave us the other half of the house. We reluctantly moved in and spent about two weeks with her until we got our marching orders from Brother Evangelist to leave Juarez.

I was excited when the news came that several of us were going to hitchhike into the interior. I had flirted with the border towns long enough; it was finally time to go into the deep parts of

Mexico and witness. Brother Kraig and I were to travel with Brother Guillermo while Brother Abel was going to travel with his wife and two children. The next day we went to the train station and found a south bound freight headed to Chihuahua. I went into the train station to use the bathroom, and as I returned to the freight train we were stopped and interrogated by the train employees.

"Why are you headed toward that train?" they asked. "It doesn't carry passengers."

"We are headed toward Mexico City."

"But you gringos can afford to take the passenger train.

Why are you doing it the hard way and taking a freight?" "Because we are Christians and we're living by faith. We don't have enough money to take the passenger train." "Orale, pues," they smiled. "Go ahead."

We laughed as we realized how strange this might seem to them. Gringos always had money and preferred the finest accommodations when they traveled. Not even most Mexicans would stoop so low that they would take the freight train! We found an empty flatbed which usually carried trailers and made ourselves cozy for the trip.

On Good Friday in 1983 we set out for Chihuahua. We traveled the 250 kilometers in a little over a day. We slowed down in one small village and observed a passion play by a group of local folk reenacting the crucifixion of Christ next to the railroad tracks. It seemed so pagan to us as we loftily condemned their superstitious practices. Perhaps one of the teenagers read my mind and therefore incited his friends to pick up stones and hurl them at us as we drove by at ten miles per hour.

That night we arrived in the Chihuahua train station where Guillermo told us to get off and follow him. He took us into the station where we saw dozens of people sprawled out on the floor, waiting for the next day's trains. He told us it would be okay to sleep there since it was Mexico and not the United States. A man came over and inquired who we were and when his curiosity was satisfied left us with these words: "Just sleep with one eye open."

We slept on the marble floor until I was startled out of my sleep to see a man leaning over to help himself to my backpack. When I awoke he sauntered off guiltily, pretending he was leaning over to pick up a garbanzo bean from the floor.

We inquired and found a bus that took us to the outskirts of Chihuahua. Eventually a truck driver stopped for us and took us down the one lane highway, stopping occasionally to place flowers at the roadside mini shrines to the Virgin of Guadalupe. The truck drivers were pious men who didn't let their faith interfere with their behavior. They would circumflex at every church and drink Corona beer with the best of them. There were no contradictions there. A good Catholic could live life as he pleased until Sunday when the Mass wiped clean the previous week's plate of mischief.

From Dean's List to Dumpsters: Why I Left Harvard to Join a Cult

We moved through the towns and villages toward Mexico City where we finally arrived after five days. The folks were hospitable, offering us lemonade as we passed by their stands, peering at us with a curiosity devoid of hostility. We were a gazing stock: gringos in long robes, sporting untrimmed beards, lugging eighty five pound backpacks, communicating in the basest of Spanish. Several times people invited us into their homes where we bathed with a bowl from a fifty gallon barrel of rainwater.

We stopped overnight in Guadalajara and found a building in progress to sleep in. After setting up our gear, about ten police rushed in with flashlights and questions demanding who we were.

Brother Guillermo used our stock line to keep out of trouble with the police, knowing that they had respect for men of the cloth. "Somos hermanos," he explained, "We're holy brothers and followers of El Señor. We travel to spread the Gospel." The police knew they were treading on dangerous ground if they messed with us, so they stepped back and began to apologize for coming in. We forgave them and offered them some tea bags which they quickly accepted. They let us sleep there and told the next watch to make sure no one bothered us. It was a little galling of us to play this charade, but it kept us out of Mexican jails.

We met Brother Abel in the Zócalo in downtown Mexico City, the plaza which was the center of the Mexican government. Brother Shor met us and took us on a long bus ride to the university district where the brothers were being housed by a prominent young medical doctor and his wife. Being Christian, they accepted the brethren as missionaries and invited them to share the apartment building they owned. Brother Shor was careful not to accentuate the differences of doctrine so that we could continue to remain there as long as possible. I felt uncomfortable, hoping we could avoid the issue and convince them we thought they were Christians, without somehow compromising our own testimony. To accept them into fellowship was to condone their lifestyle and compromise our strict "be ye therefore separate" doctrine. If they ever felt we were judgmental of them, they never showed it.

We walked out daily to take the trains and witness wherever we went. The subway in Mexico City was only one peso, the equivalent of about a half cent in 1984 dollars. We would preach to the crowd, get off, and get on the next train headed the other direction where we could enlighten them, too.

The walk to the train station often took us through the poorest areas of Mexico City where we saw emaciated pigs out for morning strolls, chickens by the dozen, fighting roosters, and mangy dogs. Women with buckets of laundry perched out on their heads would stroll by while older men pushed their insulated ice cream carts and sold popsicles to the children. We noted a few suspicious and hostile glances, but overall were treated warmly by the people. Often groups of children would run up desiring pesetas, or handouts. I regretted that I was living hand to mouth and could not give anything other than my doctrine to the children.

After several weeks in Mexico City, we headed south to Puebla, a large town with a metropolitan flavor. A year earlier I had met a young man in Chicago named Eduardo. He had arrived there undocumented from Puebla several months before. He appreciated the help I gave him (mainly food, and a place to stay) and had told us to look up his family if we were in Puebla. We did just that.

The family lived in San Francisco de Totimehuacán, a suburb about twenty five minutes from downtown. We took a bus and began to inquire as to where the house was. The neighbors denied knowing the Chetl (Eduardo's family), but finally an older man in a field, when he heard Eduardo's name, admitted that he was Eduardo's grandfather. When we explained we were missionaries and that we had seen Eduardo several months before and what we had done for him, they opened up their house and feasted us royally. Kraig and I both came down with Montezuma's Revenge, that common blend of dysentery and diarrhea that immobilizes many Americans who drink the water.

After a couple of weeks there, we had overstayed our welcome. As usual, we had taken advantage of others' kindness without realizing what a burden we were placing on them. An ashen-faced Guillermo came to me and told us the family wanted us to pitch in with our own support. I was so used to other people sacrificing for me that I couldn't feel their sacrifice. We also felt that since God was using them to meet our needs, we were really only using God's material goods, and therefore were not a burden to them.

Kraig was almost healed of his dysentery when we put him on the bus back to Mexico City. Guillermo and I decided to hitchhike and meet Kraig at the main bus station near the airport. Guillermo and I later found Kraig's long thin frame stretched out across his backpack in the bus station, staring groggily at the ceiling. He was weak and emaciated from two weeks of vomiting and diarrhea, but cheerful to see us.

We walked out of the station and took a bus to a large market area about a mile from the Zócalo. Guillermo went looking for food while we waited outside the market. Kraig drew a lot of attention since he was again lying across his backpack and staring at the Pleiades. Very kind people approached us, concerned about Kraig. They offered us medicine or told us where the farmacia was. Others suggested home remedies like drinking a lot of lemon juice or eating a jalapeño pepper. We thanked them for their kindness, but explained that we didn't use medicine because we were Christians. Several of the more spiritual people assured us that God gave medicine to mankind to help him heal, but we were too spiritually enlightened to fall for that one. I took advantage of the situation to ask people if they knew where we could stay. Several people pointed to a church down the road that put people up for the night, where we ended up sleeping when the padre got back at 8:30 that night.

We left Mexico City a couple of days later and hitched north toward Matamoros. We got rides primarily from truck drivers, and one ride almost ended our sojourn through this "veil of tears." A man with a flatbed stopped for us, but explained that we would have to ride in the bed. Weary of waiting, we agreed. We piled our backpacks against the front wall of the flatbed and grabbed hold where we could, and the terror began.

Ten minutes into the ride we knew we had made a mistake. The trucker was a maniac, passing every vehicle in his way, crossing the double yellow lines, swerving wildly back and forth, laughing when he hit a bump at sixty miles per hour as we held on for dear life. He was like a bucking bronco trying to discharge his three riders.

Forty-five minutes into the ride, my backpack started to shimmy backwards in the truck, dangerously close to the edge. Everything I had was in it. Kraig was in the middle, head down, praying fiercely. Nothing would get his attention to let us off. Finally, when we could take it no longer, I crawled out and grabbed a tent pole out of my backpack and began to slam it on the roof of the cab. The driver looked into his mirror with a huge grin and pulled over. We jumped out, furious at him, and wouldn't look him in the eye. Laughing, he screeched off, enjoying his joke immensely. Kraig broke into tears and kept his head down and sobbed uncontrollably for an hour. A few blocks away we found an empty house and bedded down, sleeping fitfully because of the mosquitoes.

Three days later, we arrived in Matamoros, where I saw something about Brother Evangelist that shook me to my foundation.

III
Section Three: Days of Restoration

29

Becoming Offended

We had hoped to keep our three-month tourist visas when we reentered the United States, but the Mexican o cials saw us as we walked past their post toward the American side. They demanded our visas, which we relinquished, and questioned us about our activities in Mexico. After a few questions they let us go and we continue toward Brownsville, Texas. As soon as we entered American airspace, an o cial from the DEA stopped us and searched our packs. We hadn't even gone through customs when he stopped us. We fit the drug smuggler profile: young single males in their late twenties, bearded, carrying backpacks, hippie-looking. We told him we were Christians, and he believed us but searched us anyway.

We passed through customs with little difficulty, onto the streets of Brownsville, Texas and back into America. We had mixed feelings about being back, but we knew we would have better care and could eat American food again.

We found a place to camp in a citrus orchard along the Rio Grande. Just across the river, about thirty yards away, we could see houses and the back of an auto mechanic's shop. We found a spot deep into the orchard, surrounded by tall grass, where we could have privacy. At night we heard the continual Mariachi festivals across the river until 10 pm, and then the glittering stars of the crisp evening sky took over as we fell asleep.

In the morning Kraig and I walked a long dirt path into town, past the orchard on our right, through a city park, and to the library. I was rewriting my notebook since Brother Evangelist instituted a new standard about notebooks. A few months earlier he had gathered a few of us together to let us know his latest command.

"Brothers," he said, looking down. "This may seem like a strange request, but I'm asking all brothers and sisters to destroy any notes about things I have said. If you have any studies written down with things I have said, or gatherings, please get rid of those things."

"Do we have to get rid of the Scriptures, too?" I asked. "Just the notes," he replied.

"Does that include notes of things that other brothers taught?"

"No, brother."

We were amazed at the request, and tried to understand why he said those things.

"Perhaps he's just humble and doesn't want us to glorify his words," one brother suggested.

"Perhaps. You know how Moonies have the Bible and Moon's book, The Divine Principles. He probably doesn't want to be glorified of man."

I accepted those explanations halfheartedly, searching for a better reason. Brother Evangelist gave us no explanation. It was difficult to accept this new order since I had spent days copying notes into my notebook, but it would be dangerous to question. So I went to the library to redo my notebook.

Another task I had to accomplish was to reestablish contact with the group. Brother Abel had lost communication with the group while in Mexico, and we were sent to the Matamoros-Brownsville area to get in contact with Brother Evangelist. I knew of two possible ways to do it: first, I could write to the house in Kansas City where I had been prior to traveling in Mexico; and second, I could write to the address in Pittsburgh near downtown where I had found the house with Kraig a couple of years earlier. I decided to write to both of them and give them the phone numbers of two pay phones that were side-by-side near the library.

In my letter to the brothers in Kansas City, I asked them to call me on a Sunday at 9:30 am. If Brother Evangelist was there, and he was calling, he was to let the phone ring until I answered it. If he wasn't there, they were to call me and let it ring one time and then hang up. This would assure me that they had received my letter and that would let Brother Evangelist know where we were and how to contact us.

In my letter to Pittsburgh, I asked them to call me at 9:35 am with the same instructions. That way I would hear from somebody and would know we could be contacted if necessary to move to another city.

At 9:30 am, the phone rang on time. Just once. And then silence.

At 9:35 am, the phone rang again, this time several times, and I answered it. On the other end was the cheerful voice of Brother Evangelist. My heart leapt for joy to hear his voice. "Good to hear your voice, brother," I replied.

"It's a blessing to hear from you, brother. Are you and Kraig doing okay?"

"Lord willing, we're doing fine. We're camped in an orchard along the river. It's a nice spot."

"Praise Elohim. I got your letter. I just wanted you to know that the brothers are no longer in Kansas City. They have forsaken that house there."

I was puzzled. How could that be? Didn't the phone just ring from those brothers?

"Okay," I replied, letting the joy of hearing from him overshadow my reason.

"Just lift up the standard while you're there. Sometimes God tries us in the little things to see how faithful we're going to be."

"Amen," I replied.

He then spent several minutes sharing some new doctrines with me that he had taught the Church, being very personable and warm. I left the phone call on cloud eight and three fourths, weighted down slightly by what had to be a lie.

I found Kraig and told him about the call and what a blessing the brother was. He rejoiced with me, but inwardly I struggled to reconcile Brother Evangelist's comment that the brothers were not in Kansas City with the fact that they had called me.

The months of isolation were doing something to me. I began to secretly wish, unknown to myself, that I could find a way out of the group. It was not that I didn't love Jesus, or that I wanted to go back to the world and enjoy ice cream and X-rated movies, or that I couldn't endure the physical elements of the life of poverty. That wasn't the problem. I began to lose my joy for life as my deepest personal needs were not being met.

I wanted intimacy with a spouse. I wanted to have friends around with whom I could grow and share my faith. I desperately needed more than one brother around with whom to fellowship. I needed the freedom to speak to a sister if she was interested in marrying me. Gradually I grew disillusioned with the group and with the way I felt they manipulated me.

During this time I got a call from Brother Evangelist. Brother Refesh (Hebrew for "mud" since he didn't feel he was worth anything), had told a brother what city he had hitchhiked from, a mortal sin. Brother Evangelist told me of Refesh's error and asked me to tell him that if he wanted fellowship, he should be quiet about where he was traveling from. This confirmed my suspicion that Brother Evangelist wasn't just dividing us up to witness; he used isolation as a way to punish people.

He also told me that when brothers go around asking brothers what camps they were in, "it creates distrust in the mind of the older brother." He was blaming others for his paranoia.

I found out later what prompted that remark. Brother Evangelist had told Brother Barnabas that there were no camps in the Northeast one winter. In conversation with another brother later, he was told there was a group in Maine that entire winter. Suspecting Brother Evangelist had lied to him, he nonchalantly asked another brother (without giving his reason so as not to "sow discord") where he had spent the winter the year before. This confirmed the lie Brother Evangelist had told. An older brother got wind of Barnabas's questions and "reported" to the Elder what brother Barnabas was doing.

My needs were not being met, and I suspected we were heading down a wrong path. I felt that marriage was a personal issue and that the standard in the Scriptures was that you married unless you were specifically called to celibacy. We taught that you were to be single unless specifically called to marriage.

I knew Brother Evangelist deliberately worded things in a deceitful way to protect himself and others. He especially used this to conceal the locations of camps we had previously visited. Many of us had been to Chicago one summer and knew of the camp there. But later in New York he told us that the brothers were no longer in the camp in Chicago. Then he sent me to Chicago a couple of days later.

"The brothers are still in Chicago," he clarified to me privately, "but not in the same house. They moved down the street. They really have forsaken the camp in Chicago." As long as he was technically telling the truth, and as long as distorting the truth was useful in hiding information from others to protect the flock, he felt he was not sinning.

Kraig and I spent several weeks in Brownsville until the call finally came, sending us to New Orleans. There I met a young man named Mike who was traveling around trying to be the best servant of God he could. A couple of days later he joined the Church. He would be my last disciple and the first one I would convince to leave the Church.

30

Blowing In The Wind

It was a beautiful August day when I set out from New Orleans to Missoula, Montana. Mike was my new charge, a young, zealous Christian whom I wanted to mold into the image of the group. I still strongly believed the doctrines and loved the lifestyle of the church and wanted to faithfully teach and disciple him.

We arrived in Missoula several days later and found the camp perched on a hill overlooking the river. Long, wide, and clean, Clark's Fork swept through the steep hills alongside the Burlington Northern railroad tracks, parallel to the freeway. As I ascended the hill toward camp, I couldn't imagine how the brothers had found a level place to camp. I envisioned the brothers dug into the slopes, the tents buttressed with mounds of dirt to keep them from sliding down onto the railroad tracks next to the river. To my surprise, the hill did eventually plateau and all the survival strategies I had been imagining were not necessary. There were brothers and sisters here, and they were engaged in putting up some ground cloths for protection from the elements.

Brother Jonathan greeted me with a big hug and humbly asked me my opinion about setting up the cover. As the "older brother" arrived from the road, things suddenly had to be done my way. Their efforts looked fine to me so I let them continue as they were. Later Brother Jonathan remarked to me how appreciative he was that I didn't come right into camp and take over like some brothers did.

Soon after I saw Brother Jonathan, Brother Yishiah approached me sober and disturbed. He was going through a trial and wanted my counsel. Although I had been with the church for over ten years, I still felt too honored and a bit overeager to give advice when asked. I had spent so many years denying there was anything good about me that I felt uncomfortable and afraid that I was out of my place to offer counsel. That was Brother Evangelist's place, and any counsel I offered had to be something that had been said by an older brother before and could not safely be counsel emanating from my own wisdom.

I agreed to speak with him later in the day, after I had an opportunity to rest up some from the wearying travel and had gotten a good meal in my stomach. I laid out my bag in the refreshing summer breeze, and closed my eyes for a nap. After an hour I awoke and began preparing the teaching for the evening gathering.

That night I preached on the need to be sold out for God and to give Him our absolute best. I faithfully exhorted about the need to bridle our tongues and to make sure our speech was edifying. Besides some procedural announcements (like what direction the sisters and brothers were to go to use the restroom), and some songs, that was the gathering. Soon afterward Brother Yishiah came to me with his trial.

"Brother Ariel, I've been going through some things that I need to talk with you about. It's been a real heavy trial, and it deals with the direction we as a church are going."

I froze. I feared the wrath of God would fall on me if I spoke evil of the Church. We had heard how Miriam had become a leper for talking against Moses. No one was exempt. To speak out against the Church was to talk against Brother Evangelist and persecute the anointed of God. Yet, although I felt I was treading where angels dare not tread, something pushed me onwards, part of me that wanted to believe something was wrong with the Church.

"Is this something against the Elder?" I queried. "We need to be careful that we're not speaking evil of things we don't understand." I warned Yishiah with some conviction, subconsciously taking on the role of Brother Evangelist, perhaps even imitating some of his gestures and vocal characteristics. But I was in a dilemma. If I cut the conversation off then, I would lose the opportunity to give my opinion and to counsel; but if I entertained rebellious words from a younger brother, I would be an unfaithful watchman by allowing my brother to stumble into sin.

"No," he replied. "But some things have happened recently that have forced me to question some things in the Church."

"Like what?" I asked, certain that whatever doubt he had I could straighten out.

"Brother David, Brother Larry, Brother Stan, and I went down to a city in northern California recently to witness to some people Brother Stan had met on the road. They had a lot of truth and we went down to tell them they had to forsake all to be Christians. We spent the weekend with them, hoping to correct them and bring them deeper into truth, but they said some things about us that have created a lot of doubt in my mind."

I began to think I had made a poor decision to talk to Brother Yishiah, but I was too curious to stop him. Besides, I enjoyed the challenge of facing convincing deceit and then exposing it with a few clever Scriptures. I sensed the challenge ahead. I also trembled as I felt I might be led onto the enemy's soil if I continued.

I forged onward. "What kind of things?" I asked.

"Do you really agree it is a sin to shake hands with people?" he began. I was stuck. For years brothers had shown by example and strongly suggested it was a better testimony not to shake someone's hand whom you had witnessed to unless they forsook all and joined the Church. I never felt comfortable with that conviction and always felt guilty whenever I shook someone's hand in appreciation for a long ride, or a monetary offering, or a meal on the road. I remember hating myself regardless of what choice I made.

"Brothers have said it wasn't a doctrine of the Church, just something to consider." My reply didn't even convince me. Once a behavior was suggested as a standard, brothers and sisters lapped it up until it gradually became accepted or fell by the wayside and became "a matter of conscience."

"I think it is rude to have someone do something for you and then refuse to shake their hand. Most people do not walk away and say, 'What a great testimony!' They get needlessly offended and close their hearts to whatever you have to say to them about the Lord."

I reluctantly had to agree. Finally someone had the courage to say it.

Emboldened, I added, "The testimony you leave is that you are a rude and unthankful person who took advantage of their hospitality. I've felt that way for a long time, but I was afraid to say anything, l didn't want to be guilty of 'speaking evil of things that I understand not.'"

I sensed we were just beginning to scale the iceberg of denial. There was more to confront.

"What happened in California?" I asked.

"The folks in the California church pointed out a flaw in our doctrine of divorce and remarriage."

"They probably didn't want to face up to the fact that divorce and remarriage are prohibited. They probably have some members of their church living in adultery," I ventured. Yishiah looked at me sternly, and I knew from this look that I shouldn't have been so quick to assume the worst.

Obviously he had been beaten by their deceit and I would have to help him through this trial.

"What have you always heard and understood our doctrine in the area of divorce and remarriage to be?" he asked.

"Well, the studies I have had teach that the only grounds for divorce is fornication. If a man marries a woman and discovers she is not a virgin, he can divorce her." That was what I have always been taught.

"And what is fornication?" he continued.

"It's sex between two unmarried people," I replied. "If one of the people engaged in the act is married, then it is adultery."

"That's where we have been wrong. Fornication is sex between two people not married to each other. It can include what you described, but it also includes adultery and incest."

I proceeded to argue with him for a while, but didn't get anywhere. He continued: "The word 'fornication' comes from a Latin word 'fornix,' meaning an arch. The prostitutes used to meet in areas which had 'fornices' in them. Eventually the word came to mean any kind of sexual impurity."

"How do you know this?" I asked. Brothers, since I could remember, did not consult dictionaries. We felt the Holy Spirit alone was sufficient to illuminate the Scriptures and through context give the proper definition of every word. To reference a dictionary was to open ourselves to the leaven of the Pharisees, which is deceit. Dictionaries were deliberately sabotaged by Satan to deceive us about the real meanings of the Scriptures. The clinching example was the way the dictionary defines love and how the Bible did. Although we never saw the dictionary's definition of 'love' we just knew it couldn't be, "Love is the keeping of God's commandments."

"I looked it up in several Greek and English dictionaries.

They all said the same things."

"Then the dictionaries are…" I began, before I realized the arrogance of what I was saying. The whole world is wrong, but the brothers alone know the proper meanings of words? How then was the Bible translated? Didn't King James' scholars have to consult dictionaries to learn the original languages in the first place? Didn't God use words common to all men so He could communicate to us in words we would understand? If we could understand them, couldn't we collect them and put them in a dictionary? I began to realize there was some serious error among us because we were just accepting the word of the older brothers.

I decided I would go to the library and check into this myself. But in the meantime I wanted to hear what else Brother Yishiah had to say.

"Anything else?" I asked. "Oh, and be sure not to say anything about this to any of the other brothers. We don't want to bring division into the Church or sow discord."

He agreed and began to share more. "There are a lot of unhealthy fears in the church. For example, do you really think someone has to be in the Church to be saved?"

"I don't know," I confessed. "I would like to think there are others besides us, perhaps some missionaries in some foreign countries or something."

"We wouldn't be able to recognize them if there were," he said. "Suppose there is a man who gave up everything and went to Africa to convert people to the Lord. And this man lived in a hut, spent the day taking care of the sick, and reading the Bible and ministering. Would this man not be a Christian if he shaved his face? The brothers would condemn this man for 'raking his face' and would have no fellowship with him."

I saw his point. We were notorious at judging people and excluding them from being Christians. To admit there were Christians outside the group meant there was an alternative to the Church. That gave us an alternative if we no longer felt led to continue with Brother Evangelist's ministry.

These things troubled me. I was not thinking of leaving the Church, these issues began to burn inside me. I had to confront the leadership about these issues and not be silent, but it had to be done orderly lest I sow dissension and bring division into the group. I also had to do it without appearing rebellious or unthankful for the Church.

There were dangers ahead. Questioning authority or disagreement with a doctrine could get you into big trouble. The greatest danger would be if you were labeled as "getting deceived." You were looked upon as a cancer in the Body and would be quietly shunned and removed from others so that your rebellion did not spread to others and destroy the unity of the Church.

We agreed to speak more later while I went on to my tent to pray about the things I had heard. I found it hard to keep silent, but did my best not to share it with the other brothers that night. When I did the gathering that night I cautiously preached about the importance of "proving all things," and making sure that things we teach and believe are doctrinally sound. I still respected the order of the Church and didn't want to rebel in any way. I wanted to reform, not destroy.

The next day I left early for the phone next to a mini market with Brother Jonathan to get a call from Brother Evangelist. After taking care of normal business and getting instruction from him, he warned me. "Brother, I want you to know that Brother Yishiah has been having some trials recently, and I do not want you speaking to him about those trials."

"Brother," I replied, "I have already spoken to him. He came to me about some things yesterday and I've tried to help him."

"What?!" he growled. "Why didn't you tell me? Brother, you shouldn't have hidden that from me. That's not good. I don't want you talking to him anymore about these things. Brother Yishiah has a lot of trouble keeping his mouth. He babbles continually and cannot study to be quiet. He has been walking proudly recently and he is getting deceived."

"Yes sir," I replied, my head spinning from the rebuke. I didn't dare tell him I agreed with Yishiah about these things.

After agreeing to check the pay phone the following morning, we headed back. As we walked along the levee toward the camp, the tall hills peering down at us from our right, we saw a police car stopped about fifty yards away. Not feeling particularly paranoid, and starting to feel like I could use my own brain for once, I approached the cars without any guile or dishonesty. The police saw us and stopped us to question us. A homeless man was with him who had been sleeping in the same woods as we were.

"Good morning, gentlemen," they said. "We've gotten some reports about some possible foul play. A young man is missing and there is a terrible stink coming out of the levee about 100 yards away. Do you know anything about this case?"

"No sir," I said, "but I would be glad to check it out for you."

Seeing no reason to deny it, I replied, "Yes, sir. We are camped about three quarters of the way up the hill."

"Are there any others with you?

"Yes sir. We are part of a small traveling Christian ministry. We've been here for a couple of weeks. There are about ten of us on that hill."

"Okay, just be careful. This is high fire season, and you cannot have any fires. A simple mistake and these woods can go in a flash. Are there exactly ten of you here? We need to know so in case there is a fire we know how many people to look for. That way no one is left unaccounted for on the hill."

I mentally counted the brethren and figured there were ten. He thanked me for my cooperation and let us go on to camp. I felt good being honest with the authorities instead of deceiving them.

The next morning Brother Evangelist called again and asked me if I had spoken anymore with Brother Yishiah. I had been obedient and had not shared more with him. Besides, Yishiah kept his distance because he was afraid he had damaged me and didn't want to be responsible for me leaving the Church. After saying some discrediting things about Yishiah, he warned me to watch out for the fowls and not to let the police know we were there.

I explained my previous day's encounter with the police, but he hastily commented, "That's not good brother. Those men are a bunch of liars. We can't trust them. They just want to persecute the Church."

His ravings at this point sounded ridiculous as he condemned my judgment. I did not share his paranoia. I felt I had done the right thing and that I didn't feel the police had lied to me. There was a stench along the levee which turned out to be a dead animal. The homeless man had been missing his friend who turned up later the next day. None of the things were fabricated, and the police hadn't raided our camp, but just seemed genuinely concerned about our welfare.

I halfheartedly said "Amen" to his comments, but became more and more disillusioned with Brother Evangelist's superior wisdom. He sounded like a madman to me at that point. When he finished his lecture I was unconvinced and more open to the idea that it was okay to disagree with church authority. He then invited Brother Jonathan and me to come to Seattle, Washington, to see him and discuss the issues with him. Telling him I believed the things Brother Yishiah had told me, I agreed to confront him about the issues.

From Dean's List to Dumpsters: Why I Left Harvard to Join a Cult

I journeyed alone from Missoula, burdened because my whole world seemed to be crumbling. I did not want to be deceived as I began to recount in my mind the happenings of the previous month. Brother Evangelist had lied to me about brothers not being in Kansas City. He had deliberately tried to deceive me. Lying was wrong. He had preached so much about it that I knew the Bible verses by heart. Furthermore, I had done the right thing by talking to the police. Brother Evangelist wasn't there and couldn't possibly make a sound judgment. He was speaking hastily without thinking. We really were deceived about the meaning of "fornication." As I traveled, I realized even more how deceived I had been and that there were some doctrinal issues that needed to be resolved.

Three days later we arrived in Seattle, having caught a freight train from Spokane, Washington, into the outskirts of Seattle. We met a brother at the Greyhound bus station and he led us to a steep tree covered hillside under the Trinity Hospital, just east of the Kingdome. Running along the hill was an eight foot chain link fence bordered by an asphalt jogging path. To get into the woods we had to grab a branch that overhung the fence, pull ourselves over, and jump into the underbrush. The path wound steeply upward through the low willows, mesquite trees, and dense underbrush. We were careful not to leave tracks as we struggled with our packs up the primitive path, stopping occasionally to listen for joggers who might come by and see us. As usual, secrecy was a high priority.

I was apprehensive about seeing Brother Evangelist because I knew he didn't trust me. But I had to confront him about the doctrine because I couldn't continue to teach things that were not true. After a five-minute hike we broke through to a clearing where several of the brothers were camped. Brother Evangelist was one of the brothers that greeted me, though less enthusiastically than the rest.

Weary from the journey, I set up my tent and took another mid afternoon nap. As I lay there, Brother Evangelist came to me and said he would speak to me later. I could see he was royally upset with me, although I couldn't imagine what I had done wrong. Later that day he sat down on the ground cloth next to me and explained. "You say you disagree with some doctrine or something?" he began.

"Yes sir. I think we as a church are in error concerning some things," I replied.

He looked genuinely hurt when I said this, and his voice sounded like one desperately trying to keep in his rage. "Brother, how would you like it if Brother Kraig came home saying he had spoken to some Moonie and believed the Moonie without checking it out first with you?" He spoke with such conviction that I was an offender that I became extremely confused.

I didn't know how to answer. I didn't feel I had done anything wrong, but that judging from his mortal wound, I should have. I had been insensitive and unloving toward him by believing this doctrine and not checking with him.

But another thought occurred to me. Didn't I have the responsibility to "prove all things" and make sure everything I taught was sound doctrine? Did I have to get Brother Evangelist's permission before I believed something? Couldn't I figure some things out for myself? And yet, I felt I should feel wrong, because Brother Evangelist obviously was offended.

"Wouldn't you want Brother Kraig to speak with you first since you have labored so long with him?" he pressed.

I agreed under those circumstances that I would want to speak to Kraig first. But these were not the circumstances with which I was faced. The Moonies believed a middle-aged Korean businessman was Christ's Second Coming. They used a different Bible and were obviously deceived, while I was referencing the Bible itself and the original Greek words to form my conclusions. Besides, Kraig was only two years in the Bible while l had been studying it for ten and a half. That must count for something.

Brother Evangelist told me he would discuss more with me later and left in a huff. In confusion I went into my tent to pray, desperately wanting to know the truth of this doctrine. I began to weep as I thought of Brother Evangelist, his torn tennis shoes, his long gray thrift store pants, and his still longer face that never smiled and rarely showed any joy. It was a picture of pity, not hatred or resentment. He was so dedicated, had so much invested in being right, and so much to lose if he were ever proven wrong. I began to weep in "repentance" as I prayed for him.

Although I felt I should feel convicted, something kept me from feeling I was wrong. I couldn't make myself feel wrong. And yet Brother Evangelist was convinced I was guilty of a great sin. My tears were really tears of sorrow for Brother Evangelist, tears of compassion for a man that I was beginning to believe was in terrible spiritual condition.

A little later, I saw him standing off alone, and I humbly approached him.

"Would you have a minute to speak?" I asked.

"Sure, brother." He seemed pensive and calmed down. "I'm sorry for what happened. It's just that there have been a lot of things over the years that I haven't agreed with and I have been afraid to say anything." He lo ked shocked.

"Why brother?" he asked, looking at me through his kindly, piercing dark eyes. "We love the truth. We've never resisted the truth."

For a moment I felt ashamed. All my fears over the years were just imagined. Brother Evangelist really was reasonable and a servant of truth. So I proceeded cautiously. "There have been some doctrines and practices that I would like to have the brothers discuss and help me resolve," I said.

"Like what?" he asked. "There are a lot of things."

"Tell me about the one doctrine you and Brother Yishiah have been having trouble with."

"Well, it pertains to the doctrine of divorce and remarriage. We are not the only brothers who have trouble with this. Would you like to know who else?" Panicking and responding in a voice lodged deep in his throat, he weakly replied, "Uh, no brother, that wouldn't be necessary."

I wouldn't be deterred. I wanted him to know the extent of the problem and who was thinking like I was. I didn't want to approach him on my own without some sense that I wasn't the only one believing this. So I told him, "Brother Larry and Brother David went down to California to witness to some professing Christians, and they questioned our doctrine of divorce and remarriage and came back with their minds changed."

I was startled by his hostile reply.

"Brother Larry, huh! That brother has been having some real trials with raising his children. They are not very sober and he has not been very diligent with them. He's also not been very faithful as an older brother in camps, not lifting up the standard. And his wife spends too much time in the sisters' room and babbles on for hours."

His next target was Yishiah. "That brother has a big mouth. He's been going around telling brothers and sisters what camps he has been in. He has not learned to have a meek and quiet spirit. He's also been reported as babbling on for hours with the brothers and sisters." I could see the rage in his eyes.

After a few harsh words about Brother David, he seemed to catch himself and offered some reconciling remarks. "What I have shared with you here is not to leave this camp. I spoke to Brother Larry about these things and he has been laboring more diligently with his children."

"Praise God," I remarked, glad to hear that in spite of Larry's weaknesses there was still redemption with Brother Evangelist.

"Why don't you write down those things on some paper and give them to me to consider. I'd like to know what scriptures you are having difficulty with."

"That would be a blessing," I said, relieved to find such a cooperative and open spirit. I embraced him and went to my tent, realizing that his obligatory hug in return had no heart in it.

I had planned to question all the problem verses I had encountered over the years, suggesting some better interpretations. But after a few minutes Brother Evangelist came over and asked me to only write about the doctrine of divorce and remarriage. I agreed, and after about ten minutes had all my texts and explanations written. He came over to the ground cloth on which I was lying, graciously received my thesis, and promised me he would look at it. That evening he came to me in haste and assured me he had read my concerns and told me he had never preached the doctrine I had been believing for years.

Washing his hands of the doctrine, he hoped this would put me to rest. It would have, except I knew there were many brothers and sisters believing the old way. He didn't comment on what he believed the right teaching was, but he did assure me that what I was arguing about was not his doctrine.

Whose was it then, I wondered, because I knew where the church stood on the issue. His comment troubled me and I began to wonder if I had learned it from some other older brother and the error was never detected before.

Then something went "snap." Why hadn't this error been detected before, whether Brother Evangelist taught it or not? It suddenly occurred to me that I had accepted the teaching on the basis of another person's authority. The brothers were so good, therefore their teachings were good. If there was an error, I reasoned, it would have long ago been detected by the other older brothers.

But obviously there was an error that had remained long- undiscovered, damaging those we preached to, like radon gas seeping unaware into an unsuspecting basement. Why weren't we questioning? Because questioning was pride, and God resists the proud. But not questioning what we were taught had led us into error. Therefore, it is okay to question someone if we are doing it to make sure what they are preaching is the truth.

Then a novel thought hit me. If we taught a false teaching for years because no one was questioning the doctrine, then perhaps there were other doctrines we needed to question.

From then on, everything was negotiable. Armed with pen and notebook, I started frequenting the public library, telling myself that Brother Evangelist had no right to forbid us to go into libraries because the Bible did not forbid it. The glorious truth that no man can forbid what God does not forbid started to set me free. I walked into the library with all confidence that I was not sinning because the Bible did not forbid me to use dictionaries and public libraries.

After several days of research I was convinced we needed to convene some older brothers and begin a serious discussion about where the church was heading. I knew we were erring in a lot of areas, but I still had no plans to leave. Brother Evangelist was to let me know that summer whether I would be allowed to marry Sister Noahh.

I looked for Biblical evidence to support his contention that we were not to buy salt, toilet paper, or laundry detergent. It was nowhere from Genesis to Revelation. So my conscience was freed from two more restrictions. Nor did Proverbs 17:18, that spoke of "not being among those who strike hands," refer to shaking hands as a greeting or as an expression of thanks. Saying "ken" and "lo," the Hebrew words for "yes" and "no," was another concoction of the elder's fertile imagination. I would no longer do that because the Bible didn't command it. It was a commandment of man. Whatever discoveries I made I wrote in my notes. My notes thickened as I began to become freed in my spirit and mind.

Brother Evangelist assured me again he had never taught the doctrine of divorce and remarriage the way I had always heard it, and then he left on the road. I was to go with Sergeant Louis daily to check for a phone call from Brother Evangelist.

The next day, as we went to the phone, Sergeant Louis could see that something was troubling me. He tried to pry it out of me, but I didn't want to say anything to him that would get me in trouble with Brother Evangelist or with God. I would not be "one who sows discord among brethren." He honored that and I assured him I had not discussed any of these things with any other brothers.

The phone rang and Sergeant Louis spoke for a while and then turned to me. I took the phone and heard the Elder's warm, reconciling voice. "Brother, I just want to assure you that we're discussing this matter with some of the other brothers. Also, remember, I don't remember ever teaching that doctrine.

It was stonewalling, but I bought it at the time. After another similar phone call the next day in which he denied ever teaching the doctrine, he called a third time. "I just want to assure you again that I don't recall ever teaching that doctrine.

I was intrigued and convinced that this was obviously a doctrinal error that he now saw and didn't want to take responsibility for. Since he seemed to wash his hands of the doctrine, I felt I should ask his permission to share it with the whole church since there were obviously some people in error. I became bold.

"Brother, since you didn't teach this doctrine, would you mind if I went around and straightened the brothers out about it?"

He paused. In a suspicious voice he replied, "That would be okay, brother."

Not wanting to spread dissension without pinning him down to approving of my exact message, I pressed him: "In other words, if a man commits adultery against his wife, she can divorce him and be remarried, right?"

And then he began defending the doctrine he never taught. "Brother, I've been speaking with some of the brothers and there may be some things that you are not considering. In Galatians the words 'adultery' and 'fornication' are used separately. They must be separate things."

He tried to correct me, but I stopped him, "Would it be okay for me to share a verse with you?" I countered.

"Uh, ken," he replied.

"Are you familiar with the verse in 1 Corinthians 4:1 where Paul says 'there is fornication among you such as is not so much as named among the Gentiles, that a man should have his father's wife?' If a man is sleeping with his father's wife, he is either committing adultery or incest. How could this be two virgins having sex?"

I expected a thoughtful response and perhaps a comment like, "That's a good point, brother. Let me consider that verse and get back to you." Instead, he revealed his true nature; "Yes, I am familiar with that verse. You know brother, you have to work on being more humble. We have brought you out of a lot of pits. Remember those folks in Portland where you almost got deceived? Brother Chris had to labor hard to get you to realize your mistakes."

Everything he said was in anger, bitterly accusing me of pride and arrogance when all I did was try to reason with him about a doctrine.

31

More Evidence To Leave

I began to fantasize about what I would do if I were ever to leave the Church. How would I support myself? I had visions of moving back on the farm with my mother. I'd rebuild part of the woodshed and renovate the interior to include a warm room for my continued Bible study. I could support myself from the dumpsters, and not be in my mother's hair. I wondered if there was any chance for me to rekindle the glory days of my baseball career and turn professional. I batted .405 in high school with some power to hit the long ball. Or perhaps I'd put a piano in the shed with me and practice eight hours a day and become a virtuoso. I had given up these things to follow Brother Evangelist, and I was beginning to think they were not so evil after all. In his eyes I was backsliding, in mine, my real personality was emerging.

I realized if I forsook the Church, I would have to entirely rethink my convictions. Many of them were too good to abandon. There was wisdom and good sense in the disciplined lives we were living. My life had benefited from hours of prayer and communion with God. The Bible, properly interpreted, was a real joy and source of strength and guidance. I had no intentions of ever going out of the group and becoming a drunken fornicator or Satan worshiper. I was just seeking some breathing room to follow God on His terms. I walked dazed from the phone call that morning and began to assert my individuality. I had become a weak person, whimpering and simpering to the beat of Brother Evangelist's drums. After a decade of hitchhiking in the snow; honestly confessing my sins and shortcomings, nights spent seeking shelter from the rain, blizzards, and sleet; sleepless nights on Burlington Northern freighttrains rollingthrough the Rockies; scorching days on interstate on-ramps where the heat from the road radiated to 135 degrees Fahrenheit…he still didn't trust me! I was not committed enough. Still immature,

I needed his wisdom to see things correctly!

His arrogance astounded me. I was proven faithful and had labored many years studying the book on which he based his authority. Could I not understand the Word of God myself? Was Brother Evangelist infallible? Was my character to be impugned because I disagreed with him on a doctrine?

Was I evil because I believe differently than he did on some verses? Enough of his pride! I was offended.

As I walked toward downtown, the words of an old Bob Dylan song came back to me and I began to sing it, first guiltily, and then slowly with great assurance. There was no sin in the words, and it comforted me as I walked toward the Seattle City Library:

How many roads must a man walk down Before they call him a man?

How many years must the white dove sail Before she rests in the sand?

And how many times can a man turn his head And pretend that he just doesn't see?

The answer my friend, is blowing in the wind, the answer is blowing in the wind.

"How many roads…" I had done and experienced much in a decade of self denial. When would I be called a man?

"How many times can a man turn his head…" How long would I deny the truth about the group? How many more times would I shut my eyes and accept things I knew were wrong?

By the end of that afternoon, I had filled twenty-three pages of my notebook with disagreements with the Church's doctrine. I realized the early church was a local church, and they were housed permanently. The brothers represented a vagabond group with no permanence and no long term relationships to affect others for Christ.

We were also guilty of taking good principles and applying them in extreme ways. Sure, women should be dressed in modest apparel, but the sisters were so covered and plain they actually drew attention to themselves in public. Sure, we shouldn't lay up treasures in heaven, but surely Christians were allowed to own more than a backpack and a notebook!

After I realized we were following a bunch of non-binding commandments created by Brother Evangelist, I began to get some historical perspective on the group. How long had "the Church" been functioning in America? Since 1971. What was there before then that looked like and believed our "straight and narrow" doctrine? None. Any in Europe during the Reformation? No. They had houses and jobs and didn't live by faith the way we did. What about the Dark Ages? All those people were Catholics and without salvation from God. So, how was I so lucky? Why did God hide His truth for centuries and eons, from nations and cultures, only to divulge it to us? God must not really love the world if so few are allowed to know this truth.

That evening, Sergeant Louis told me I would be going to the phone with him the next day. Brother Evangelist called and had settled down some and after exhorting me to stay humble, asked me if I wanted to go on the road. He obviously didn't want me to be around the other brothers since I harbored such spiritual poison. I agreed to leave town, wanting to get away from Sergeant Louis and his heavy handed leadership. He had mellowed some outwardly over the years, but he still did not consider me a peer and treated me like a weak and foolish brother.

From Dean's List to Dumpsters: Why I Left Harvard to Join a Cult

Brother Mike and I hopped on a bus to ride out of town to an on-ramp for I-80 East. We split up and headed separately to Boise, Idaho, where we agreed to go to the main library every day at noon after we arrived, until we found each other. After catching my first ride, and out of sight of Mike, I did a strange thing. I tucked in my long shirt that looked like a lab coat. I looked modest enough without having to be a spectacle.

When I arrived in Boise, I headed for the university district where I found a sandbar in the middle of a small stream. I stashed my backpack and went looking for Mike. The sandbar had some foliage and low hanging willows, perfect for hiding my tent. Across the stream was the southern edge of Boise State, and a joggers' path. The water was about three feet deep, but in the heat of the day it was refreshing to ford across it. The mosquitoes were manageable and the ground soft enough to sleep on. It seemed the ideal spot.

I had to walk across a large park filled with picnic tables and a band shell in the middle. About a half a mile away was the public library to do further research and meet Brother Mike.

Mike arrived in good spirits and told me about his trip east. Everything had gone smoothly and he was glad to be in. I told him where the camp was set up, and I had him wait for me in the park while I looked for food.

I went to the local Chamber of Commerce and obtained a free map of the city, and using the Yellow Pages had plotted the location of the nearby supermarkets. But first I had to go to the post o ce and send a letter to Seattle with the phone number for Brother Evangelist to call. In line with me at the post o ce was a kindly man who seemed interested in who I was and what I was doing. We had a cordial conversation and I discovered he was a Christian. He was heading to the store also and he offered to take me there.

When we arrived at the supermarket, he began to ask me about myself. I began with my usual spiel about the hypocrisy and lukewarmness of the churches, and he agreed with me. Then I discovered he was an independent thinker devoted to searching the Scriptures. Everything he believed he checked against his own Bible study to make sure he was believing the truth. He spent hours and hours studying the Bible and knew it as well as I did.

We spoke for an hour and, as we departed, he gave me his phone number. After asking me how much money I had ($3.00), he pulled out his wallet. Saying he always prays about what to do with his tithe, he gave me $40 because he felt God was telling him to give it to me. He told me to thank God, and we shook hands as he departed. I bought cereal, bananas, and milk for the next day, and canned goods for dinner that night. The following day I went to do research at the library. The issue of paranoia intrigued me. I wondered if Brother Evangelist was paranoid, so I began my study. The twenty-pound dictionary informed me that paranoia is an unsound fear characterized by megalomania and dissembling. I looked up megalomania and discovered it describes a person consumed with an extremely unrealistic and grandiose idea of himself or herself. Then I looked up the other characteristic. A paranoid person uses deception for protection, and this fit him to a tee. I grieved for Brother Evangelist.

That explained why we weren't allowed to know the location of other members. He was protecting himself. That's why he often preached on "the fear of man." That was the one sin he couldn't conquer. That's why he lied to me about brothers not being in Kansas City. He was afraid I could trace him down if he didn't control what I knew about the whereabouts of other members. That's why he scattered us in groups of three and two, spread thin over the whole country. He didn't want us to get together and overthrow him. That's why he didn't allow dissension, and why he wanted us to destroy our notes. It jeopardized his rule over the group. That's why we were not allowed to visit parents. They might track him down and get him. All these "standards" were really to protect the paranoid megalomaniac who was convinced he was so important that anyone who disagreed with him was jeopardizing the work of God. Only he could be trusted with the role of leading God's Church.

Brother Evangelist lived in great fear. He couldn't even trust those closest to him. He let very few know him intimately, and was reluctant to reveal his past. Occasionally he would send out morsels of self-revelation to his hungry admirers, but would usually stop short of revealing anything significant, wanting not to "preach himself, but Christ crucified." All his years of "being quickened to the warfare" was nothing more than his heightened fears of paranoia. There had been some persecution, yes, but not enough to justify, calling all police liars and assuming people who didn't know us were out to get us.

All through the years l had chided myself for not being "quickened to the warfare," like Brother Evangelist. There were a few older brothers who adopted the same frame of mind, but struggle as I would, I could not convince myself that we were constantly in imminent danger. I saw no purpose in constantly looking over my shoulder for people following me back to camp. Nor did I think most people who gave us rides were actively pursuing the Church.

I pitied him more. I remember him standing at the windows of temporary housing throughout the night counting the police cars that drove by and reporting that to an older brother. Then there was the time the police raided our camp and he told Brother Alan to step out and pretend he was Brother Evangelist if the police asked for him. Alan obeyed, and the police took one look at him and laughed, saying, "You're not Brother Evangelist!"

As these revelations came pouring in, I began to get extremely confused.

Could I straighten out the Church? Would the brothers listen to me? Was I receiving a strong delusion and being "purged" from the Church? What was happening?

I looked in my pocket and found the telephone number of the man I met at the post o ce. I trusted his judgment and integrity. He answered the call and I told him I needed to speak to him about something very important and that it dealt with whether or not I was in a cult. We agreed to meet in an hour at the local Big Boy Restaurant.

He ordered coffee and the conversation got underway. I described how Brother Silas' daughter had died and Brother Evangelist kept Silas from having fellowship with the rest of the Church because he didn't trust him. In his time of need Brother Evangelist turned his back on him. "That man ought to be horsewhipped," he said. "What a cruel heart! That man has no business being a pastor."

I agreed. I shared more of my doctrine and what I had been learning, and he agreed with everything. Finally, I was emboldened enough to get his opinion. "Am I in a cult?"

"MAN, YOU'RE IN A CULT WITH A CAPITAL C. GET OUT OF THAT THING AS FAST AS YOU CAN!"

I was relieved to hear the truth, and we prayed together and parted ways. I told him I would keep in touch and would be leaving the group soon.

I met Mike a little later in the park and began to share my doubts with him about the church. He listened intently and asked the logical question after believing me: "Now what do we do?" I told him I was going to call my mother and tell her I was coming home. He then confessed that he had been sneaking off and calling his parents for the last two months.

I found a pay phone near the library and dialed my mother. She answered, and when I said, "Mom, this is Jim. I've been deceived. The group is a cult. I'm coming home," she replied, in tears, "Thank God. I was so worried about your soul."

"I was worried about your soul." Perfect words. A confirmation from God that Brother Evangelist had lied to me about my parents' love. She worried about my soul. Brother Evangelist had told us parents are only worried about our flesh and they don't care about your souls which was another sweeping generalization based on his paranoia.

My mother explained that she had prayed for me every night for the last ten years. "When are you coming home?" she asked.

I wasn't sure. I felt like an invisible hand was holding me from committing to leaving. My mind lapsed into and out of the doctrine as I felt a strange brew of security and fear: security in being with the brothers and holding onto the familiar, and fear of losing my salvation. Years of conditioning had convinced me that those who forsook the Church would either die spiritually, go insane, or lose their souls. You could not forsake the Church and have God. They were a package.

Beside that, I still had much of my identity wrapped up in being a member of the endtime Church. I loved the brothers and sisters and found it hard to digest that I would have to leave this nomadic lifestyle if I left the Church.

"I'm not sure when I'm leaving," I told her a little while later. "There are some people I would like to get out first."

"Do you think that's safe?" she asked. "I'm not sure."

"The longer you think about it, the weaker you may become. I think it would be smart to get away from their influence and then decide."

That seemed to make a lot of sense. I told her I would call her later and she tearfully made me promise. I think she felt like I was hooked but not yet landed. As I walked along the stream in the park behind the Boise Library, I questioned whether I could convince some of the older brothers to stand up with me against Brother Evangelist. The Elder seemed so lonely, so sincere, so isolated, so burdened, so burned out. I would want to do it in love for him and for those like me who were following his leadership with the sincerest of hearts. Perhaps the Church could be healed.

I had no doubt what would happen to me if I left the Church. I would be shunned. Things in my past including my relationship with Sister Esther would be brought out and used to support the accusation I had lost my understanding. Younger brothers and sisters would shake their heads in horror at the judgment God had prepared for me. Many would be depressed and would shed tears. But they needed to forget me, learn from my mistakes, heed the proper warnings that my life ultimately would teach, and make sure they didn't turn away from God in the same way. I had been purged and needed to be flushed from their minds. If anyone would see me in public, I would be shunned. Gatherings would be held and the brethren would be warned to avoid me because I had become offended. If Brother Evangelist suspected I was in a certain city, he would encourage the brothers and sisters to avoid that city, or not to "tarry" too long there.

How ironic. This is what I did whenever someone else left the church, and I was always ready to accept Brother Evangelist's explanation. Now it was my turn. I was resigned to my fate, although not certain the best way to proceed. I considered hitchhiking back to Seattle to explain to the brethren there why I left, before the Elder could turn them against me. Perhaps some of the older brothers might listen and we could confront Brother Evangelist. As I passed through the park I came across a Christian music concert in progress. I sat down and listened, this time with an open heart, allowing myself to believe these people were true servants of God as I had been trying to be. As I allowed myself to enjoy the music, not fearing that I was compromising the Gospel by accepting these musicians as brothers and sisters, anguish began to sweep over me. Tight chords of guilt and condemnation, legalism, and bondage began to snap as my previously secure world view crumbled. I cried over my notebook, cradling my eyes in my arms, trying not to be too conspicuous. The tears felt good as the grip of bondage slowly broke away. A young man in the crowd named Dave saw me crying and came and put his arm around me to console me. When he asked me what was wrong, I showed him my notes, and how I was in a cult and wanted to get out. He lovingly a rmed my conclusions and took Mike and me home with him that night.

From Dean's List to Dumpsters: Why I Left Harvard to Join a Cult

In Dave's house Mike and I began to feel already separated from the Church. We discussed the Church and our plans for the future: I tucked my long shirt in, took a shower, and packed up all my belongings.

I called my mother collect that night and she arranged for a flight for me the next day, leaving Boise, Idaho, at noon and arriving at Washington National Airport that night. She also had a letter from Brother Barnabas, the brother who had joined the Church a few months after me in Portland, Maine, and who had left the Church several months before. Since he had visited my mother's house in 1982 when we first came back to visit, he still had her address. He had written to me in care of her, outlining why he had left and what scandals and dishonesty were occurring in the Church. My mother told me about the letter and asked if I would like her to read it to me. I agreed.

For once, the accusations against the Elder were believable. He spoke of things I had experienced and could relate to. In it he documented lies he had been told, how he had been falsely accused of being rebellious, how Brother Evangelist had sabotaged and ruined a relationship he had with a sister, and how he and a couple of other brothers no longer in the Church had been purged. He gave me names and phone numbers of former members I could contact who could verify the eider's patterns of manipulation and deceit. Barnabas' letter confirmed my decision. I was not alone in seeing Brother Evangelist's abuses of authority. I was seeing the truth.

The next morning Dave invited Mike and me to his church, an evangelical church of several hundred people, singing praises and worship songs loudly and joyfully. Dave introduced me to several of the members and, when they heard we were leaving a cult, they were exceedingly happy for us. We sang along with the congregation, reading the words projected on the huge movie screens up front, still nurturing some doubts that we might be compromising with the enemy. Nevertheless, as we continued to worship and listen to the sermon, we gradually began to feel at peace in the congregation.

After church, Dave took me to the airport and Mike and I hugged each other at the gate. Mike asked if he could have my notes and I reluctantly agreed, giving him my address to send them to when he was finished. He still didn't know what he was going to do, but it was no longer my responsibility. I had a sick sense I would never see my notes again, which later proved to be true.

As the plane took off, I felt like I was beginning life again, freed from the tyranny of a man who had carved out his own hell in the midst of Heaven.

32

Epilogue from the First Edition

Over ten years have passed since I boarded the plane in Boise to start a new life. Much has happened since August 30, 1986, when I stepped off the plane at D.C. National and rode silently home with my mother and her best friend Kris. My mother was both forgiving and very angry at the way I had disappeared with hardly a peep for ten years. I was not ready to face their pain as I felt I had enough to deal with on my own.

A psychologist wanted to get the family together for therapy, and this I felt may be too threatening. I didn't want to sit in a room with my brothers and sisters and have them spew their rage against me. I was tired of guilt and needed a rest. Besides, being a cultie just out of the group, I had little respect for the mental health industry. I wanted them to understand how badly it hurt me to forsake them and that it was nothing personal, I was just obeying what I thought the Bible was teaching.

I flirted with the idea of returning to Harvard, but realized I did not have the resources to pull it off. I didn't even have the resources that day to eat. I was thirty years old, with little job experience, a ten year gap in my resumé, one-third of my bachelors degree completed, uncorrected 20/400 vision, and two changes of socially laughable clothes.

Fortunately, my parents pitied me. My mother dug up an old pair of wire-rimmed glasses I wore in high school which were too weak, but better than my unaided vision, and gave them to me. My sister-in-law, a beautician, trimmed my beard and made me look a little less like a homeless person. My dad bought me some contact lenses and offered to purchase me a suit (which I was not ready to accept since I still thought suits were too vain and worldly).

Wherever I went I felt compelled to tell people of my cult experience. Their reactions outwardly were very positive and they were filled with questions about how I joined and how I got out. I returned to school in January of 1987, thanks to a scholarship given to me by an anonymous donor through the Cult Awareness Network. I traveled to churches and youth groups and told them of my experience. I called the parents of members of the Church and updated them about their children.

From Dean's List to Dumpsters: Why I Left Harvard to Join a Cult

One family, who had a son in the group, wanted to know what I knew about their son because his mother was dying of cancer. I wrote her a long letter, staying up late into the night, chronicling details of her son's marriage and life in the group. Although her son had been told through a letter that his mother was dying, he didn't feel it was the Lord's will to contact her in her last days. The family wrote to me and thanked me profusely for the letter which I had written. They said it brought his mother comfort in her dying moments to know that her son still loved her and he was doing fine. My letter was the only news they had about their son in over ten years. I have learned he has visited his family recently.

Through the Presbyterian church I joined, I got a job working at Safeway Stores while I finished my degree at the University of Maryland. In December of 1989 I graduated "magna cum laude" with a Bachelor's degree in language and literature. I met my wife Luchy that year and we were married in November of 1989. We moved to California in 1990, where I earned my teaching credential and now work as a middle school math teacher. In July of 1993 my daughter Rebekah was born, and a son, William, in July of 1998.

After I left, several brothers and sisters followed. Brother Shor called me one day out of the blue and told me he had finally awakened to the deceit and manipulation of the group. He gradually recovered, got married, and earned a degree in occupational therapy.

Sister Noahh, tired of the constant "fear of man" taught by the group, left the group in 1988 with another sister and walked the entire length of the state of Oregon before settling down and marrying another former member. Brother Joel returned to the Midwest, got a college degree, and raised his six kids on a farm. Brother Bob disappeared from the group after suffering severe depression and has not been heard from in many years.

Esther and Michaiah got married in 1985, just a couple of months after she left the Church. They have three boys and a flourishing ministry delivering wheelchairs to the disabled in Third World countries.

Brother Byron, the inventive one, settled in the Portland area, got married, and has a daughter. Brother Silas moved to the Midwest and settled with his family, where Rhoda, the oldest, got married. Alan, Juliet, and Annie moved to San Diego after a period of floating around the country looking for "fellowship." Alan purchased a condominium and worked for Federal Express as a customer service representative.

Life goes on for those who leave the Church. Some have been so burned by their experience that they do not trust God or religion anymore. Some come out and drift, looking for a similar group, but one that is different enough to suit their style of Christianity. Others put religion on the back burner and then return to it years later, perhaps when they have children or suffer a death in their family. A fortunate few leave Brother Evangelist's group and do not get offended by religion. They realize Jesus is still the truth, that the Bible is still the Word of God, and that life without Him is meaningless and empty. These find fellowship and remain faithful to Christ, learning to adapt their Christianity to whatever circumstances they are in.

I thank God I have not forsaken Him. There are times when I wish I could return to communal life, live simply and by faith, and be totally free to serve God without the encumbrances of having to provide for my family. But I also know that "the Church" was an aberration, a good idea taken to an extreme, leading to a loss of individual freedoms and preaching a gospel that only the young, healthy, and single had any hope of following.

I no longer view myself as such an elitist. Thank God for His grace which goes beyond the huddled few who still wander the country in groups of three and four, and who still answer to the gospel of Brother Evangelist. There, but for the grace of God, continue to go I.

I am often asked if I have any regrets about my ten years with Brother Evangelist. I have a few. My strongest and most virile days were spent in celibacy. I lost ten years of building a career. I do not have the time left to build a large family or experiment with a variety of careers. I deeply offended, worried, and hurt my family. I missed seeing my younger brothers and sisters grow up. I didn't attend my brothers' and sisters' weddings. I gave up a Harvard education and the advantages it afforded.

On the other hand, I have experienced things few people get to experience. I have seen miracles of God. I have built a deep and effective prayer life. I have learned how feeble I am and how great God's grace is. The years spent studying the Bible have given me a foundation for life that most Christians would envy. God has more than "restored the years which the locust has eaten," (Joel 2:25) by giving me a wonderful wife and family, good fellowship at church, a fulfilling job, sufficient economic resources, and season tickets to the Dodgers.

God did not depart from me when I left the group. He is still there when I seek Him. Although I do not have the time to seek Him as I did when I was unemployed and single, I still maintain a relationship with Him and see His influence and blessing in my life. The fears of falling away and going to hell for leaving Brother Evangelist have proven to be idle threats of a paranoid man wishing to keep control over my life. Although he still roams the country and makes his converts, his power over me has been broken, and I am glad. I pray for him and for those still following him. God alone can break their bonds.

Sadly, their minds are like concrete thoroughly mixed and permanently set. But the best way to influence people for God is to intercede with God in prayer for people. This I will continue to do, and I recommend it for everyone who has lost a child or friend to a cult. It brought me out when there was no hope. It can wake up others, too.

IV
Appendix

33

An Open Letter to the Brothers and Sisters

From Jim Guerra, 2004

Dear Brothers and Sisters in Yeshua,

I know that before writing to you I already have three strikes against me. Why should you listen to me? I no longer travel from city to city with a backpack, nor do I submit myself to brother Evangelist's ministry. In your minds I have fallen away, lost my understanding, and have become a fowl wanting to turn you away from following Yeshua and his teachings. (Matt. 13:4) Nevertheless, even Balaam's ass had something to say which was useful. (Num. 22:28) I pray you consider the scriptures and the observations I am setting before you.

What has happened to the church since it started out in 1971 as just a traveling Christian ministry? How has it gotten to its current state, where members are distrustful of one another, secretive, deceitful, self-righteous, hateful toward their families, unwilling to be corrected? Very simply. Your leader is not accountable to anyone.

Let me explain. We all believe that correction is necessary for every follower of Christ. (Prov. 15:10) That correction may come from various sources: the Holy Spirit convicting us through the Word, (John 16:8) a brother or sister convicting our hearts with truth or a testimony, or even an unbeliever who sees through us and speaks truth (the Balaam's ass syndrome). Without correction we err.

What happens when the elder errs? He does err, you know. (Even the Apostle Peter had to be rebuked.) (Gal. 2:13-14) Brother Evangelist is a sheep just like the rest of us. (1 Pet. 2:25) If he gets proud, the Holy Spirit cannot convict him. There goes one source of correction. Brothers and sisters cannot correct him; that would be "rebuking an elder." (1 Tim. 5:1) Another source down the drain! What's left is a Balaam's ass like me. A few dismissing words about me and that source is gone, too.

From Dean's List to Dumpsters: Why I Left Harvard to Join a Cult

Is it true that everyone who speaks against the church that brother Evangelist has set up is motivated by pride or a desire to justify themselves? What if the church really has fallen into a pit of deception?

Organizations are like people. We often cannot see what is wrong with our own behavior. (Ps. 19:12) So it is with groups in general. (Luke 6:41) Insiders, particularly the leaders of a company, often cannot see their organization clearly. To improve they often hire outside consultants. You may have employees that have been overworked and under appreciated by their superiors, but who are afraid to say anything for fear of losing their jobs. Or perhaps the leadership is blocked into looking at a problem in only one way, and needs an outside perspective to find solutions. (Matt. 15:14)

The church is no different. As a former member, I see much that needs correcting. Precisely because brother Evangelist does not receive reproof I am no longer with the brethren. The church is erring greatly and desperately needs correction, (Prov. 10:17) but unfortunately has become an old and foolish king who will no more be admonished. (Ecc. 4:18)

I realize that the brethren inside the church humbly receive correction from their older brothers. You are receptive to that kind of correction. But what you cannot hear are the global reproofs you so desperately need to improve as a church. You need to hear reproof that illuminates your organizational and doctrinal errors.

Yeshua did this to the churches in Asia in the book of Revelations. (Rev. 2-3) Each church was displeasing the Lord in some way but did not realize it. He lovingly rebuked them, albeit sharply in some cases. They needed a voice from outside the church to illuminate the errors of the entire church. From whom on the outside do you receive rebuke and correction? If the whole church is led astray, how do you get corrected?

Below is a list of errors that crept into the church and you self-corrected. I give it to you as an example of how the entire church can err. However, there are many other things that have not been corrected that are causing unnecessary trials and tribulation to group members and families, and which you are too proud to correct.

Errors in the Past Which You Acknowledge

1. "Wearing glasses is not of faith." Perhaps that was never said, but was strongly implied by the group. Why else would so many of us struggle with our vision for years when a simple pair of glasses solve the problem?
2. "Brothers don't go into libraries." This was a typical overreaction to a brother reading a heretical book and getting deceived. That made as much sense as forbidding brothers to eat because someone ate a bad hamburger.
You now go into libraries and do research, whereas for years this was considered a forbidden and carnal practice. (Commandments of men) (Matt. 15:9)

3."Lord willing, we will not be buying laundry soap, salt, or toilet paper." Although perhaps some good practice to get ready for the mark of the beast, faith does not come by not buying, but by hearing the word of God. (Rom. 10:17) This is man's attempt to exercise faith, and not God's commandment. (Col. 2:20-23)

4."Sisters shouldn't ride bikes. It's not modest." (An opinion expressed to me by some older brothers, including Daniel.)

5."Having a bank account is laying up treasures on earth." Jonathan Schmidt, why is your money in the bank? (1 Tim. 6:17)

6.Changing opinions of dressing modestly. You went from plaid shirts, to robes, to shirts around the crotch, to shirts below the knee. What is modest? (Rom. 14:23)

Some Errors that Have Not Yet Been Corrected

1."Forsaking all means leaving your family and traveling." The Book of Acts and the Epistles all reveal that the early church was a series of local churches, with some people sent out to establish other local churches.

2."Single sisters should submit to the brothers." "Women should submit to their husbands", (Eph. 5:22) or stay in their parents' house and submit to their parents, until they are of age and can take care of themselves.

3."No one is to rebuke an elder. If I am erring, God will correct me." (Misinterpretation of 1 Tim. 5:1) In the verse which brother Evangelist quotes to keep himself from being questioned, "elder" means someone older in the flesh than you; it does not mean an elder (presbuteros) of a church or an overseer. Nowhere in the Bible is there a record of a church with only one elder. The Bible supports the ideal that every member of the church be accountable, including the elders. (1 Peter 5:3)

Why, after 27 years, is there no one equal to Brother Evangelist? Why has he structured the church so that everyone is accountable to him, but that he is accountable to no one? Who corrects brother Evangelist when errs, or do you so idolize him that you think he is above erring? Has no brother under his discipleship grown enough to be trusted to be an equal? What will happen to the church when he dies? (1 Tim. 5:19)

Presbuteros are not to be falsely accused, but may be accused of wrongdoing before two or three true witnesses. This was written to protect the flock from the abuses of leadership.

You will note also in the following verses that elders are exclusively spoken of in plurality in the New Testament, never as one man running the entire show. You will also notice that there were councils of elders in the early church government, and individual elders that served with other elders in the church were to be given honor. God's plan is not for one elder to rule over a flock, however lovingly, without accountability to other elders and pastors in the church. (See Acts 11:30; 14:23; 15:2, 4, 6, 22, 23; 16:4; 20:17; 21:18; 22:5; 1

Tim. 5:17, 19 (an elder, not "the" elder!); Titus 1:5 (Elders in every city); Heb. 11:2; Jas. 5:14; 1 Pet. 5:1; Rev. 4:4, 10, etc.)

4. "Marriage is not for everybody." That's true. Neither is celibacy. Forcing a majority of brothers and sisters to remain single contrary to their calling to marriage quenches the Spirit of God and creates unnecessary and burdensome trials for the brothers and sisters. (Matt. 19:12; 1 Cor. 7:2; Heb. 13:4; Gen. 2:18; 1 Cor. 7:9; 1 Tim. 4:1-3)

Concerning the response that the church does not forbid marriage, one only has to ask around to see how many people have been discouraged from it, denied permission, or told that it was not God's will. When the devil wishes to bring discord and confusion into a church, he meddles with its view on sexuality. Some groups err by being sexually promiscuous, others err by making it impossible for a person to express their sexuality in a lawful (marriage) way. Although the church has no doctrine against marriage, you do have a practice of forbidding it. Which is worse: what you believe or what you do? (1 Tim. 4:1-3)

A. It is not good for men and women to be alone. God acknowledged this in the Garden when Adam was still in perfect fellowship with God. "We are complete in Him," (Col. 2:10) true, but Paul was not referring to marriage in this passage, otherwise why would Paul want the younger women to marry, bear children, and guide the house? (1 Tim. 5:12-14) Paul was pro-marriage and motherhood and saw it as a way for women to avoid idleness, gossip, and spiritual deterioration.

B. Marriage is the rule, celibacy the exception, in the Bible. Celibacy is voluntary, and marriage is not to be forbidden in the church. Those who would discourage and forbid marriage are submitting themselves to the doctrine of devils Paul warned about. (1 Tim. 4:1-3) Although the church has no doctrine against marriage, the elder has a practice of forbidding it and an attitude against it. If you don't believe me, ask yourself if you would marry if you were free to marry any brother or sister you wanted. Chances are, if you are honest you would marry in a heartbeat.

C. Even now there are brothers and sisters in the church who wish to marry but are waiting for permission from brother Evangelist. Some, no doubt, have waited for years. Did you know that this is none of his business? Where does the Bible give him that kind of power over your personal lives? (1 Pet. 5:3) What are the limits to his power? Does he truly have total say in all matters personal and private? Why do you have to give account to the Lord for your actions, if most your actions are dictated by him? (Rom. 14:10-12)

5. "Your flesh relations are your foes." This false doctrine is the root of your "persecution." Search your own hearts. Do you feel good about disappearing from your family and not contacting them for years? Have you for one moment considered the unnecessary pain you have inflicted on them? Although you have gone with the group willingly, the effect on your parents is the same as if you were kidnapped. You left suddenly, many times, without an explanation. You are out

of contact for years, leaving them to wonder if you are alive or dead. You selfishly focus on your own salvation and leave them in a cruel and unloving manner.

Which of you willingly forsook your families? You were given the non-choice of loving God or loving your families. Rejecting your families is not loving them. Those verses about a man's foes make more sense in Muslim countries where a convert to Christianity is rejected by his or her family and treated as being dead. You have reversed it. A family is assumed to be the enemy and the believer rejects the unbeliever! This is not God's love.

Conclusion

There are many ways you can respond to this letter. You may dismiss it all by saying that I fell away and that I am trying to destroy the church. Perhaps you may call it all a bunch of deceit and not even consider what I have written. Your older brothers may read this on the Internet and tell you not to read it because it is "sowing discord." (Since when is reproof considered "sowing discord."? The next time brother Daniel or brother Leonard corrects you, look him in the eye and tell him that he is sowing discord!)

Perhaps you won't consider this because you don't want to receive an accusation against the elder. But read the rest of the verse…"except it be before two or three witnesses." You must receive an accusation if it is true! Remember what John the Apostle said about Diotrophes in 3 John? (John must have received many accusations against Diotrophes to lead him to warn others about that elder gone astray.)

Undoubtedly you could find sin in my life, too. But that has no bearing on the truth of what I have written. I am willing to be called a Balaam's ass, if you will only have the humility to consider what I have written and not dismiss it in your pride. Your souls are at stake.

In Yeshua,

Jim Guerra (Brother Ariel)

Epilogue

Epilogue to the Second Edition, by Jim Guerra

Life has sped by and I am o cially retired from a long and happy teaching career as a math teacher in the Claremont Unified School District in California. The group suffered the loss of its leader, Jim Roberts, on December 6, 2015. He died of an untreated cancer; untreated because he refused to seek medical attention but put his faith in God. I pray he finds grace before God as we all need it on that Day.

Life continues for the group, as they are still living according to their doctrine of "forsaking all", although much has changed in the leadership. They have made some excellent decisions to reconnect with their families, allow marriage, and spread the leadership among three of the seasoned members, to get away from the unquestioned and unaccountable mono-leader at the head of the fellowship. The brothers and sisters continue to love God and serve a counter-culture life in preparation for Jesus' return.

Philip Haney, who served in the group as the humble and wise "Brother Aaron", traveled throughout the Middle East as an agricultural entomologist, and became familiar with Islamic and Jewish culture, learning to read and speak both Hebrew and Arabic. After returning to the United States, concerned about the goals of radical Islam, Philip became one of the founding members of Homeland Security after 9/11. During his tenure with Homeland Security, he collected data on known Islamist groups that had infiltrated our country and were responsible for several terrorist attacks on American citizens, including the Pulse Nightclub massacre and the San Bernardino shootings. Politicians within the government forced him to delete much of his tracking data and hampered his work, leading to these atrocities.

Phil wrote his book, "If You See Something, Say Nothing", was pushed out of the Department of Homeland Security and went to Congress as a whistleblower against the government's secret program to protect terrorists under the guise of civil rights. Phil traveled the country, was interviewed on major talk shows, and worked diligently to alert Americans to the danger he had uncovered. Sadly, while working on his second book, he was murdered, and his body was dumped on the roadside in northern California. The killer was never found.

Mark Richard, aka Brother Michaiah, established a wheelchair ministry in Guatemala where his workers and supporters have assembled and distributed over one million wheelchairs worldwide in developing and poorer countries, free of charge. In the last couple of years, he engineered and patented a series of new wheelchairs and carts that are inexpensive to make, highly durable, and conform easily to any terrain. He calls them his "Bumblebee Brand" and they are making life in difficult terrain much easier for those with disabilities.

Sandy Richard, his wife, sadly passed away with lung cancer. She was an outstanding woman who supported Mark in his ministry, raised his three boys, and lived a selfless life of excellence. She will be missed.

My kids remain in California while my wife and I moved to sunny Southern Florida where I am tutoring and writing in my retirement. I continue in my faith as a youth leader at Christ Fellowship in Port St. Lucie, and am grateful for those whom He has brought into my life.

Afterword

By Rebekah Guerra Day, Daughter of Jim Guerra

Growing up, my father and I would often have long conversations about his time in the group. When I was a child, he would share anecdotes to teach me that despite the difficulties and the trials that he faced, God was indeed still there with him. God was always watching over him, caring for him, and protecting him during every moment of those ten- and-a-half years, even though he would consider it to be one of the darkest decades of his life.

As I progressed into my young adult years, those stories began to take on a deeper and more personal meaning. My own difficult life experiences provided me with a greater understanding of what it was like to believe that I was doing the right thing by pursuing my passions, values, mission, and calling. Yet, I still encountered so much pain along the way.

Ultimately, even though I felt as if I was making my best effort, I was still hurting so much, and it was because I was not genuinely making choices that aligned with my goals. My traumatic experiences, inadequately treated mental health issues, and a lack of wise counsel and accountability to help keep me on track clouded my judgment and impacted my decision-making. As a result, I did not know what I needed to do to get myself to the place of success and personal fulfillment that I had sought for so long.

Despite the support of my family and friends, and to an outsider, near-ideal socioeconomic circumstances, I still experienced a pervasive struggle with cognitive dissonance, a mismatch between my values and my actions. As a result, I continued to engage in self-destructive behavior, actively rejecting the inner voice that screamed at me constantly that the way I was living was never going to empower me to achieve my goals. Through the patience and support of behavioral health professionals and loved ones, and with an extensive examination of every facet of my existence, I eventually realized that forces beyond my control were leading me down this dark path. I worked on forgiving myself for my past indiscretions, made efforts to make amends with those who I had wronged who were open to engaging with me, and resolved to make intentional choices to take actions that would align with my life's calling. Only then was I able to start to find some peace.

Just as my father described in his narrative about the cult, even those who society deems to be intelligent, with excellent research and critical thinking skills, sound judgment, and a wise mind, can fall victim to the deceit and manipulation of malicious individuals and groups. Sometimes when we want something so badly, we can betray what we know deep down to be true in favor of the options that sound attractive at the moment. This betrayal of self is particularly dangerous in the face of compelling and seemingly evidence-based arguments in favor of what will turn out to be a destructive path. In our modern era, where there is so much information available at a click of a button on every topic imaginable, it is difficult to cut through the noise to find the truth.

This noise presents itself in thinking patterns as "shoulds": These are the things I feel like I'm supposed to do. This path is what society tells me I should do to be accepted and successful. Despite doing my best to fall in line with these expectations, I still felt so much pain, and longed so deeply for the ability to encounter the joy and satisfaction that I thought would come out of pursuing my calling.

Now that I am reading my father's book with fresh eyes at the age of thirty, having certainly been through my fair share of struggles, I'm grateful that I'm finally starting to recover and move forward. I'm working in a field that allows me to ardently pursue my lifelong passion for engaging and supporting disadvantaged communities. This work challenges me to demonstrate that I can rise above my struggles and dedicate myself honestly to uplifting communities that historically have been cast aside by our civic institutions.

I know now that despite all of my painful experiences, I still had someone watching over me, and I was always protected. Even though my circumstances were quite dark at times, I was always safe in the end. To me, that's what my dad's story is about: despite the darkness in our circumstances, we have a protective force in our lives to keep us safe. I appreciate my father's story because it applies broadly to people in many situations, including those who are not believers. Given the proper support, no person is a lost cause.

I often grapple with the ethical dilemma of why I get the opportunity to thrive and succeed, when so many others on this planet don't get nearly the same privileges. However, the universal message does resonate: with perseverance, experience, vulnerability, community, and self-advocacy, we can reclaim our agency and break free from situations like the one my father discusses in this book. I'm grateful that I have had this opportunity to help him revise and edit and reformat this Second Edition, nearly two-and-a-half decades after its initial publication. It has been a pleasure to revisit the stories he told me when I was a child and understand them within the overarching context of his experiences in the cult.

If you ever talk to him about his story, you would be fortunate to absorb his wisdom. I haven't always appreciated his story, but now more than ever, I'm grateful that I get to see it through his eyes, and I get to apply that same wisdom to my own experiences. This revision process gave me a new perspective on the wonderful man I am lucky to call a father. So, I hope that in reading this, you can find a piece of that wisdom that can apply to your challenges. Just because something or someone looks perfect and says the right things, doesn't mean that those ideas aren't worth a closer look. It's easy for things to seem attractive when wrapped up in a shiny package, when the reality can often be much darker than that. Thank you for taking the time to read, and I hope this book brings you peace and encouragement.

Acknowledgment

I would like to acknowledge my daughter, Rebekah, for her hard work and brilliant counsel in helping me revise and republish this book. Without her help, it would never have been completed!

About the Author

Jim was the second oldest of four children, the son of Charles and Marilyn Guerra. As a sophomore at Harvard, Jim was building for a future as a lawyer when he was recruited into a Christian cult. After spending ten years in the cult, Jim returned to Maryland and completed his education graduating Magna Cum Laude from the University of Maryland. He married his wife, Luchy Binet, and has two children with her. Jim has spent time teaching others about cults, and has appeared on the Maury Povich Show, and was interviewed by Charlie Rose and other local news outlets, about his experiences in the "Brothers." Jim is currently in his 33rd year as a public-school math teacher, and roots for the Dodgers and any team that is playing the San Francisco Giants.